Early Modern Cultural Studies

Ivo Kamps, Series Editor

Published by Palgrave Macmillan

WOMEN'S WORK IN EARLY MODERN ENGLISH LITERATURE AND CULTURE

Michelle M. Dowd

palgrave
macmillan

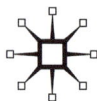

WOMEN'S WORK IN EARLY MODERN ENGLISH LITERATURE AND CULTURE
Copyright © Michelle M. Dowd, 2009.

First published in 2009 by
PALGRAVE MACMILLAN®
in the United States—a division of St. Martin's Press LLC,
175 Fifth Avenue, New York, NY 10010.

Where this book is distributed in the UK, Europe and the rest of the world,
this is by Palgrave Macmillan, a division of Macmillan Publishers Limited,
registered in England, company number 785998, of Houndmills,
Basingstoke, Hampshire RG21 6XS.

Palgrave Macmillan is the global academic imprint of the above companies
and has companies and representatives throughout the world.

Palgrave® and Macmillan® are registered trademarks in the United States,
the United Kingdom, Europe and other countries.

ISBN-13: 978–0–230–61345–4
ISBN-10: 0–230–61345–4

Library of Congress Cataloging-in-Publication Data

Dowd, Michelle M., 1975–
    Women's work in early modern English literature and culture /
    Michelle M. Dowd.
        p. cm.—(Early modern cultural studies)
        ISBN 0–230–61345–4 (alk. paper)
        1. English literature—Early modern, 1500–1700—History and
    criticism. 2. Working class women in literature. 3. Work in literature.
    4. Labor in literature. 5. Housekeeping in literature. 6. Working class
    women—England—History—17th century. 7. Literature and
    society—England—History—17th century. 8. Women—England—Social
    conditions—17th century. I. Title.

PR428.W63D68 2009
820.9'9287—dc22   2008035854

A catalogue record of the book is available from the British Library.

Design by Newgen Imaging Systems (P) Ltd., Chennai, India.

First edition: April 2009

10 9 8 7 6 5 4 3 2 1

Printed in the United States of America.

For my parents, Frank and Pat Dowd

Contents

Figures

FOREWORD

In the twenty first century, literary criticism, literary theory, historiography, and cultural studies have become intimately interwoven, and the formerly distinct fields of literature, society, history, and culture no longer seem so discrete. The Palgrave Early Modern Cultural Studies Series encourages scholarship that crosses boundaries between disciplines, time periods, nations, and theoretical orientations. The series assumes that the early modern period was marked by incipient processes of transculturation brought about through exploration, trade, colonization, and the migration of texts and people. These phenomena set in motion the processes of globalization that remain in force today. The purpose of this series is to publish innovative scholarship that is attentive to the complexity of this early modern world and bold in the methods it employs for studying it.

As series editors, we welcome, for example, books that explore early modern texts and artifacts that bear the traces of transculturation and globalization and that explore Europe's relationship to the cultures of the Americas, of Europe, and of the Islamic world and native representations of those encounters. We are equally interested in books that provide new ways to understand the complex urban culture that produced the early modern public theater or that illuminate the material world of early modern Europe and the regimes of gender, religion, and politics that informed it. Elite culture or the practices of everyday life, the politics of state or of the domestic realm, the material book or the history of the emotions—all are of interest if pursued with an eye to novel ways of making sense of the strangeness and complexity of the early modern world.

JEAN HOWARD AND IVO KAMPS
Series editors

ACKNOWLEDGMENTS

It gives me great pleasure to begin this book on work by acknowledging the labors, guidance, and support of those who have contributed so generously to it. I am particularly fortunate to have had the advice and support of Jean Howard during the many years that it has taken to bring this book to fruition. Jean has selflessly devoted enormous amounts of time and energy to this project, and her meticulous readings of each chapter combined with her always thoughtful, patient, and rigorous mentorship have enabled me not only to write the book but also to become a better critical thinker and scholar. I am continually amazed by her consummate professionalism, warmth, and attention to detail, and I am deeply grateful for all of her guidance and generosity. My thanks also go to Julie Crawford, who offered insightful critiques paired with infectious enthusiasm for the project in its early stages, helping me not only to hone my arguments but also to enjoy myself in the process. David Kastan, Anne Prescott, and Jim Shapiro graciously shared with me their vast knowledge, humor, and advice as I was first formulating and developing the ideas for this book. I also owe a debt to Fran Dolan, whose intellectual generosity and astute advice have been invaluable. She has been wonderfully supportive of the project and has continually challenged and inspired me to find pleasure in the complexities of early modern texts. Ken Gross, Rosemary Kegl, and Jarold Ramsey taught me Renaissance literature as an undergraduate, and I remain grateful to this day for their thoughtful mentorship.

At Columbia, I was fortunate to be a part of a wonderful cohort of graduate students who gave me valuable feedback on earlier versions of this project, including Tiffany Alkan, John Bird, Alan Farmer, Tom Festa, James Fleming, Jessica Forbes, Ellen MacKay, Doug Pfeiffer, Zachary Lesser, Ben Robinson, and Adam Zucker. Naomi Reed and Anna Trumbore Jones deserve special thanks for their friendship and their unwavering support during the dissertation-writing process and beyond.

At the University of North Carolina at Greensboro, I am privileged to be part of an outstanding department of generous colleagues who have consistently supported my work on this book. Particular thanks go to Russ McDonald, who read large portions of the manuscript and offered sage advice on numerous subjects, and with whom I shared many happy hours playing cello–piano duets. Jennifer Keith read several chapters and helped to improve them immensely, and both she and Jim Evans offered invaluable advice on eighteenth-century texts. Other colleagues to whom I owe special thanks are Denise Baker, Chris Hodgkins, Ali Schultheis, Stephen Stallcup, Annette Van, Amy Vines, and Anne Wallace. Janet Boseovski, Stuart Marcovitch, Dave Lefkowitz, and Alli Wetterhahn have all helped to make Greensboro home for me, and I am delighted to have them as friends.

While writing this book, I received financial support from the Folger Shakespeare Library, the Gillman Shakespeare Fellowship, and the Bennett Memorial Fellowship at Columbia. At the Folger, I benefited tremendously from the expertise and guidance of Barbara Diefendorf, as well as from the assistance of Georgianna Ziegler and Heather Wolfe. A New Faculty Research Grant and a Summer Excellence Research Grant from UNCG enabled me to travel to archives in England and provided funding for my research assistant, Michelle Coppedge, who helped me track down essential bibliographic information. A 2006–2007 Barbara Thom Postdoctoral Fellowship at the Huntington Library allowed me to spend a blissful year in Southern California completing the book. I am immensely grateful to Roy Ritchie for his kindness and hospitality, as well as to the excellent staff at the Huntington, especially Susi Krasnoo, Sue Hodson, and Mary Robertson, for all of their assistance.

Many other colleagues have provided me with helpful criticism and advice at various stages of the project. I would like to thank the wonderful group of scholars I worked with at the Huntington, especially David Armitage, Joyce Chaplin, Jonathan Earle, Jared Farmer, Lori Anne Ferrell, Will Fisher, Amy Froide, Heidi Brayman Hackel, Karen Halttunen, Deb Harkness, Cynthia Herrup, Heather James, Peter Lake, Rebecca Lemon, Josh Piker, Cara Robertson, Francesca Sawaya, and Leslie Tuttle. I am also grateful to Doug Brooks, Graham Bradshaw, David Evett, Katie Field, Erin Kelly, Erica Longfellow, and Michael Neill for offering insightful comments on earlier versions of the project that were presented at conferences and elsewhere. Julie Eckerle, Stephanie O'Hara, and Tom Rutter deserve special thanks not only for reading portions of the manuscript but also for being such supportive friends and colleagues while it was being completed. Mary Campbell, Thea Davis, Sydney Foster, and Kerry Hotopp have encouraged my literary studies for many years and have enriched my life in ways both big and small.

At Palgrave, I would like to thank Farideh Koohi-Kamali for her interest in and continued support for the project. Brigitte Shull patiently answered all of my editorial questions and was enormously helpful in getting the book ready for publication. Ivo Kamps and the anonymous reader for Palgrave provided amazingly cogent and thoughtful responses to the manuscript, and I am extremely grateful for their detailed readings and suggestions for revision.

An earlier version of chapter 1 appeared as "Labors of Love: Women, Marriage, and Service in *Twelfth Night* and *The Compleat Servant-Maid*," in the *Shakespearean International Yearbook* 5 (Aldershot: Ashgate Publishing, 2005), 103–126; and part of chapter 2 previously appeared as "Leaning Too Hard Upon the Pen: Suburb Wenches and City Wives in *Westward Ho*," in *Medieval and Renaissance Drama in England* 15 (Madison, NJ: Fairleigh Dickinson University Press, 2003), 224–242. I thank Ashgate Publishing and Associated University Presses for permission to reprint this material here. The cover image, a kitchen scene from Nicholas de Bonnefons's *The French Gardiner*, trans. John Evelyn (London, 1658) is reproduced by permission of The Huntington Library, San Marino, California.

Finally, I owe an enormous debt of gratitude to my parents, Frank and Pat Dowd, to whom this book is dedicated, for their love, support, and guidance over the years. Mike Cowie has shared his life and his wisdom with me, and I thank him for always reminding me what really matters. He has truly made working on this project a labor of love.

A Note on the Text

When quoting from early modern manuscripts and printed texts in original or facsimile editions, I have retained original orthography except for silently expanding contractions, changing long s to short, and modernizing the letters i, j, u, and v where necessary. Dates in parentheses indicate the year that a work was first published, unless otherwise indicated.

INTRODUCTION

For female laborers in England, the seventeenth century was a period of remarkable economic change. The population of England was growing exponentially, the country was witnessing substantial expansion in trade and consumerism, and, as the economy shifted gradually from a feudal economy to one more consistently based on wage labor, guilds were increasingly being replaced by labor contracts and by more casual economic arrangements. But in the midst of this burgeoning consumer economy characterized by a newly diverse workforce, William Shakespeare wrote *Twelfth Night*, a play in which two female servants rise dramatically in social station *not* through their financial expertise or proficiency at domestic skills but through their ability to secure promising marriages. Maria's clever manipulation of Malvolio leads to her marriage to Sir Toby, and Viola famously ends the play fortuitously positioned as Orsino's "fancy's queen" (5.1.387), substituting the role of mistress for the discarded role of subordinate page.[1] Nor was this kind of idealized narrative unique to Shakespeare. Though more acutely aware of the economic realities of early modern culture than Shakespeare's romantic comedy, Isabella Whitney's poetic miscellany *A Sweet Nosgay* nevertheless deploys a similar narrative trajectory, one in which female servants progress steadily toward marriage regardless of financial difficulties. Given the diversified and wage-driven economy in which these texts were written, what might have been the cultural significance of such fanciful fictions?

Women's Work in Early Modern English Literature and Culture argues that the social, religious, and economic changes that transformed early modern English culture prompted the development of new and sometimes surprising narratives about women's work.

Reading texts from both the public theater and the pens of early modern Englishwomen, this book demonstrates that narratives about working women profoundly shape the texts in which they appear, including works such as *Twelfth Night* and *A Sweet Nosgay* that do not seem at first glance to engage with questions about women's labor. These fictional stories play an integral role in a society that was both transformed and deeply troubled by women's increasingly diversified labor within England's proto-capitalist economy. Idealized stories about female servants whose work ends neatly in marriage, for instance, offer a reassuring fantasy of social order to those who might be concerned about women's ambiguous position within a volatile service economy—one that was newly based on yearly contracts and variable wages. These narratives thus serve a crucial social function, namely, to construe and define the limits of female subjectivity within a shifting and contested labor market. In addition to service, this study considers several types of work—including midwifery and wet-nursing, housework, and educational work—that changed significantly during the seventeenth century, generating new discursive formulations of women's economic, political, and religious authority. This book investigates literature's role in this historical transformation, revealing how popular texts shaped the cultural understanding of women's work in early modern England.

Englishwomen's work took a variety of forms in the seventeenth century, as popular literature of the period makes clear.[2] In the ballad *A Womans Work is never done*, for instance, the female speaker describes the wide range of daily tasks for which she is responsible. These include cooking a meal ("some wholesom mess") to feed her husband and children, sweeping and cleaning the house, breast-feeding her "one sucking Childe," and making the beds "until [her] back, and sides, and arms do ake." The repeated refrain of the title highlights the inevitability and even monotony of many of these tasks; in one stanza the speaker laments: "Sometimes I knit, and sometimes I spin, / Sometimes I wash, and sometimes I do wring, / Sometimes I sit and sewe by my self alone" before concluding with the recurrent axiom "And thus a Womans work is never done."[3] Ballads such as this one portray women's daily tasks as diverse, time-consuming, and rigorous, ranging from needlework to cooking to breast-feeding.[4] The varied nature of women's labor in the period is further borne out by historical and demographic studies, which reveal that the characteristic diversity of women's employment was directly linked to the gendered division of labor. In contrast to early modern men, women of the period changed occupations more frequently throughout their

lifetimes, meaning that they were more likely than men to participate in multiple sectors of the labor economy over the course of their
lives. Working women, according to Katrina Honeyman and Jordan
Goodman:

> were generally more prone than men to long periods of underemploy-
> ment and unemployment, and enjoyed few of the security buffers built
> into men's work. In industrial activities women were more dependent
> upon monetary wage payments than were men. With little other com-
> pensation, women workers were particularly vulnerable to the vagaries
> of the early modern economy. This reinforced the irregular rhythm
> of work.[5]

Though the intermittent nature of employment would have affected
women lower down on the social scale most dramatically, and often
with dire financial consequences, it also meant that middling class
and even elite women were often directly involved in England's labor
economy at some point in their lives, even if their work was temporary. Indeed, women from all social levels participated in paid and
unpaid forms of labor, and a high number of them (particularly in
London) were "wholly or partly dependent on their own earnings
for their living."[6] Women's labor was thus crucial to the functionality
of early modern social institutions as diverse as the family, the retail
marketplace, and the church.

The seventeenth century witnessed several significant historical
developments that greatly influenced how women worked and how
their labor was culturally understood. One of the most fundamental changes to early modern England's labor force was its dramatic
increase in size. The population of England exploded during the sixteenth and seventeenth centuries, doubling between 1520 and 1680,
when it reached about 5 million.[7] In tandem with this growth in population, early modern England saw a substantial increase in trade and
consumerism as English families became more dependent on goods
produced outside of the home. The number of imported goods rose
dramatically during this period, a development predicated on both
the increase in England's purchasing power and on "the growth of
English commercial and colonial power, which brought much lower
prices for some products."[8] Furthermore, as the economy shifted
gradually to favor contractual, wage-based models of labor, the guild
system largely gave way to more varied and informal working arrangements, particularly for female workers.[9] England's rapidly developing
consumer economy combined with the sheer size of its population

thus both demanded and produced a larger, more diverse workforce. Many of these workers were drawn toward urban centers, most notably London, looking for either subsistence-level work or for potentially more prosperous work as apprentices, servants, or midwives.[10] This urban migration, together with the variety and unpredictability that characterized much employment in the period, helped to create a labor force that was socially and geographically mobile.

These economic and demographic changes were particularly relevant to women who worked as servants, midwives, and wet nurses, as we will see more fully in chapters 1 and 2. Such women could often pose potential challenges to household governance due to their anomalous place within early modern social hierarchy: they were expected to possess and demonstrate a range of skills and forms of cultural authority, and yet they were also subordinate to the master or family for whom they worked. These kinds of implicit contradictions make it tempting to view such female workers as a testament to a "crisis" of order and gender relations, a term that some scholars have used to describe the period between 1550 and 1700 in England. However, I instead follow Martin Ingram, Laura Gowing, and others in resisting such terminology as ultimately unhelpful in describing how social and economic change occurs.[11] As Gowing argues, "Gender is *always* in contest: gender relations seem to be continually renegotiated around certain familiar points."[12] Work is clearly one of these points, a vexed social and economic issue that has prompted the renegotiation and reformulation of gender relations at various historical moments both well before and well after the early modern period. And yet, though I resist labeling this era a definitive time of crisis, I nevertheless contend that in the ongoing process of imagining work as a specifically gendered category of analysis, the early modern period was one of particular urgency. As in earlier centuries, the implicit mandates of a patriarchal culture meant that women's subordination had to be repeatedly advocated and culturally reinforced. But demographic changes and a fundamental transformation of the nature of England's workforce brought concerns about women's work and cultural authority to the fore in new and pressing ways. As a result, I argue, women such as servants and wet nurses, whose jobs often called social boundaries into question, emerged as key figures in early modern writers' attempts to comprehend and discursively manage a changing social order.

Women who worked more exclusively within the household experienced similar upheavals during this period, though these changes were linked as much to religion as they were to economics or demographics.

Though the changes it heralded certainly did not happen overnight, the Reformation was unquestionably instrumental in shaping and reimagining gender relations in the late sixteenth and seventeenth centuries. Following the Reformation in England, women assumed positions of greater authority within their households, working as spiritual stewards and teachers. A key component of Protestant domestic ideology, this heightened emphasis on women's familial and spiritual roles altered the nature of gender relations within the household. And yet, as I discuss more extensively in chapters 3 and 4, this gradual increase in domestic influence for housewives and mothers did not remain uncontested. Instead, moralists and writers of the period struggled to define the precise scope and nature of women's household labors and the necessary limits to female agency in the home. The redefinition of women's religious and domestic role in the post-Reformation household fundamentally transformed not only the balance of power and practical duties within the home but also the spiritual opportunities available to women who labored to maintain the economic and moral well-being of their homes and families.

Women's working conditions, their cultural authority as laborers, and their occupational opportunities were thus changing significantly over the course of the seventeenth century. These changes were slow and uneven; they do not, for example, attest to a medieval "golden age" for women workers or a sharp decline in women's working conditions in the early modern period.[13] Nor were many of these changes recognized as such until decades or even centuries later. That is, it would be misleading to work backward from the Industrial Revolution in order to trace the "prehistory" of England's capitalist workforce, since the seventeenth-century labor economy obviously did not recognize itself as a precondition to later historical developments. Nevertheless, new forms of women's labor and new concerns about women's position within England's developing consumer economy clearly emerged during the seventeenth century.[14] And by the eighteenth century, as I discuss more specifically in the individual chapters that follow, women's work was beginning to look very different indeed, being characterized by a more rigid gendered division of labor, the feminization of many occupations (including service and housework), and a general decline in professional opportunities, such as midwifery.[15] My analysis thus focuses on how texts from the period engaged creatively with a labor economy that was shifting in subtle yet notable ways. Instead of emphasizing a strictly teleological narrative of historical change at the expense of contradictory discourses, I am interested in retrieving and exploring the often idiosyncratic and contested narratives that were created to make cultural sense of the role of women workers within the dynamic economy of early modern England.

This leads me, then, to comment on the specific role of literary narrative in this process. What can fictional stories tell us about women's work? How did such narratives shape the ideologies of labor that were circulating and developing during the seventeenth century? By the beginning of the seventeenth century, the increased availability of printed texts and the popularity of London's public stage meant that more representations of working women were available and reaching a broader audience than ever before. In analyzing a variety of these texts, I argue that the social upheavals of early modern England helped to generate new stories about women's work. In turn, these literary narratives both facilitated and problematized cultural change through the histories of working Englishwomen that they imagined. During a time in which women were taking on a wide range of occupational positions and were acquiring new forms of authority within post-Reformation culture, these stories discursively resolve some of the most pressing concerns associated with women's labor. Often these concerns revolve around questions of agency. For example, how can women's duty to educate and socialize their children best be articulated in a culture governed by the dictates of coverture, in which a wife was officially "covered" by her husband's legal identity? In struggling to find answers to these kinds of cultural questions, writers from the period create narratives that imagine and delineate emerging, and often limited, forms of subject-hood for female laborers. That is, in the process of defining women's work, these texts inevitably produce innovative depictions of working women, ushering in new ideas about women's marketable skills, domestic authority, and professional responsibilities. In tracing specific narrative developments over the period, I am interested in the role of popular literature and, specifically, recurring narrative structures in the cultural redefinition of women's labor. This book thus reveals how early modern literature carved out an imaginative space for the female worker, fundamentally transforming cultural perceptions about women's place in English society.

This study follows recent scholarship interested in developing a field of inquiry begun by Alice Clark in her groundbreaking book, *Working Life of Women in the Seventeenth Century*, first published in 1919.[16] Clark's analysis, which first documented the lives of early modern female laborers and the shift in their economic position during the seventeenth century, has been joined by an outpouring of historical and literary studies in the last few decades that have continued to investigate early modern women's active participation in various sectors of the labor market and analyze how that work was reimagined in various kinds of early modern texts.[17] Most of these studies, including Natasha Korda's *Shakespeare's Domestic Economies: Gender and Property in Early Modern England* and Wendy Wall's *Staging Domesticity: Household Work and English Identity in Early Modern Drama*, have emphasized the material and economic histories of early modern women labor or have explored women's work in order to query the nature of domesticity. By contrast, I shift focus away from domesticity as a primary category of analysis. While recognizing the domestic location of much of women's work, I expand the categories of labor to include those occupations, such as service, midwifery, and education, that often took place outside the bounds of individual households. In addition, I take an approach that is less invested in the materiality of early modern culture per se than in the process by which narratives throughout the period participated in delimiting the scope and nature of women's work. In thus taking narrative and gender as its primary terms of analysis, this book considers how form—the structure and design of textual discourses—actively engages with history to determine how women were constituted as working subjects in seventeenth-century England.

By focusing on narrative, my project aims to integrate feminist historicist methodologies with formalist ones.[18] Like many who have studied early modern women, I read representations of female workers in terms of their complex intersections with economic, social, and literary contexts, and I demonstrate the ways in which differences in class, age, religion, and geography affect the stories that are told about working women. But I also contend that these feminist concerns are intimately related to the narratological structures of individual texts. This study thus seeks to expand the interpretative possibilities of formalist inquiry by building on the work done by practitioners of what has come to be known as the "new" or "historical formalism." This methodological approach to literary analysis was initiated by the work of Raymond Williams and Fredric Jameson to interrogate the ways in which form mediates between the content of a text and its historical contexts.[19] The value of this critical method is that it proposes to examine "every text as a complex and unique interaction of historically specific formal and contextual ideologies."[20] Textual form and its (many) social contexts are not treated as independent categories but as mutually constitutive and culturally productive. Historical formalism thus attempts to understand more precisely, in Jameson's resonant phrase, "what happens when plot falls into history."[21]

However, Jameson's evocative pairing of these two categories fails to capture the full complexity of their relationship. As suggestive as his formulation is, it implies that plot and history are mutually exclusive domains; plot remains outside of history, at least until it "falls" into it. But one of the primary aims of this study is to demonstrate that the stories circulated about early modern women workers *are* the trace history of those workers in the sense that those stories actively produce the definitions, subject positions, and discursive contexts by which those women were called into being as working subjects in early modern England.[22] Embedded within history, plot, in other words, is also constitutive of that history, even if that process is often messy and contested. The stories that I examine throughout this book—however fanciful, conventional, or convoluted they may sometimes seem—are thus historical to their very core, as they are always engaged in the process of positioning the female worker within the complex and shifting economy of seventeenth-century England. Taking individual narrative strands rather than larger generic categories as its primary focus, my own practice of historical formalism is also narrower in scope than the approaches to genre developed by Williams and Jameson. By combining some of the theoretical methods of narratology with the general analytical premises of new formalism, I concentrate on the ways in which narrative structures within individual texts—and the stories held in common between different texts—have historical and material consequences.

Narratologists often refer to the two key categories of "story"—a sequence of events—and "discourse"—the narration or representation of those events. While classic theories of narrative, dating to the 1960s and the work of the French structuralists, emphasize that story is necessarily prior to and independent of discourse, poststructuralist or "postclassical" narratology resists this distinction, stressing instead that an individual event can often be "a product of discursive forces rather than a given reported by discourse."[23] Furthermore, more recent theories of narrative share with new formalism more generally the conviction that narrative dynamically engages with its historical moment. In the words of David Herman, "stories are what they are not because of their form alone, but because of a complex interplay between narrative form and the contexts of narrative interpretation, broadly construed."[24] In using the term "narrative" to analyze stories about women's work found within individual texts, I thus suggest first that these stories do have a sequence of events, not so much in terms of definitive plots, but in terms of standard features and episodes that get repeated and redeployed. In chapter 3, for instance, we see that women's housework is frequently represented through a narrative of proof and introspection so that the pious housewifery of a heroine can be manifested to readers. Though this is not a "plot" in the traditional, narratological sense, it is a notable recurring pattern that helps to shape stage plays, women's private diaries, and the stories of housewifery that they tell.

Additionally, I find the category of narrative useful for describing the process by which early modern literary texts engage with a historical moment marked, as we have seen, by large-scale social, economic, and religious changes. As Hayden White, following Roland Barthes, has ably articulated, narrative often arises out of a desire to "have real events display the coherence, integrity, fullness, and closure of an image of life that is and can only be imaginary."[25] In this sense, he argues, historical texts and literary texts share the same propensity for narrative, for a satisfying formal structure to make sense out of individual events. White's emphasis on the coherence of narrative has been challenged by poststructuralist and feminist critics who have rightly argued that not all narratives follow the plan of "well-made stories," nor do they always achieve the "integrity" and "closure" that White describes.[26] Like these critics, I do not assume narratives to be internally consistent. In tracing recurring stories and narrative structures in this book, I do not suggest that these narratives are invariable, single, or even predictable. They always make room for alternative stories or suggest precisely what must be excluded from a given narrative to make it function in a certain way. Similarly, I am not proposing an archetypal theory of narrative, such as the one developed by Northrop Frye, which tends to flatten out historical differences in favor of universal aesthetic categories.[27] Instead, I argue that it is precisely in the gaps, fissures, and inconsistencies within individual stories that we can locate the sedimented traces of social struggle and the points of tension within early modern ideological debates about women's work.[28]

But at the same time, White suggests that the *desire* for narrative coherence, or at least for narrative intelligibility, is notable in and of itself. Though this desire is inevitably thwarted by the unpredictability of texts themselves, it helps to explain the processes by which literary texts both respond to and feed back into the culture of which they are a part. I base my arguments in this study on the premise that the act of storytelling, the literary process of relating early modern women's work in narrative form, is rooted in part in the desire to represent, explain, or clarify these figures, even if that attempt is predetermined to fail. During a time in which the position of women within the English labor economy was in need of clarification and definition, these narratives perform an important social function by offering reassuring fantasies, posing potential solutions, and managing perceived dangers. In the end, these stories also delimit the forms of cultural authority available to working women in seventeenth-century England.

By incorporating feminist, historicist, and formalist methodologies, this study seeks to articulate the productive capacity of early modern narratives about women's work. I attend throughout to both the commonalities and shared narratives that link individual texts and to the nuanced rhetorical, structural, and representational details that signal fissures or tensions within those larger narratives. In doing so, I also subtly depart from some literary scholarship on early modern England that tends to read textual discourse as a direct signifier of societal preoccupations and unease. While the process of unearthing the cultural resonances of literary narratives is a valuable one, this methodology often implies that one should read *through* the text to get at the social meanings and discords that lie behind it. Instead of reading representations of women's work as transparent textual demonstrations of cultural anxieties, I treat these narratives as culturally useful fictions that not only absorb and respond to early modern culture but also develop with a certain degree of autonomy and according to an internal logic that enables them to contribute actively to the processes of cultural definition and social change. Popular literature from the period displays a unique ability to construct engaging *stories* about what is going on in the world, to produce fictional narratives that can influence cultural ideologies. As such, these texts do not merely register social problems; they help to solve, contextualize, and even, on occasion, exacerbate those problems.

Conceptually, this study begins with drama, with the canonical and obscure plays produced for the public theater between 1590 and 1640 that have long been considered among the most important literary texts of the period.[29] Drama is a particularly energized and tension-filled genre. It is a medium unusually invested in representing actions—including women's actions—and the controversies, paradoxes, and possibilities that those actions engendered. Its stock and trade was the dramatization of conflict, and, as numerous studies on the early modern theater have demonstrated, it was remarkably successful at staging social, religious, and political conflicts for a large and diverse audience.[30] As such, early modern drama is an especially rich and productive genre to consider in a study that aims to investigate not only representations of women but narratives about how women's labor was constructed, challenged, and debated in the period.

But if this book begins analytically with the stage, it does not end there. That is, though I choose drama as my primary literary focus, I also decenter these texts and resist the urge to privilege them as sole sites of inquiry by reading early modern plays alongside texts by women in which they represent their own labors through didactic, fanciful, or semiautobiographical means.[31] In arguing that seventeenth-century writers created specific stories about working women in order to define and articulate the cultural position of these figures during a period of social, religious, and economic change, I am interested in the patterns and commonalities that often (and often surprisingly) span gendered and formal divides. I thus attend to the nonfictional accounts and prescriptive treatises written by early modern women alongside the works of male dramatists—rather than study these two groups of texts in isolation, as is often done—in order to broaden and complicate our understanding of women's labor in the period and to continue efforts to resituate early modern women writers within literary contexts not determined solely by gender.[32] In my chapter on housework, for example, I consider representations of women's quotidian domestic chores in the plays of Thomas Heywood and William Rowley alongside those in the personal diaries of Lady Margaret Hoby and Anne Clifford. Though these texts differ significantly in style, form, and audience, they all depict women's housework in spiritual terms, thereby creating similar discursive links between women's successful domestic management and their ability to manage their own souls. Reading early modern texts across gendered lines thus enables me to pinpoint the narratives that appear with notable frequency throughout the culture—narratives that appealed to early modern writers and readers as they debated, defined, and categorized the work of seventeenth-century women.

Putting these texts in conversation with each other also emphasizes the historical fluidity of early modern print culture and the connections between male and female authorship that could be made on a quotidian basis. A Londoner who attended a production of *The Fair Maid of the Exchange* in the afternoon may well have spent her evening perusing a popular advice book such as Dorothy Leigh's *The Mothers Blessing* or consulting Elizabeth Clinton's *The Countesse of Lincolnes Nurserie*.[33] Attending to women's writing, which was actually published in greater numbers *after* 1640, also allows me to push a bit on the chronological limits of the Renaissance public theater, thereby demonstrating how similar narratives get reformulated and redeployed in texts from both slightly earlier and slightly later periods.[34] Particularly in my opening chapter on servants, in which my chronological scope is notably broader than in later chapters, I look at texts written by women that fall just outside of the 1590–1640 timeframe in order to emphasize representational trends that persist throughout the period as well as changes that occur in England as the seventeenth century gives way to the eighteenth. Similarly, examining stories about women workers from the end of the seventeenth century and into the early eighteenth century, as I do in my epilogue, allows me to discuss some of the factors that distinguished the period of 1600–1700 from the era that followed it.

Most of the female-authored texts I consider could be loosely characterized as "extraliterary"; they include diaries, practical guides, miscellanies, and mothers' legacies. In these texts, women represent themselves as workers; they describe and reimagine their own labors as servants, housewives, or educators. In other cases, they offer pre-scriptive guidelines to women in the labor economy, advising them on how to choose a good wet nurse or how best to behave as a ser-vant. However, though it may be tempting to do so, I do not endow these extraliterary sources by women with a mystical ability to bring us nearer to the "real," to the way in which women "really" worked or what their lives "really" looked like. A woman's diary, though dif-ferent in form, scope, and intended audience from a stage play, still offers a highly mediated discursive representation of women and the work they performed. To emphasize this point, I intentionally shift the directional nature of my reading throughout the book in order to resist the notion that these two groups of texts offer categorically distinct points of access into early modern culture. In some chapters, I begin with the analysis of a play; in others, I start with readings of women's writing. Nowhere in this book, then, will readers be able to find an objective portrait of working women or a text that definitively aligns with the actual experiences of these women. To put it most sim-ply, this is not a history of women's work. Readers of this book will find instead an emphasis on narrative as a vital social force, with real consequences for how women's working lives were understood and envisioned in early modern England. *Women's Work in Early Modern English Literature and Culture* is neither a book about the stage nor a book about women's writing per se but rather a book about the ways in which these two sites of cultural production jointly participated in the process of narrating the seventeenth-century female worker.

In each of the chapters that follow, I pinpoint and discuss some of the most significant stories that early modern writers told about women's work. My approach in each chapter is to highlight a primary narrative that gets repeated with some consistency during the period. In chapter 2, for example, I discuss the work of midwives and wet nurses and argue that early modern texts frequently represent these forms of labor by creating narratives based on spatial separation and distancing. In this case, the recurring narrative pattern is predominantly a cautionary one; rhetorical structures safely segregate midwives and wet nurses from birth mothers and thus compensate for the fluid social and economic boundaries that attended early modern wet-nursing and midwifery practices. However, I also analyze the narratives that are left out or marginalized by these dominant stories, the alternatives that are discursively available, and the discrepancies present. In the case of midwives and wet nurses, we see glimpses of other narratives in which these female workers are not simply banished to the margins but rather are assigned cultural agency by virtue of their physical mobility and their ability to control access to bodies and origins. In many cases, such competing stories can be found within the same texts. Juliet's Nurse in *Romeo and Juliet*, for example, is represented both as the sole authority on Juliet's weaning and as a meddling figure who must ultimately be distanced from the Capulet family. It is in the tension between these narratives that we can see the processes of historical change and discursive transformation. By analyzing narratives that are in conversation and often in conflict with each other, I account for the textual practices that helped to define women's work over the course of the early modern period.

The individual chapters of this book take up four types of women's work that saw profound changes during the seventeenth century. Ranging from domestic service to the education of children, these occupations engaged the vast majority of early modern Englishwomen. Indeed, most women would have taken on at least one of these tasks at some point in their lives. Without articulating a precise or rigid chronology, I have organized my chapters to coincide with the general trajectory of women's experiences in the labor market. That is, I begin with service in chapter 1 primarily because service would have been the first occupation held by many early modern women. I then move on to types of work—wet-nursing and midwifery, housework, and educational work—that women would have usually performed later in their lives, perhaps after leaving an initial position in service. This organizational structure is meant to be suggestive rather than absolute.[35] In emphasizing the work women did over the course of their lives, I follow a model offered by Barbara Harris in her study of the "careers" of late medieval women in *English Aristocratic Women*

1450–1550: Marriage and Family, Property and Careers. Harris argues that Yorkist and early Tudor aristocratic women combined work, domestic business, and politics throughout the course of their lives. Instead of dichotomizing women's activities into "either public or private" by separating women's political and economic engagements from the traditional reproductive and domestic duties associated with the female "life cycle," Harris emphasizes the "full extent and political significance of their contribution to their families, class, and society."[36] By avoiding the reductive binaries of public and private, domestic and political, this kind of critical methodology encourages a more nuanced reading of women's lives and the stories that were told about those lives. In the chapters that follow, I take a similar approach to the "careers" of women in the early modern period, demonstrating how the complexities of their working lives, broadly defined, were conceptualized in seventeenth-century texts.

I begin in chapter 1, "Labors of Love: Female Servants and the Marriage Plot," with representations of domestic service, one of the most common forms of women's work in early modern England, and one that placed vast numbers of young women from all social levels into unstable, temporary positions. Service as an institution was changing considerably during this period, as employers were becoming more reliant on an economically diverse and geographically mobile workforce that could be engaged for increasingly shorter periods of labor. Despite a general expectation that women would leave service to get married, many female servants found it extremely difficult to save the requisite money for a dowry and, as a result, often experienced significant disruptions and hardships both during their term of service and after it was officially completed. I argue that these social and economic developments during the period prompted the creation of new literary narratives. Texts such as Shakespeare's *Twelfth Night* and Isabella Whitney's *A Sweat Nosgay* offer their readers teleological narratives in which service ends neatly in marriage, and in doing so they reassuringly restore the continuity between women's service work and their role as future wives.

These tales were socially satisfying in that they mitigated very real concerns about the financial hardships often faced by female servants. However, these stories also frequently depict the agency of female servants in terms of their economic wherewithal and the mastery of skills. This was an important development, as it heralded the further changes to the institution of service that would occur by the eighteenth century, when service would become a more professional and permanent occupation that demanded unique skills and training.

This chapter thus traces two concurrent trends in the representation of women's service in seventeenth-century literature. It explores the ways in which the fanciful, teleological marriage narrative gradually began to forge a discursive link between female servants and an authority that could be gained through practical, marketable skills. And it also examines the surprising resilience and cultural utility of the marriage plot as late as 1677, when Hannah Woolley published her practical guide *The Compleat Servant-Maid*.

The second chapter, "The Spatial Syntax of Midwifery and Wet-Nursing," considers representations of women's reproductive work. Both midwifery and wet-nursing were occupations that witnessed historic highs in both employment numbers and social prominence during the seventeenth century, and yet women who held these positions were often treated as suspect since their jobs depended on a degree of proximity to and physical intimacy with mothers, children, and other household members who were usually above them in social station. Midwives and wet nurses thus often needed to mediate between different class positions and between the different social spaces that those positions signified in order to carry out their work. If the story of early modern servants was that of a vexed narrative trajectory leading precariously toward marriage, the story of midwives and wet nurses was often a story about space, and specifically about the imprecise divisions between social spaces that attended these occupations. This chapter argues that texts from the period attempt to clarify the ambiguous social, economic, and spatial positions of wet nurses and midwives by creating narratives of separation and compartmentalization that assign these figures to clear-cut social spaces within early modern English culture. I examine how stage plays such as John Webster and Thomas Dekker's *Westward Ho* use the physicality of London's geography to reestablish separations between mothers and midwives, and I consider how Shakespeare's *Romeo and Juliet* and a popular prescriptive treatise, Elizabeth Clinton's *The Countesse of Lincolnes Nurserie*, similarly deploy rhetorical strategies to erect divisions that segregate mothers from the wet nurses they hire.

In each of these texts, midwives and wet nurses accrue cultural authority through their geographical mobility and their ability to mediate between social categories. In recognizing and often legitimizing these forms of agency, these narratives insist that maternal authority is located in multiple sites; it is not restricted to the birth mother alone. In part, this narrative dispersal helped to legitimize the labor practices of well-to-do seventeenth-century families who hired both midwives and wet nurses in large numbers. Birth mothers and their hired help could thus exist discursively in a fragile symbiosis within the early modern reproductive economy. But we can also see in this chapter that early modern narratives participated in a gradual and contested historical process whereby maternity was consolidated and naturalized in the figure of the birth mother by the eighteenth century. In other words, the stories that push wet nurses and midwives to the narrative margins would eventually succeed in eliminating these figures altogether.

Certainly not all early modern women received money or goods in exchange for their labor, and the next two chapters of the book consider forms of women's work—housework and the work of educating children—that were almost exclusively unpaid.[37] These types of labor are consequently more amorphous in nature than service, midwifery, or wet-nursing and less clearly defined in terms of occupational categories. In examining stories about housewives and female educators in the second half of the book, I also shift attention to the ways in which religion and spirituality became deeply intertwined with early modern discourses about women's work within the post-Reformation household. Though religion is an important category of analysis for me throughout this study, it becomes particularly so in chapters 3 and 4, where I demonstrate that meditative practices of introspection and guidelines on parental duties for the moral and spiritual upbringing of children had profound affects on how early modern texts narrated women's housework and pedagogical duties. Both of these chapters consider the expanded authority ascribed to women within the household in post-Reformation discourse, but they also demonstrate that prior to the consolidation of women's spiritual and domestic roles in the eighteenth century, the nature and scope of women's duties within the home were imprecisely defined. Early modern writers construct narratives about women's household labors that seek both to clarify these duties and to elucidate the very nature of female domestic authority.

Chapter 3, "Divine Drudgery: The Spiritual Logic of Housework," argues that women's daily household labors were frequently represented in spiritual terms. Seventeenth-century Englishwomen were increasingly expected to maintain authority over their households and to produce domestic order through both physical labor and spiritual devotion. But these expanded expectations for women's domestic duties coincided with Protestantism's heightened focus on introspective piety and self-scrutiny. The result was an epistemological gap: women's pious housewifery was essential to household order, but as piety could only be internally regulated, it became difficult to monitor or guarantee this order. I argue that early modern texts create narratives that make visible an essential link between women's housework and personal piety, often deploying evidentiary narrative structures in which the unseen aspects of introspective piety are made clear to audiences and readers. By representing the invisible links between piety and housework, these texts, including the diaries of Lady Margaret Hoby and Lady Anne Clifford, and Thomas Heywood and William Rowley's *Fortune By Land and Sea*, tell a reassuring story about housewives' abilities to ensure practical and spiritual order within their homes. Or, in the case of Heywood's *A Woman Killed with Kindness*, they caution audiences about the disorder that may result if pious housewifery is neglected.

These narratives also begin to construe the housewife's subjectivity in terms of her successful management of her domestic duties and her own soul. As we will continue to see in chapter 4, this ideological demarcation of domesticity, work, and piety as inherently feminine domains would take place in the eighteenth century. We can, however, witness this formulation beginning to take shape in earlier, seventeenth-century texts in which housewives accrue authority by virtue of their selective, and pointedly gendered, skills of pious housewifery. This is not to say that stories about housewives remain constant over the period. Indeed, as women's household duties become part of a well-defined sexual division of labor later in the eighteenth century, the epistemological gap between introspective piety and its outward manifestation in orderly housewifery no longer warrants such pressing concern. But by focusing on the previous century in which such clear divisions were not yet imaginable, this chapter emphasizes seventeenth-century writers' efforts to clarify and categorize women's housewifery by creating evidentiary narrative structures that celebrate expedient and spiritual housework or denounce it when it fails. In doing so, these stories offer the semblance of stability and epistemological clarity even when these were absent or, at best, uncertain.

The fourth chapter, "Household Pedagogies: Female Educators and the Language of Legacy," examines texts that represent women's work as educators and socializers of children. I consider how writers including Shakespeare and Dorothy Leigh struggle to articulate women's educative functions (their "household pedagogies") within a discourse of coverture, in which a wife's agency was ostensibly subsumed under that of her husband. In theory, women's specific duties to educate their children were occluded by general mandates that parents be jointly responsible for their children's upbringing. In practice, however, women in post-Reformation England were increasingly expected and enjoined to play key roles in the economic, spiritual, and educational lives of their families. I argue that stories about female educators attempt to resolve this paradox and offset the potential for female agency within the discourse of coverture by linking women's pedagogy to inheritance via narratives that emphasize seamless transition and transference. In doing so, they suggest that direct generational transmission is crucial to both humanist pedagogy and patrilineal inheritance practices.

At a time in which maternal authority in the household was increasingly assumed yet not clearly delimited, these stories create an appealing and straightforward narrative of female pedagogy in which such instruction is linked with patriarchal interests and limited in scope and duration. However, I also demonstrate that in constructing such orderly narratives, these texts are simultaneously struggling with the primary paradox of coverture, namely that the restraints it places on female agency in theory are consistently undermined in practice by the quotidian demands of post-Reformation English society. The intimations of women's domestic initiative that we see in texts such as Elizabeth Grymeston's *Miscelanea, Meditations, Memoratives* and Shakespeare's *All's Well That Ends Well* suggest more sustained subject positions for female educators, though they also inadvertently foreshadow the separate-sphere ideology of the eighteenth century, in which moral education, domesticity, and femininity become conflated. By tracing these narrative discrepancies, I explore the process by which popular stories articulated the scope of women's educative functions under coverture.

In an epilogue, I consider the sermon given at Anne Clifford's funeral in 1676 and William Congreve's turn-of-the-century play *The Way of the World* as discursive evidence of the changing ideologies of women's work in the late seventeenth century. Looking to this later period helps contextualize and frame the narratives about working women that circulated in the earlier part of the century, offering a diachronic perspective on literary representations of early modern women's work. Furthermore, though sexuality is often heralded as a key component of modern subject-hood, my epilogue suggests that the ideological category of "work" played an equally significant role in the construction of the early modern female subject. As such, analyses of women's work and their textual manifestations will yield current and future dividends to scholars interested in theorizing and historically situating women's subject formation in early modern England.

Not meant to be exhaustive in its coverage of either seventeenth-century women's work or of the texts that represented it, my study presents a suggestive series of case studies rather than a thorough overview or a comprehensive meta-narrative. By considering both drama and women's writing and focusing on four types of women's work that saw significant practical and ideological shifts over the course of the seventeenth century, however, I hope to suggest some of the significant ways in which popular literature participated in the process of historical change and brought into being new subject positions for female workers. Above all, *Women's Work in Early Modern English Literature and Culture* is an argument about narratives and about the processes by which those narratives constructed powerful and long-lasting cultural ideologies that came to define the working lives of early modern women. It unravels and illuminates the stories that helped to make the female worker culturally legible during a period of social, economic, and religious upheavals. This study thus attests not only to the social significance of women's work during this period but also more broadly to the dynamic force of fictional narrative in early modern England.

CHAPTER 1

LABORS OF LOVE: FEMALE SERVANTS
AND THE MARRIAGE PLOT

When William Shakespeare's *Twelfth Night* was first performed around 1600, the institution of service in England was in the process of shifting rapidly, though uneasily, from a feudal model founded primarily on loyalty and obligation to a wage labor system based on the protection of property rights.[1] This is not to say that the period witnessed a shift from the emotive to the economic, as service was always both an economic relationship between masters and subordinates and a complexly personal set of social interactions. However, the nature of this relationship began to change as England developed an increasingly commercial labor system during the sixteenth and seventeenth centuries. Under the feudal ideal of "universal service," laborers offered their services to masters and mistresses in return for protection. Social hierarchy tended to be more rigidly maintained, and both the possibility of upward mobility and the efficacy of personal ambition were significantly limited for servants in domestic positions.[2] As a social institution, the feudal model of service pervaded medieval and early modern culture, and the structures of submission that service engendered permeated virtually all types of social interactions, forming an "unbroken chain of service" that led from the peasant to the monarch and included people from all ranks of society.[3] Formal relationships between masters and servants were understood (at least in theory) in terms of allegiance and honor and could often last for many years. Indeed, as Shakespeare memorably dramatizes in Kent's faithful service to King Lear, the bonds of feudal service could last for the entire span of a servant or master's life.

By the beginning of the seventeenth century, however, this model of service was gradually giving way to a wage labor system in which servants negotiated yearly contracts with employers. As a result, servants increasingly came to depend upon marketable skills in order to obtain new positions or rise in the social hierarchy. The causes of this shift were complex, but during Shakespeare's lifetime the transition away from living-in workers and extended periods of service was fueled in large part by changes in the structure and formation of elite households. Between 1590 and 1620, the size of aristocratic households was sharply reduced—"from an average of one hundred or so each to three or four dozen"—resulting in the replacement of long-term domestic servants with "short-term hirings on a cash basis."[4] As Michael Neill has argued, "In this world of progressively demystified relationships, most household service was coming to seem like a form of wage-slavery, more and more difficult to reconcile—whatever Kent would have us think—with honor or gentility."[5] Contemporary social commentators such as Walter Darell and I.M. expressed similar sentiments, lamenting the decay of aristocratic hospitality and largesse and noting with disdain the increasingly mercenary nature of service.[6] In his idealized and nostalgic treatise, *A Health to the Gentlemanly Profession of Servingmen* (1598), for instance, I.M. laments: "What estate, degree, or calling, can then be more miserable, then the profession of a Servingman: Heere to day, and gone to morow" (J4v). The principles of hospitality and fraternity that supposedly governed the institution of service in earlier days have given way in I.M.'s account to more pecuniary motives, leading to more transitory and unfavorable circumstances for household servants. This fundamental transformation of the service economy is neatly summed up by Orlando's response to his old servant Adam in *As You Like It* (written in 1599):

> O good old man, how well in thee appears
> The constant service of the antique world,
> When service sweat for duty, not for meed!
> Thou art not for the fashion of these times,
> Where none will sweat but for promotion,
> And having that do choke their service up
> Even with the having. It is not so with thee. (2.3.56–62)[7]

In Orlando's wistful commentary, "meed" and "promotion" have replaced "constant service" and "duty" as the primary characteristics of dependent household labor. The "fashion of these times" requires that domestic servants be motivated by money, not by personal devotion. Amidst a growing consumer culture, the feudal concept of universal service endured in nostalgic sentiments such as Orlando's, but it was steadily being replaced by an emerging ideology of service that emphasized ambition, production, and profit. No longer a long-term commitment based on loyalty, the institution of service in seventeenth-century England demanded an economically diverse and geographically mobile work force that could be employed for temporary labor.[8]

This ideological shift had particular significance for women since domestic service was by far the most common occupation for early modern Englishwomen between the ages of fifteen and twenty-four, and women were increasingly replacing men as servants in middling and wealthy households.[9] The temporary nature of wage-based service also had different consequences for women than for men: women were expected to work as servants not in order to gain occupational training per se (as was the case for men) but in order to learn the domestic skills that they would need as wives and to delay their marriages until they were economically and socially prepared for them. Removed from their birth homes and the watchful eyes of parents, female servants occupied ill-defined positions as sexually vulnerable and potentially disorderly singlewomen who were expected to follow an imprecisely defined trajectory that often ended with marriage. However, the cultural expectation that women's departure from service would coincide exactly with the beginning of marriage was frequently undermined by demographic and economic realities. Many female servants experienced a significant gap between the end of their service in their early to mid-twenties and their marriages in their late twenties—a gap often necessitated by poverty—and the lack of sufficient financial resources prevented many female servants from ever marrying.[10] Women's service thus might have had a presumed trajectory in the period, but it was a trajectory with an uncertain duration and ambiguous ending. In the decades surrounding *Twelfth Night*'s first performance, the economic and sexual uncertainties that had come to characterize women's service cried out for solutions, however temporary, provisional, or fanciful those solutions might be.

England's difficult and extended transition from a feudal to a wage-based labor system prompted the creation of new literary narratives about female servants, a process that began in the late sixteenth century and continued throughout the seventeenth century. I argue in this chapter that texts from the period frequently turn to narratives of marriage—progressive and usually romanticized plot structures in which the telos of female service is marriage—in order to offer a palatable solution and a literary order to a form of women's work that was notoriously indeterminate. As an idealized "end" of service, marriage provides a tidy conclusion to a messy and unpredictable social situation while also ensuring that the agency and skills women could acquire while in service are safely transferred to their subsequent occupation as wives. But in offering these solutions, early modern texts simultaneously begin to redefine the scope of female authority by incorporating emerging discourses of skill, marketability, and professionalism into their stories about female servants. The teleological impulses of these narratives, in other words, cannot entirely elide the various forms of cultural authority that these texts imagine for women in service, even if those subject positions are often articulated fleetingly or with reservation. Examining Shakespeare's *Twelfth Night*, Isabella Whitney's *A Sweet Nosgay* (1573), and Hannah Woolley's *The Compleat Servant-Maid* (1677) as pivotal texts in the literary history of early modern female servants, I both trace the particular forms of subject-hood that these texts bring into being and explore the striking resilience and adaptability of the marriage narrative throughout the period despite significant historical changes in women's service work.[11]

FROM SERVICE TO MARRIAGE: BECOMING "FANCY'S QUEEN"

Of all of Shakespeare's comedies, *Twelfth Night* offers the richest possibilities for investigating narratives of female service. Women in service anchor both of the play's two plots: the main plot by Viola (Orsino's cross-dressed page) and the Malvolio subplot by Maria (Olivia's lady-in-waiting). Though the play ultimately insists upon a romanticized progression from service to marriage, this progression is not identical for both characters. While both Viola's and Maria's paths to marriage via service are strikingly disengaged from economic imperatives, Shakespeare dramatizes their respective relationships and influences at court quite differently. In Maria's story in particular, we begin to see a new form of authority emerging for female servants within the rapidly shifting economic contours of seventeenth-century society.

Viola might at first seem an odd choice to include in a discussion of female service since her role in Orsino's household is performed in the guise of a man; it is Cesario, not Viola per se, who serves as a page in Orsino's court. Indeed, most recent critics of the play read Viola and her servant's disguise in relation to narratives of cross-dressing.[12]

Yet, it is significant that Viola makes the choice to enter service while still a female character; at the level of dramatic narrative, Viola follows the culturally sanctioned progression of an aristocratic female domestic servant: she is separated (albeit unexpectedly) from her family, she enters service at court, and she eventually leaves service to get married. Furthermore, the audience is always aware that Viola is a female servant and in possession of, in Jean Howard's phrase, a "properly 'feminine' subjectivity."[13] Viola's structural trajectory in the play thus closely resembles other narratives of female service, but Shakespeare's idealization of her route to marriage is noteworthy both for its historical erasures and for its conservative deployment of the formal conventions of romantic comedy.

Viola's foray into domestic service is coded as privileged from the moment that she decides to disguise herself and become a page at Orsino's court. Though the word "servant" in its modern sense conjures up images of menial labor, it implied a much broader social spectrum in Shakespeare's England. Women from nearly all ranks of early modern society worked as servants in domestic settings; whereas wealthy girls might be employed as ladies-in-waiting at court or as domestic servants in the homes of relatives, poorer girls might be employed in homes that could afford only one live-in servant.[14] For most early modern women, in other words, service was a virtually inevitable corollary to youth.

Viola's exact social position is never clearly delineated in the play, but her initial discussion with the sea captain suggests that she is nobly born. Despite narrowly escaping a shipwreck in which the "ship did split," Viola is still able to reward the captain with gold for his optimistic news about her brother (1.2.9, 18).[15] Furthermore, her decision to enter into service is couched in the rhetoric of choice rather than need. Though the scene seems to imply that Viola chooses her disguise as a practical matter of protection, this motive is not immediately present in Viola's language.[16] Upon hearing the captain speak of Olivia, Viola exclaims:

> O that I serv'd that lady,
> And might not be deliver'd to the world,
> Till I had made mine own occasion mellow,
> What my estate is.   (1.2.40–43)

Viola's entrée into service is thus not conditioned by economic need or the hope of social promotion, as was the case for the vast majority of early modern servants, but by a desire for a temporary respite from the world until the appropriate time when her "estate" may be revealed. Nor does the motive for Viola's service change when the captain encourages her to shift her focus from Olivia's household to that of Duke Orsino. Viola rather ambiguously instructs the captain to "[c]onceal me what I am, and be my aid/ For such disguise as haply shall become/ The form of my intent" (1.2.53–55). The fact that Viola's "intent" cannot be extracted from this scene without a good deal of speculation means that the audience is left with only the vague rhetoric of choice, unencumbered by irksome practicalities. The formal elision of need from Viola's narrative—an elision predicated upon her economic wherewithal at the outset—allows her service work to be from its inception subordinate to her own desire.

Viola profits from both her class standing and from an exceptionally rosy work environment while in service to Orsino. As a page in Orsino's court, she gains the privilege of access and social connection that accompanies her physical nearness to the Duke, a form of early modern "networking" that could significantly benefit those women who served at court.[17] Orsino selects Viola/Cesario as his emissary to Olivia precisely because of her intimate knowledge of his affairs. As he tells her: "I have unclasp'd / To thee the book even of my secret soul" (1.4.13–14). Perhaps even more striking than Viola's intimacy with Orsino is the rapidity of its development. In Viola's first scene in the Duke's court, Valentine informs her that "if the Duke continue these favours towards you, Cesario, you are like to be much advanced: he hath known you but three days, and already you are no stranger" (1.4.1–4). Compared to the typical service experiences of young seventeenth-century Englishwomen who spent seven to ten years in service with little hope of social mobility because of the prevalence of yearly contracts, Viola's narrative of service and preferment is ludicrously accelerated.[18] Indeed, her progress as a servant is romanticized even beyond the scope of the class privilege that attends her nobility; when the Duke tells her to "[p]rosper well in this, / And thou shalt live as freely as thy lord, / To call his fortunes thine," he holds out the promise of a status equality that not even the most fortunately positioned royal servant could expect (1.4.38–40). The excessive idealism of Viola's trajectory as both a comic heroine and a female servant produces a specific fantasy of service characterized by swift advancement and rich rewards that far exceed the typical expectations of servants in wealthy households.

Though Viola's service does lead to her rapid social advancement, there is no indication in the play that she profits monetarily from this social promotion. Though the Duke promises Viola a share in his "fortunes" if she serves him well, and though her financial status is undoubtedly bettered by her eventual marriage, her progress to that marriage via her service is conspicuously devoid of financial recompense. At the end of her first visit to Olivia, the countess offers her money, saying "spend this for me" (1.5.287). But Viola responds by saying, "I am no fee'd post, lady; keep your purse; / My master, not myself, lacks recompense" (1.5.288–289). Viola shifts the word "recompense" from an economic to an emotional context, simultaneously insisting that her own labor be located outside of a money economy. Viola's pose of economic disinterestedness again runs counter to historical narratives of service in which young women worked for many years precisely in order to save up enough money for a dowry. Even well-to-do servants depended upon financial recompense that was often in the form of wages, and saving this money for a dowry was particularly vital to women in the period because they were expected to depend upon husbands rather than on their own occupations for financial maintenance. Seemingly removed from a wage-based labor system, Viola's narrative of service hearkens back nostalgically to a feudal model of allegiance that was steadily eroding at the time of the play's first production.

Twelfth Night as a whole, however, is not completely oblivious to the financial components of service, even service at court. Feste, Olivia's clown, is absolutely aware of the financial aspects of his position, and he requests and receives money throughout the play. Sir Toby pays Feste to sing in Act 2, as does Orsino, and Sebastian pays him to leave him alone in Act 4. When Orsino comes to Olivia's court in Act 5, Feste manages to get three payments in gold from him by arguing, "the triplex, sir, is a good tripping measure" (5.1.35–36). Even Viola/Cesario pays Feste his "expenses" in Act 3 (1.44). The play thus accepts the economic foundations of wage-based service for Feste but not for Viola or, more to the point, not for Viola as a servant who will eventually marry her master. Viola's marriage to Orsino depends upon a model of "willing service" and a substitution of romantic desire for economic imperatives.[19] Even Malvolio—whose longing for his mistress most closely parallels Viola's desire for Orsino—stands in direct contrast to Viola because his fantasies of marriage are explicitly connected to his desire for social advancement and the financial and political wherewithal that would accompany such a promotion. Malvolio's daydreams depend on an imaginative logic in which power is the ultimate aphrodisiac; he fantasizes "[c]alling my officers about me, in my branched velvet gown," and then, "after a demure travel of regard, telling them I know my place, as I would they should do theirs" (2.5.47–48, 52–53). Unlike Viola's romanticized trajectory from service to marriage, Malvolio's desire to "wash off gross acquaintance" (2.5.162–163) as he moves up the social ladder from steward to "Count Malvolio" (2.5.34) is not only highly eroticized but also clearly linked to his economic and social ambitions.[20] In part, then, *Twelfth Night* marks the shift from feudal to wage-based service through a process of formal displacement; the play transfers the financial logic of service from Viola to other characters, such as Feste and Malvolio.

The fantastic quality of Viola's story also suggests that Shakespeare tells her tale at the expense of other less economically promising scenarios. In Viola's transformation from page to Orsino's "fancy's queen," (5.1.387) the play offers a romanticized narrative of female service and upward mobility that is structurally contingent upon the suppression of other narratives—namely, narratives of limited upward mobility, prolonged service, and financial hardship. For instance, historians have demonstrated that "[t]he custom of late marriage was closely linked to the prevailing low rates of wages for maidservants," due to the fact that women "were expected to save out of their earnings for a dowry, but with maidservants' salaries at rock-bottom, they found it difficult to save anything at all."[21] Purportedly writing from the position of maidservants in London, the anonymous authors of *A Letter sent by the Maydens of London, to the vertuous Matrones & Mistresses of the same* (1567) reinforce this more common narrative of extended service and economic difficulty by complaining frequently of the "small stipend or wages" that maidservants receive while in domestic positions.[22] What is absent from Viola's story, in other words, is every bit as significant as what is present. Hayden White has argued that "every narrative, however seemingly 'full,' is constructed on the basis of a set of events that might have been included but were left out."[23] In a similar manner, Viola's story symptomatically betrays its ideological underpinnings by leaving out the social instabilities of service that troubled early modern lawmakers and public officials.

Viola nevertheless emerges in the play as an erotic, desiring subject who acquires a limited agency by virtue of her pleasing speech and rhetorical prowess. In her capacity as Orsino's servant, Viola inadvertently seduces Olivia with her "poetical" speech and "comfortable doctrine" (1.5.196, 225). Her monologue at the end of 2.2—in which she confesses that her "state is desperate" for her "master's love" (36)—enables her to articulate her own erotic attachment to the Duke, as does her veiled discussion with him in 2.4 about her fictional "sister" who concealed her love and "with a green and yellow

melancholy...sat like Patience on a monument, / Smiling at grief"
(114–116). In pleading for her master's love, Viola pleads for her own
romantic desires using language borrowed from an older, courtly tradition of romantic service. Neatly collapsing together Viola's story as
a servant with her story as a lover and future wife, Shakespeare spins
a tale of erotic rather than economic subject-hood.

Significantly, Viola's eroticized subjectivity never devolves into disruptive sexuality. In avoiding this dangerous slippage, Shakespeare
deviates from the familiar story of the hypersexualized female servant
that pervaded historical and literary narratives throughout the period.
Tales about lecherous maidservants who used their occupations as
covers for sexual escapades, for example, were common in popular
literature as early as the thirteenth and fourteenth centuries.[24] By the
seventeenth century, as Susan Amussen has demonstrated, female servants were understood as "sexually available" within the households
in which they worked and were often not protected by "normal community controls on extramarital sex."[25] Jacobean dramatists represent
this system of sexual subordination in urban plays such as *The Fair
Maid of the Exchange* (1607), which I discuss briefly later in the chapter, and in tragic and tragicomic figures such as Diaphanta in Thomas
Middleton and William Rowley's *The Changeling* (first performed in
1622) and Winifred in Thomas Dekker, John Ford, and Rowley's
The Witch of Edmonton (first performed in 1621). The maidservant
Winifred, for example, is subject to the sexual advances of both her
master, Sir Arthur Clarington, and Frank Thorney, a gentleman's son
also in Sir Arthur's service. But though the play begins with Winifred's
marriage to Frank—a marriage that serves to legitimate their unborn
child, transforming Winifred "[f]rom a loose whore to a repentant
wife" (1.1.193)—this union quickly turns into a bigamous one when
Frank marries again later in the play.[26] Marriage in this text, then,
is hardly a celebratory end to service or even to sexual improprieties, but a convenient arrangement that foregrounds Winifred's social
powerlessness. Similarly in *The Changeling*, Diaphanta's substitution
for Beatrice in Alsemero's wedding bed contorts and parodies the
marriage plot, characterizing the waiting-woman as unreliable and
sexually voracious when she partakes too excessively in her sexual rendezvous, "devour[ing] the pleasure with a greedy appetite" (5.1.3).[27]
Ultimately, Diaphanta is killed because her unruly desires threaten to
expose Beatrice and De Flores's schemes. In representing the sexual
vulnerability of the female servant, these popular fictions thus produce moralistic and cautionary messages about sexual disorder and its
potentially disastrous effects on the household.

In *Twelfth Night*, however, Shakespeare carefully sidesteps the issue of sexual impropriety by constructing Viola's subjectivity in relation to her erotic desire, yet locating that desire within a safe trajectory of marriage. The marriage plot safely eliminates the threat of the sexually unruly female servant just as Viola's fantastic success in the service hierarchy erases the economic tensions that increasingly characterized the service work of early modern women. Defying the economic logic of both service and marriage, Viola's story in *Twelfth Night* reassures its audience that women in service will secure good ends for themselves in patriarchal marriages that are seemingly untainted by a sexual division of labor. Safely sequestered from both sexual and financial risk, Viola appears to move seamlessly from privileged servant to "fancy's queen."

HUSBANDS, HOUSES, AND "SERVICELESSE" MAIDS

My reading of Viola assumes the importance of those sets of events, themes, and narrative structures that are *not* included in Shakespeare's text. Viola's fantasy of service is reassuring to an audience concerned about the potential (and potentially disruptive) mobility of female servants precisely because it symptomatically displaces less desirable narratives of domestic labor. But this reading necessarily presumes that more unsettling stories of women in service circulated in early modern culture, haunting the margins of plays such as *Twelfth Night*. Where might we find such stories? Is it possible to complicate the romantic narrative of female service that Shakespeare offers his audience? What does female service look like outside of Illyria? Before returning to *Twelfth Night* to examine the role of Maria, I want to take a step back from Viola's fancifully progressive tale to consider another text that depicts women's service work in more troubled terms. Doing so helps to fill in the gaps in Shakespeare's narrative and allows us to supply Viola's unwritten subtext through competing discourses of early modern women's service.

Almost thirty years before *Twelfth Night*'s first performance, Isabella Whitney published *A Sweet Nosgay* (1573), a heterogeneous collection of verse and prose works. In one of the short poems included in the anthology, the verse epistle "A Modest Meane for Maides," Whitney offers advice about obedience and piety to "two of her yonger Sisters servinge in London" (C7v).[28] In the epistle she adopts the role of experienced advisor and educator—a role that seems to come naturally to Whitney, since she claims in the *Nosgay* to have worked as a domestic servant in London. Though Whitney's claims may or may not be "accurate" in autobiographical terms (and since we have no information about Whitney's service aside from the *Nosgay*, the only arguments in support of her claims are circular ones), the rhetorical persona that she adopts in "A Modest Meane" successfully conjures up a fictive how-to session for her sisters, and perhaps for other servant readers. The authorial stance that governs the poem thus helps to bring into visibility a particular narrative of service in an urban household.

In the opening stanza of "A Modest Meane," Whitney offers advice about how to succeed as a servant:

> Good Sisters mine, when I
> that further from you dwell:
> Peruse these lines, observe the rules
> which in the same I tell.
> So shal you wealth posses,
> and quietnesse of mynde:
> And al your friends to se the same,
> a treble joy shall fynde.   (C7v)

Whitney offers her sisters a simple formulation: follow the rules and read my advice and you will gain wealth and peace of mind. At first glance the poem seems to sketch out a trajectory that appears remarkably similar to Viola's idealized progression from service to rich rewards. But "A Modest Meane," like the *Nosgay* as a whole, is structured around a thematic core of risk, loss, and failure that is far removed from the idyllic world of Orsino's court. In the opening lines of her address to the reader earlier in the anthology, Whitney adopts the persona of a servant who has recently lost her position in a London household:

> This harvest tyme, I harvestlesse,
> and servicelesse also:
> And subject unto sicknesse, that
> abrode I could not go.
> Had leasure good, (though learning lackt)
> some study to apply:
> To reade such Bookes, wherby I thought
> my selfe to edyfye.   (A5v)

Whitney represents herself as a "harvestlesse" and "servicelesse" maid who has lost her household position and has fallen into poverty. She continues to draw attention to poverty throughout the *Nosgay*, in the section of 110 verse couplets (or "philosophical flowers") borrowed directly from the Senecan-style aphorisms in Hugh Plat's *The Flouers of Philosophy* (1572) and in the prose and verse epistles written by Whitney and those friends and family members with whom she shares personal problems and advice.[29] In a letter addressed to her brother, for example, she laments that she "least, / of fortunes favour fynd" and that she has not been blessed with "goodes" (C6r), and later in the letter she links her deflated financial prospects to the loss of her service position: "The losse I had of service hers, / I languish for it styll" (C6r).[30]

These expressions of economic loss are in part characteristic of the complaint genre that Whitney adopts in her text. Wendy Wall argues that Whitney's *Nosgay* "offers a revision of, or an alternative model to, the Petrarchan topos of plenty and lack."[31] The speaker's nostalgia, most palpable in the concluding "Wyll and Testament," written as a farewell to London, enables her to rewrite the figure of the abandoned lover endemic to early modern sonnets and to transform loss into rhetorical empowerment. But the rhetoric of poverty in the *Nosgay* is also specific to her discourse about women's service. The tropes of poverty and nostalgia in Whitney's text establish her previously held service position as both financially necessary and dangerously subject to the whims of fortune and employers. For Whitney, service seems *not* to lead to marriage, but to a "servicelesse" period filled with sadness and economic hardship, a failed narrative that contrasts sharply with Viola's story of social advancement and romantic fulfillment.

The posture of poverty that Whitney adopts in the *Nosgay* authorizes her entrée into print and justifies her position as a knowledgeable guide in the affairs of domestic service. But it also throws her promises of wealth and "quietnesse of mynde" in "A Modest Meane" into question. Though Whitney does not state explicitly why she lost her own service position, there is no indication in the text that this loss resulted from not "observing the rules." In the poem to her brother, a mere two pages before "A Modest Meane," Whitney specifically claims that she has been left with nothing and that she "languishes" for the loss of her mistress's service (C6v). In the poem that immediately precedes "A Modest Meane," again to her brother, Whitney claims that she herself will have "no joy at all" because she lacks "lucke" and "happy chaunce" (C7r). Whitney's choice to present herself as an impoverished out-of-work servant who has neither money nor joy thus produces a striking contradiction in the *Nosgay*. Whitney's service did not lead either to wealth or "quietnesse of mynde," the very things that she promises her sisters in London. This discrepancy between Whitney's fictional persona and the advice she offers her sisters in "A Modest Meane" suggests that the attainment of wealth or "quietnesse" through service is neither inevitable nor necessarily permanent.

In "A Modest Meane," Whitney also emphasizes the heightened sexual vulnerability of women in service positions. She advises her sisters:

> All wanton toyes, good sisters now
> exile out of your minde,
> I hope you geve no cause,
> wherby I should suspect:
> But this I know too many live,
> That would you soone infect   (C8r).

As Ann Rosalind Jones has argued, though the reference to "infection" is ambiguous, it takes on sexual overtones when placed in the context of the "wanton toyes" that Whitney's sisters must "exile." Rather than circumventing these images of danger and infection, as Shakespeare does in *Twelfth Night*, Whitney underscores the sexual risks that accompany the position of a serving maid in London.[32] The poem indicates that sexual self-restraint is essential for the female domestic servant who wishes to remain free from suspicion, but it further implies that these women are vulnerable not only to tarnished reputations but also to more tangible forms of "infection," such as sexual violence, abuse, or pregnancy.

Whitney's warnings about sexual vulnerability, her nostalgia for lost service, and her rhetoric of poverty paint a picture of domestic service that is vastly removed from Viola's idyllic existence in Illyria. But Whitney's disheartening narratives are not isolated strands; they are embedded within the larger formal structure of her verse and prose anthology. In Whitney's case, this structure assumes a rhetorical force greater than the sum of its parts. By looking at the larger structure of the text, we can begin to nuance and even revise the nostalgic image of service that Whitney establishes in individual poems such as "A Modest Meane." Taken as a whole, the *Nosgay*'s recurring tropes of collection and management overwhelm its individual moments of despair and caution. Indeed, the act of anthologizing enables Whitney to redirect and transform her speaker's nostalgia into an oddly reassuring narrative of success and advancement.

The individual poems within the *Nosgay* are often studied individually, but the design of the text as a whole is crucial to the construction of Whitney's narrative of service. Whitney's choice of title, for instance, both connects her work with Plat's *Floures* and draws attention to her own work as an anthology. Taken from the Greek *anthos* (flower) and *legein* (to collect), the word "anthology" literally means a collection or bouquet of flowers, a meaning that was present in sixteenth-century English usage and that the *Nosgay* cites explicitly.[33] By drawing attention to this literal meaning in her title, Whitney produces a particular understanding of herself as both author and laborer. Writing about the early modern connotations of the word "anthology," Douglas Pfeiffer argues that the metaphor of the bouquet effectively shifts the agency associated with the book's production toward the collector or editor. He writes, "Nature, not artifice, produces the 'slips' that are then picked and arranged, often loosely or casually. By extension of this guiding botanical figure...any labor involved in the creation of the work is redirected from the author to the collector or gatherer of the volume."[34] In the *Nosgay*, Whitney is both the collector of Plat's "floures" and an author of her own poems. She thus cedes narrational control as an author but gains it back through her labor as a collector. The anthology form complicates the stories of service that it frames by realigning the author/servant persona that Whitney adopts. This subtle shift in meaning enables a decidedly more encouraging narrative of service to emerge in the text.

In structuring her text as an anthology, Whitney chooses a literary form that is ideally suited to the role of a servant. As a gatherer of the words of others—who include Plat, Whitney's relatives, and friends such as George Mainwaring and Thomas Berrie—Whitney orders and manages things that do not belong to her, just as a servant orders and watches over the goods of her master or mistress. In his commendatory poem, Thomas Berrie praises Whitney as she "who framde her Plot in Garland wise / So orderly, as best she might devise" (A8v). Berrie admires Whitney precisely because she is able to order the various texts that constitute her "Garland," another word that plays figuratively on the literal meaning of "anthology" and Whitney's authority as a collector. In her "farewell to the Reader," which follows the section of aphorisms, Whitney describes her work as an anthologizer:

> Good Reader now you tasted have,
> and smelt of all my flowers:
> The which to get some payne I tooke,
> and travayied many houres.   (C5r)

"Getting" the various flowers for her anthology takes "payne" and "many houres" of labor; Whitney lays claim to the specific skills of ordering and gathering that are requisite to her book production and characteristic of her former profession.

In "A Modest Meane for Maids," Whitney advises her sisters in service to develop similar skills of domestic management and organization. She instructs them to care for their masters' goods and "see that their Plate be safe, / and that no Spone do lacke" (D1r). This focus on the protection of the home and family property signals—as early as 1573—an emerging interest in servants' development of the managerial skills that would become essential to England's growing consumer economy. Household goods synecdochally represent family well-being, but they also gradually supplant personal allegiances (at least in economic theory) as the primary motive for faithful service. Thus, as a nostalgic substitute for female domestic service, the anthology format of the *Nosgay* allows a metaphoric revisitation of the nascent skills of domestic management that are gaining economic value in the late sixteenth century. Yet this relatively new narrative of property rights is held in check in the *Nosgay* by its dominant emphasis on piety and personal loyalty. The poem frequently reminds Whitney's sisters to pray and "give thanks to God" and to perform their master's business modestly and efficiently (C8v). Aside from the brief references to spoons and plate in "A Modest Meane," then, Whitney never fully articulates a discourse of marketable skills. Rather, the skills required of female servants as careful property managers are represented most forcefully *not* in Whitney's practical advice to her sisters but in the anthology format itself, where the gathering and organizing of texts effectively substitutes for the gathering and organizing of family goods.

But if Whitney is able to regain some of her lost service position through her role as a collector of other's texts, she is also able to position herself as a manager of *her own* texts. As both author and anthologizer, Whitney takes on the role of a mistress or housewife whose "household cares" include managing her own goods. The textual "goods" that she both possesses and manages temporarily fill the void of her "servicelesse" poverty.[35] Through this dual role as author and collector, Whitney manipulates her speaker's nostalgia and enacts a textual recovery of her lost service position. The literary form of her *Nosgay* thus allows Whitney to recover her position as a servant while simultaneously figuring herself as a mistress. This doubled process of textual recovery and refiguration produces a fantasy of social advancement and autonomy that might reassure servant readers such as her sisters that they too may rise, phoenixlike, out of poverty and into more auspicious positions.

What is surprising, then, about the *Nosgay* is the way in which a romanticized narrative of upward mobility develops within such a forthright and even cautionary text. Even more striking, the marriage trajectory that Whitney seems to ignore in her story of "servicelesse" maids reappears in subtle ways throughout the anthology. We could speculate, for example, that Whitney's symbolic assumption of the position of mistress through her act of anthologizing implies that she has taken on the duties of a housewife, thereby transferring the skills she developed as a servant to her husband's home. But the *Nosgay* offers more tangible representations of the service-to-marriage trajectory. In the opening epistle to the reader, as we have seen, the speaker specifically describes her interest in studying and writing as coincident with her "servicelesse" situation. At the end of the verse epistle "To her Sister Misteris A.B.," Whitney writes:

> Good Sister so I you commend,
> to him that made us all:
> I know you huswyfery intend,
> though I to writing fall:
> Wherefore no lenger shal you stay,
> From businesse, that profit may.
>
> Had I a Husband, or a house,
> and all that longes therto
> My selfe could frame about to rouse,
> as other women do:
> But til some houshold cares mee tye,
> My bookes and Pen I wyll apply.   (D2r)

The parallel structure in lines three and four constructs an analogy between Whitney's writing and her sister's "huswyfery." But in the second stanza, Whitney creates another figurative substitution by suggesting that her work as a writer is temporary until she finds a husband, "or a house." Husbands and houses might be two distinct alternatives to Whitney's writing career, or "Husband" may be a synecdoche for "house," implying that these two possibilities go hand in hand. In either case, Whitney envisions an endpoint to her labor that corresponds with marriage and domestic management. Like the service it substitutes for, Whitney's writing is a temporary position that will end when she marries and can take on the "cares" of housewifery "as other women," such as her sister, do. The act of writing thus takes over the role of female service in the progressive narrative that culminates in marriage. Whitney's verse enables its speaker to reclaim in textual form some of the service labor that she has lost, and it repositions marriage (if only fleetingly and through figurative substitution) as the ultimate terminus of that labor.

Whitney's *A Sweet Nosgay* undoubtedly complicates the idealized narrative of women's domestic service represented by Viola in
Twelfth Night. But, in substituting a narrative of writing and ownership for the far messier narrative of "servicelesse" poverty, the *Nosgay*
also offers its readers (including, we must suppose, Whitney's sisters
serving in London) an oddly dematerialized and rather conservative
narrative of social control. Whitney's promises of rewards and social
advancement are, at least to some degree, expedient fantasies because
they encourage servants such as her sisters to remain in their positions and hope for the best. And yet, despite the textual energy that
Whitney expends advocating for servants and offering advice for profitable advancement, successful servants are nowhere to be found in
the *Nosgay*. Rather, the text slips treacherously between two definitions of "success": Whitney's success and autonomy as a writer and
anthologizer must stand in for her (missing) accomplishments as a servant. Whitney's literary achievement—the prominent "success" of the
Nosgay—is singularly unavailable to her readers, including her sisters
in service who must be content to "peruse these lines." The formal
processes of substitution in the *Nosgay*, like the formal displacements
in *Twelfth Night*, thus privilege the linguistic over the financial; the
act of collecting and writing offers Whitney and her readers a rhetorical solution but not an economic one.

Yet even as early as 1573, Whitney's text begins to hint at the
importance of practical skills such as household organization and
writing-literacy that would become even more essential to women in
service over the course of the seventeenth century. The *Nosgay* thus
participates in a small but significant way in the process of imagining, defining, and limiting women's agency as domestic laborers
in late sixteenth-century England. And though Whitney's narrative
of service is structured quite differently from Shakespeare's several
decades later, the two texts share an emerging discourse of skill and
a particular interest in the skill of writing. In *Twelfth Night*, this discourse is most apparent in the story of Maria, where the act of writing
coincides with female authority and independence rather than with
figurative reassurance, as it does in the *Nosgay*.

"WHICH IS SHE?": WRITING MARIA'S NARRATIVE

Let's return now to Illyria and examine it from another perspective.
Maria, the other half of *Twelfth Night*'s doubled focus on female servants, seems to follow a narrative trajectory that is in many ways similar to Viola's. As Olivia's lady-in-waiting, Maria shares with Viola the

privilege of serving in an aristocratic household and may herself have come from a noble family. She also, like Viola, ends the play with a promising marriage—to Olivia's kinsman, Sir Toby.[36] Furthermore, Maria's route to marriage via service is conspicuously distanced from economic imperatives. The first hints of Maria's marriage prospects come in Act 2 of the play, immediately following the pivotal scene in which Malvolio discovers the love letter, supposedly from Olivia, that Maria has forged. Sir Toby talks with Fabian and Sir Andrew Aguecheek about Maria's clever prank:

> *Fabian*: I will not give my part of this sport for a pension of thousands to be paid from the Sophy.
> *Sir Toby*: I could marry this wench for this device.
> *Sir Andrew*: So could I too.
> *Sir Toby*: And ask no other dowry with her but such another jest.
>   (2.5.180–185)

In this exchange, Maria's clever manipulation of Malvolio rhetorically acquires economic value; Fabian values it more than "a pension of thousands," and Sir Toby finds its value equal to that of a marriage portion. Yet, by allowing Maria's "jest" to substitute for her dowry, the play downplays the importance of the financial components of marriage in the lives of early modern women in service at all social levels. Near the end of the play, Fabian articulates the link between "jest" and marriage even more explicitly, explaining to Olivia: "Maria writ / The letter, at Sir Toby's great importance, / In recompense whereof he hath married her" (5.1.361–363). As in the discussion of Maria's dowry in the earlier scene, the citation of the language of economic "recompense" operates at the level of metaphor, exposing the fact that this marriage negotiation is only indirectly connected with money matters. Maria's wit is her only dowry. Wit was not, of course, an insignificant attribute; indeed, it was increasingly seen (particularly in the drama) as a valued commodity in seventeenth-century England. However, despite Maria and Sir Toby's comic banter, wit was rarely understood as a sufficient substitute for a dowry. Here we can turn to other forms of literary evidence that articulate the insufficiency of wit as a substitute for a marriage portion. For example, in her autobiographical poem dated November 10, 1632, Martha Moulsworth makes this insufficiency explicit. Describing her upbringing by her father, Moulsworth writes:

> Beyond my sex & kind
> he did with learning Lattin decke mind [*sic*]

And whie nott so? the muses ffemalls are
and therfore of Us ffemales take some care
Two Universities we have of men
o thatt we had but one of women then

———

O then thatt would in witt, and tongs surpasse
All art of men thatt is, or ever was
But I of Lattin haue no cause to boast
ffor want of use, I longe agoe itt lost
[Lattin is not the most
marketable mariadge
mettall
Had I no other portion to my dowre
I might have stood a virgin to this houre   (29–40)[37]

Moulsworth slyly puns on the word "Latin" to call attention to the fact that neither Latin (the scholarly language) nor "latten" (a non-precious metal alloy) nor indeed the "witt" that women could potentially gain through university education are "marketable mariadge mettall"; none of these is sufficient for a dowry.[38] Wit might enable Moulsworth to write a learned and clever poem, but it is no substitute for money or property in the marriage market. As was true of Viola, Maria's plot progression relies in part on the formal displacement of the economic—in this case through metaphor. Reading Moulsworth's narrative of marriage alongside Shakespeare's highlights the fact that Maria's plot is founded on a particular fantasy of early modern female service in which wit becomes a dubious place holder for economic value.

Though both Maria and Viola progress through service to marriage through similar routes that rely in each case upon a formal suppression of the economic, Maria's service is more complexly realized in the play than is Viola's. To begin with, Maria's entrée into service, unlike Viola's, is absent from the play. Viola's ability to choose her service is, as I have argued, part of the play's romanticization of her labor, but Maria's labor is not subject to this same reading. Because Maria is always already a servant, the play refuses its readers and audience members any sense that her work is either freely chosen or part of some strategic plan. And while Viola dons the guise of service as a respite that is conceived as temporary from its inception, Maria's work is only readable as temporary after her marriage to Sir Toby. Though Viola and Maria ultimately share similar fates, Maria is never given a space in the play from which to reflect upon her service or, indeed, to choose and script her service, as Viola is.

Given this seeming lack of dramatic agency, Maria nevertheless proves to be the more problematic of *Twelfth Night*'s two female servants. Several incidents suggest that Maria's servitude is neither stable nor clearly delineated. Indeed Maria's story in the play—her convoluted progression toward a comic ending—defines her subjectivity not in terms of courtly love rhetoric or erotic desire, as we see with Viola, but in terms of potentially undisciplined independence and the acquisition of marketable skills. As many critics have pointed out, for example, Maria's proposed plan to gull Malvolio results in Sir Toby's calling her "Penthesilea," a reference to the Amazon queen with whom Achilles fell in love (2.3.176). Sir Toby's allusion implies not only Maria's fierce nature but, as Cristina Malcolmson has argued, her potentially unruly "female independence."[39] Certainly, as a singlewoman, Maria poses a greater threat to patriarchal social order than she would as a wife. Indeed the 1563 Statute of Artificers, which stated that local officials could order unmarried women aged twelve to forty into service, was based on the principle that unmarried and masterless women were inherently disorderly.[40] If service was intended to regulate and control the activities of young singlewomen, Sir Toby's reference to the Amazons suggests that service and disorderly independence can coexist for Maria—at least, that is, until her marriage to Sir Toby resecures her within patriarchal order.

It is Maria's literacy skills, however, that ultimately characterize her as a witty and resourceful servant worthy of reward via marriage. Maria's plan to deliver a forged message of love to Malvolio parodies Viola's own role as Orsino's servant, a role that requires her to serve as Orsino's love emissary. Maria manipulates the required functions of service for her own amusement and, indirectly, her own profit; it is, after all, Maria's witty treatment of Malvolio that eventually "earns" her an upwardly mobile marriage. Maria's letter-writing, the essential plot device that leads to Malvolio's gulling, simultaneously advertises Maria's skills as a servant and showcases the status confusion that the acquisition of such skills could provoke. In manipulating the role of servant as love emissary, Maria functions within the bounds of her subordinate position in Olivia's household. However, when Sir Toby asks Maria what she will do to get revenge against the prideful Malvolio, her response suggests that her writing skills may begin to invalidate traditional notions of social subordination:

> I will drop in his way some obscure epistles of love, wherein by the colour of his beard, the shape of his leg, the manner of his gait, the expressure of his eye, forehead, and complexion, he shall find

himself most feelingly personated. I can write very like my lady your niece; on a forgotten matter we can hardly make distinction of our hands. (2.3.155–162)

Maria here offers herself as indistinguishable from her mistress; the similarity between Maria's and Olivia's handwriting disallows a visual sign of status difference.

An earlier scene in the play foreshadows exactly this type of visual and hierarchical perplexity: the first contact between Viola/Cesario and Maria produces a similar status confusion that temporarily blurs the distinctions between mistress and servant. When Viola first comes to Olivia to plead on behalf of the Duke, Maria is also present. Upon entering, Viola asks, "The honourable lady of the house, which is she?" (1.5.169). Though Olivia's face is covered by a veil, recognition is not really the issue, since Viola (as she herself admits) has never seen either woman before and, more importantly, since the two women's relative class status should be apparent from their dress. In addition, both women are presumably dressed in mourning garments, which were governed according to very specific and complicated sumptuary regulations during the early modern period. As Edith Snook argues, "because details of mourning dress were regulated by the crown, in keeping with sumptuary laws generally, mourning was an occasion upon which social status was palpable."[41] Olivia and Maria's mourning attire, then, should heighten rather than diminish the status distinction between them. Even if we read Viola's misrecognition as a rhetorical game or clever ploy, the theatrical *effect* of this misrecognition remains the same. The question "which is she?" momentarily collapses the boundary that separates Olivia from her lady-in-waiting—a boundary determined by duty and obedience if not necessarily by wide differentials in social rank. Like Portia's question to the court in *The Merchant of Venice* ("Which is the merchant here? and which the Jew?"), Maria's question raises the disturbing possibility that social categories are not immediately readable from visual or sartorial clues.[42] Of course audience members are not in a position to make this same error, since they have been introduced to both characters prior to Viola's entrance. But by staging the spectacle of Viola's misrecognition, even if done to allow the audience the privilege of being in "the know," Shakespeare begins to articulate Maria's ability to unsettle the social hierarchy of Olivia's court.

In the case of Maria's ability to "write very like" Olivia, however, status confusion takes an explicitly textual form. Indeed, it is precisely the form and shape of Maria's writing that is at issue, and the intriguing and elusive "forgotten matter" that provides Maria the basis for her claim suggests that Maria's service has blurred status boundaries in the past, most notably through her ability to write. Maria's writing-literacy, an increasingly valuable skill for servants in affluent early modern households, ironically makes her appear more "like" her mistress. Being a good servant, in other words, could actually erode the expectation of difference upon which traditional feudal service was based.

Maria's epistolary skills and her particular ability to "write very like" Olivia raise problems of status differentials that can be detected in early modern practices of teaching writing to girls and, more particularly, to female servants. Women in seventeenth-century England were often taught to write by translating or copying texts; copying was thus an institutionalized component of women's writing-literacy. But copying also had a social function; the texts that women were encouraged to copy were frequently ones that inculcated self-restraint and piety. In *A Very frutefull and pleasant boke called the Instruction of a Christen Woman* (translated into English by Richard Hyrde in 1529 and published in at least eight subsequent English editions during the sixteenth century), Juan Luis Vives sets very precise standards for the writing models used to educate young women.[43] Vives insists that women's models for learning to write should neither be "voyde verses nor wanton or tryflyng songes" but "some sad sentence prudent and chaste taken out of holy scripture or the sayenges of philosphers" (E2r). Eve Sanders also notes the importance of training women to write through the practice of copying carefully chosen texts. Sanders argues:

> though the lines of demarcation were not immovable...original composition generally was construed as masculine whereas other kinds of writing, chiefly the transcription and translation of devotional texts, could be considered as appropriate feminine tasks given a proper pedagogical justification...Women were encouraged to copy texts that would cultivate in them the desired traits of restraint and modesty.[44]

Thus, copying and following literary models were the socially sanctioned practices by which early modern women learned to write. The lack of distinction between Maria's and Olivia's hands can, therefore, be read as the example par excellence of Maria's proper inculcation of self-restraint and subservience. By using Olivia as her "copy text," Maria produces a literary document that mirrors her own secondary position in Olivia's household.

Yet, it is not at all clear that Maria uses her act of copying to develop "the desired traits of restraint and modesty." Indeed, her epistolary performance reminds its readers that early modern women's writing was often associated with immodesty and social mobility in addition to self-restraint. We can see these contradictions being teased out in the late seventeenth-century writings of Hannah Woolley. Woolley, who wrote several books on domesticity in the 1660s and 1670s, is a particularly interesting writer to consider in the context of *Twelfth Night* because of the specific, detailed advice that she wrote for female servants.[45] Having gleaned "Thirty years Observations and Experience" from working in elite households, Woolley published in 1677 *The Compleat Servant-Maid; Or, The Young Maidens Tutor.*[46] In this text, Woolley offers young women a treasure trove of practical advice about how to succeed in almost any service position, including that of waiting-woman, chambermaid, or scullery maid. One of the practical skills she advocates is writing-literacy, an essential part of the female servant's oeuvre by the late seventeenth century when competition for the best positions had grown increasingly fierce. In a section entitled, "Directions for Writing the most Usual and Legible Hands for Women," Woolley begins by instructing women how to make and hold their pens, but then moves on to specific instruction in writing particular hands. In her instructions for "Mixt Hand," a composite of secretary and italic, Woolley tells would-be successful servants to "diligently mind your Copy, and observe the true proportion and agreement of Letters" (B9v).[47] Not only does she advocate copying in the body of her own text, but she also provides a sample for readers to copy on their own (figure 1.1). Strikingly, the copy text Woolley provides encodes a lesson in submission within its trite verses:

> Honors are Burthens, and riches have wings
> But virtues wise Ofspring affect better things
> Quietnesse and Contentment are the most
> Soveraigne Ingredients in temporal Felicity.

The "recipe" for success that Woolley offers her readers inscribes the same virtues of "quietnesse and Contentment" that authors such as Vives encouraged writing women to cultivate earlier in the period. In offering this handwriting model for female servants, Woolley advocates not upward mobility, but social contentment.

However, I would argue that Woolley's choice of copy text is also motivated by the potential challenges to social order that women's writing often presented. By teaching social resignation within a lesson

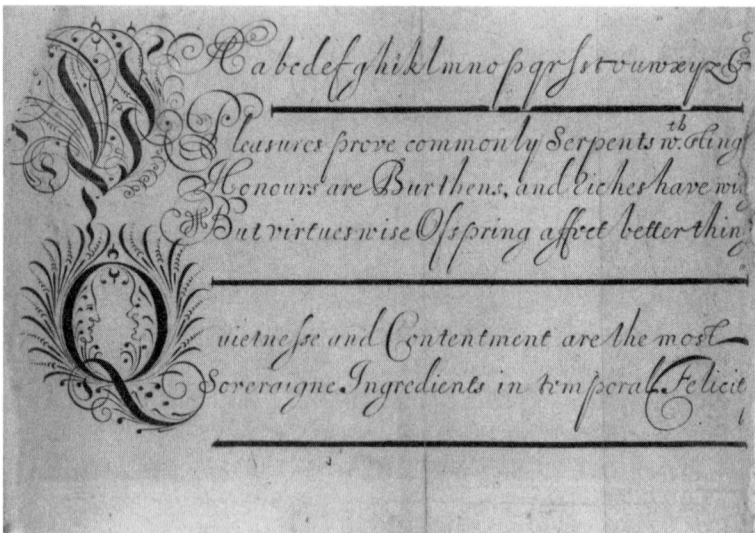

Figure 1.1   Hannah Woolley, *The Compleat Servant-Maid* (London, 1677), B9r.
Source: British Library Board. All Rights Reserved.

on writing, Woolley attempts to mitigate the cultural authority and agency that women could gain along with their newly acquired writing skills. Despite methods of teaching that reminded women of their subordinate status, Sanders argues: "some women nevertheless turned writing into a means of developing and expressing their own autonomy...Women who managed to acquire writing-literacy, in spite of strictures that made it more difficult for them to do so, were advantageously positioned to seek privileges and curry favor."[48] Handwriting in the period was both "that which made possible full participation in the new print culture and that which served as a symbolic guarantor of individual difference, privacy, and possession against the mechanical usurpations of print."[49] The "hand" of a woman such as Maria, that is, articulated her character, ability, and even independence within an increasingly mechanized and commercial economic climate. Woolley's handwriting model thus offsets the transgressive potential of a female servant's writing-literacy. Though its language reminds its reader to be submissive, its placement in a book of practical skills suggests that those women who follow it successfully might become "advantageously positioned" within the service hierarchy. The tension between practicality and its potentially disruptive ends becomes visible in the formal disjunction that characterizes Woolley's advice.

In this context of women's writing-literacy, Maria's own letter-writing in *Twelfth Night* takes on a host of contradictory and potentially subversive meanings. When Malvolio first picks up the forged letter, he exclaims, "By my life, this is my lady's hand: these be her very C's, her U's, and her T's, and thus makes she her great P's. It is in contempt of question her hand" (2.5.87–90). Maria has learned her writing lesson well; she is able to duplicate Olivia's handwriting successfully. This duplication, as I have suggested, signals her subordination, but it also enacts a dangerous replication of the dominant discourse of mastery. Olivia's signature loses its "quasi-magical authority" and "individual presence" when Maria is able to reproduce it successfully.[50]

Malvolio goes on to read the letter: "*To the unknown beloved, this, and my good wishes.* Her very phrases! By your leave, wax. Soft! and the impressure her Lucrece, with which she uses to seal: 'tis my lady!" (2.5.93–96). Ironically, the part of the letter that Malvolio cites as proof of Olivia's identity (her "very phrases") is its most conventional. Indeed, Woolley later in the century included in *The Gentlewomans Companion* (1673)[51] and *A Supplement to the Queen-Like Closet* (1674) sample letters for various occasions, complete with their proper, formulaic opening addresses, as did many such guides in the period. Though Malvolio's certainty in identifying the letter as Olivia's is partly a sign of his foolishness (as is his inability to comprehend that Olivia's wax and seal could be used by someone else), the fact that the most "identifiable" feature of this letter is the part most easily replicated suggests the ease with which roles of mastery can be counterfeited. The play denounces Malvolio for both imprudence and pride; he mistakenly believes the end of the letter, which promises that he will "alter services" with Olivia, and he behaves haughtily toward his fellow servants. However, Maria's act of letter-writing literally allows her to "alter services" with Olivia and positions her within a similar narrative of social disorder. The formal elements of the letter—the shape of the letters, the formulaic opening, even the wax seal—encode Maria's transgressive ability to mimic the discourse of mastery with the skills that she has learned as a servant. It is thus all the more necessary for Olivia to restore proper hierarchy at the end of the play, when she tells Malvolio that "this is not my writing, / Though I confess much like the character: / But, out of question, 'tis Maria's hand" (5.1.343–345). Olivia literally reinscribes the difference between mistress and servant that Maria's writing has temporarily thrown into question.

Twelfth Night thus offers its audience two plots of female service (Viola's and Maria's) that each end in advantageous marriages. Each of these narratives relies on the mystification and formal displacement of the economic components of both service and marriage to secure the play's comic ending. Viola's narrative nostalgically conjures up images of feudal service, courtly love, and a safe scenario in which female desire results in patriarchal marriage. Though Viola's route to marriage is in part structurally conditioned by the "generic contract" (to borrow Fredric Jameson's phrase) that romantic comedies such as *Twelfth Night* share with their audiences, her particular narrative also provides temporary solutions for very real social problems.[52] At the turn of the seventeenth century, a liminal moment in the history of early modern service, Viola reassures her audience that the sexual vulnerability, economic uncertainty, and social instability that characterized wage-based domestic service can all be overcome by romantic love. Foreshadowing in some respects the late seventeenth- and eighteenth-century versions of the Cinderella myth, in which plots of marriage and upward mobility come to characterize a uniquely bourgeois fantasy of self-improvement, Viola's narrative neatly encloses her labor within a narrowly defined marriage trajectory.[53]

In Maria's story, however, Shakespeare presents a broader range of social possibilities that evoke new forms of cultural authority for female servants in early modern England. Though she eventually marries, Maria (unlike Viola) never articulates feelings of love or a desire to wed. Rather, the play grants her agency in conjunction with the specific skill of writing that she manipulates for her own purposes and pleasure in her letter to Malvolio. What we see in Shakespeare's play, as in Whitney's earlier *Nosgay*, is an emerging narrative about the female servant whose subject-hood depends upon her acquisition of marketable skills and proficiencies in a commercial labor economy. However, the practical skills that service mandated always held out the possibility of upward advancement, and the play chooses to resolve this discrepancy within the ideological underpinnings of service by suturing Maria's agency (like Viola's) to a marriage trajectory in which her literacy leads not to her economic independence or occupational promotion but to her marriage to Sir Toby. In constructing the idealized world of labor relations that is Illyria, Shakespeare performs a logical sleight-of-hand, suggesting that the authority that servants such as Maria and Viola can gain through their labor necessarily leads to its own undoing in the "solemn combination" of marriage (5.1.382).

SKILLFUL SERVANTS, SKILLFUL WIVES

By the end of the seventeenth century, women's service in England was beginning to look quite different than it did nearly a century earlier when *Twelfth Night* was first staged. No longer a transitional form of labor performed almost exclusively by adolescents, household service was rapidly becoming a professional and more permanent activity that demanded specific skills and training. These differences were particularly notable by the beginning of the eighteenth century, following a period of large-scale changes such as the decline in real wages and a developing gendered division of labor that transitioned women out of agricultural work and into domestic settings. As a result, domestic service became a highly feminized form of work, performed mainly by women of the lower classes.[54] The social instability that characterized women's service work at the beginning of the seventeenth century thus gave way to a more rigid class structure, and relationships between masters and servants became "more obviously exploitative."[55] Demographic shifts and the continuing pattern of shrinkage in the size of noble houses caused a sharp reduction in employment opportunities coincident with a marked increase in competition for the best positions.

At the same time, the role of the early modern housewife was in a similar state of flux. In *Shakespeare's Domestic Economies*, Natasha Korda argues that the growth of mercantilism and the commodity form in early modern England ideologically transformed the role of the housewife from that of a domestic producer to a savvy consumer. Beginning in the late sixteenth and early seventeenth centuries, the increased availability of consumer goods together with the heightened social value attributed to these goods significantly repositioned the housewife in relation to domestic labor. Women still needed to engage in productive activities for the family economy, but they also needed to develop skills such as arithmetic and household organization in order to properly manage and keep marital property. By the mid- to late eighteenth century, wider discrepancies between social classes and the increased size and ornamentation of homes led to a disaggregation of women's domestic labor; the work of housewifery would eventually be performed almost solely by servants, while wives took on more explicitly managerial roles.[56] However, in the seventeenth century, including the decades following the Restoration, housewives were still expected to perform (as well as manage) daily housework in order to maintain their homes and their household property, tasks that increasingly demanded commercial expertise, economic literacy, and a wider range of skills related to *both* production and consumption. Indeed, late seventeenth-century household guidebooks written for female servants and for wives provide almost identical lists of required skill sets for both groups of women.[57] Ironically, then, while servants over the course of the seventeenth century were becoming more distinguishable as an employable lower class proficient in specific domestic tasks, early modern housewives were finding themselves in need of developing and mastering many of the same practical skills.

We can begin to see the ideological relationship between skillful servants and skillful wives being worked out in the urban comedies so popular on the London stage in the early decades of the seventeenth century. Much more so than a romantic comedy such as *Twelfth Night*, these plays advertise the rise of trade in England, the growth of a consumer economy, and the impact of these economic developments on the lives of men and women from the urban middling classes.[58] *The Fair Maid of the Exchange*, most likely written by Thomas Heywood, for example, tells the story of Phillis Flower (the "fair maid" of the play's title), the daughter of a wealthy merchant who lives in her parental home but is sent out to work as a sempster at the Royal Exchange in London. Phillis thus fits into the early modern category of a "craft servant"; she would not be entered into a formal apprenticeship, but would be sent out less formally to work for a master or mistress for whom they would usually provide domestic chores while also learning and carrying out more specific tasks, such as lacemaking.[59] Part of Phillis's service involves the delivery and sale of textiles; in the first scene of the play, Phillis and her coworker, Ursula, are bringing "sutes of Ruffes," "stomachers," and "that fine peece of Lawne, / Marck'd with the Letters CC. and S." to a gentlewoman client (1.28–30).[60] However, she also works in the shop of an anonymous mistress who never appears on stage but who is alluded to throughout the play.[61] In scene 8, Phillis enters the shop at the Exchange and berates a boy who is "cutting up square parchments":

> Phillis: Why, how now sirra, can you finde nought to doe,
> But waste the parchment in this idle sort?
> Boy: I do but what my Mistris gave in charge.
> Phillis: Your Mistris! in good time: then sir it seemes
> Your duety cannot stoope but to her lewre:
> Sir, I will make you knowe, that in hir absence
> You shall accompt to my demaund   (1160–1166)

Phillis clearly is a privileged servant in her mistress's shop; she is in a position of authority over the boy, who must follow Phillis's "demaund" in his mistress's absence. Furthermore, she is in charge both of producing textiles in the shop and of selling them to interested customers at the Exchange.

Though a sexual economy pervades the play and Phillis is frequently positioned as an object to be bought and sold (a figurative device common to many city comedies), Heywood downplays Phillis's economic proficiency, much as Shakespeare and Whitney subordinate financial motive in their texts.[62] In describing Phillis's laboring hands, for instance, her suitor Frank Golding is at pains to remove them rhetorically from the space of her work at the Exchange. After his first encounter with Phillis in her shop, Frank exclaims: "I saw her hand, and it was lilly white, I toucht her palme, and it was soft and smoothe: and then what then? her hand did then bewitch me, I shall bee in love now out of hand" (4.503–506). Frank falls in love because of the seductive beauty of a working woman's hands. However, Phillis's hands are both "lilly white" and "soft and smoothe," adjectives that seem especially inappropriate given Phillis's occupation in the textile industry.[63] These hands retain no sign or stigma of physical labor. Indeed, Frank's love for Phillis is founded on an insistent repudiation of the economic conditions of her service. Frank rather reluctantly decides to accouter himself like a lover, saying: "shall I defie hat-bands, and treade garters and shoostrings under my feet? shall I fall to falling bands and bee a ruffin no longer? I must; I am now liege man to *Cupid*" (4.509–511). Though Frank's newly found sartorial indifference is a commonplace of Petrarchan rhetoric, the particular objects that he rejects are the types of textiles manufactured and sold in Phillis's shop. In linguistically defying hatbands and garters, Frank also defies the material components of his beloved's labor.

Once Frank acknowledges his love for Phillis, his language becomes inflected by the tropes of pastoral, classical myth, and courtly love poetry. In one scene, Frank enters singing to himself:

> Ye little birds that sit and sing
> Amidst the shadie valleys,
> And see how Phillis sweetly walkes
> Within her Garden alleyes;
> Goe pretie birds about her bowre,
> Sing pretie birdes she may not lowre,
> Ah me, me thinkes I see her frowne,
> Ye pretie wantons warble.   (7.904–911)

As a sempster at the Royal Exchange, Phillis is nowhere near "shadie valleyes" or "pretie birds"; Frank's deployment of the pastoral mode removes Phillis from the Exchange and relocates her in "Garden alleyes." The requirements of this embedded genre romanticize Phillis's service by severing its link to a commercial locale. In a later scene, Frank, disguised as a drawer named Cripple whom Phillis loves,[64] encourages her to:

> [h]ie thee unto the odoriferous groves…
> There of the choisest fragrant flowers that grow
> Thou maist devise sweete roseat Corronets,
> And with the Nimphs that haunt the silver streames,
> Learne to entice the affable yong wagge;
> There shalt thou finde him wandring up and downe,
> Till some faire saint impale him with a crowne   (12.2021, 2024–2029)

Even though Phillis has come to Cripple in this scene to retrieve a handkerchief that she had given him to draw, Frank's turn to the rhetoric of pastoral and classical myth situates Phillis and her labor outside of the city economy. Heywood thus replaces the distinctly urban narrative of Phillis's service with a pastoral narrative of romantic love in which hatbands and ruffs are supplanted by "sweete roseat Corronets."

The pastoral mode, by removing her from the marketplace entirely, intervenes in part to disentangle Phillis from the illicit sexual potential of her work. But it also emphasizes romantic love at the expense of economic engagement. Though Phillis does eventually marry Frank, the dowry that she brings to that marriage comes not from her service as a sempster but from her family inheritance. And yet, though the play deflects the economic wherewithal incumbent on Phillis's service position, it nevertheless develops an implicit connection between the labor of unmarried female servants and the domestic work of wives. Phillis's anonymous mistress clearly makes her living as a sempster through the same skills that Phillis herself is learning. During her daughter's marriage negotiations, Mistress Flower displays a remarkable degree of control over the financial resources in her household. She privately assures Frank that she will "search my coffers for another hundred" to add to Phillis's dowry, demonstrating her economic bargaining power independent of her husband's wishes.[65] The presence of these female characters in *Fair Maid* suggests that there may be more continuity between Phillis's craft service and her post-marital labors than the pastoral language of the play's romantic plot acknowledges.

The marriage trajectory that shapes the romantic plot of *Fair Maid* serves a slightly different social function than it does in *Twelfth*

Night or *A Sweet Nosgay*. For Heywood, this progressive narrative addresses the dual need for skillful servants and skillful wives in England's developing consumer economy. Heywood's emphasis on Phillis's service and practical training in the play—however deflected and idealized—continues the discourse of skill hinted at in earlier texts and begins to reimagine the subjectivity of the female servant in terms of marketplace economics. But the play also casts doubt upon the marriage plot that it deploys, suggesting that service did not always end neatly in marriage but rather offered a form of social continuity by successfully preparing young women to be the competent and economically proficient wives that seventeenth-century English society increasingly demanded. Even though it seems to draw a sharp dividing line between the work of single women and married women, a narrative such as Phillis's succeeds in appending the female servant's agency to a romantic teleology while simultaneously addressing the new social need for stories that explain, demarcate, and even celebrate the economic proficiencies of housewives.

The discourse of skillful service and occupational proficiencies that emerges in *Fair Maid* and earlier texts becomes much more pronounced by 1677, when Woolley published *The Compleat Servant-Maid*. Before concluding, I wish to return to Woolley's practical guide in order to consider in more detail how its specific historical position affects the story of women's service that it tells. Given the move toward a more rigid class structure in the second half of the seventeenth century, one would expect Woolley to offer a radically different narrative about young women in service positions. As a pragmatic text designed for use by women serving in elite households, *The Compleat Servant-Maid* would presumably concentrate on the economic details that Shakespeare, Whitney, and (to a lesser extent) Heywood omit from their narratives and would propose significant alternatives to the marriage trajectory. However, *The Compleat Servant-Maid* demonstrates quite surprisingly that marriage narratives about female servants continued to be deployed late into the seventeenth century despite significant changes in the service economy. Though the generic form of Woolley's text provides a space from which to offer the types of practical advice that we would not expect to find in a romantic comedy such as *Twelfth Night*, *The Compleat Servant-Maid* nevertheless offers its readers a version of the service-to-marriage trajectory that develops and reworks the discourse of skill that Shakespeare articulated much earlier in the figure of Maria.

Organized according to the different positions that a female servant could hold and the various tasks that each type of servant would be expected to perform, *The Compleat Servant-Maid* reads like a "how-to" guide for getting through a day as a servant in an elite household.[66] Woolley's test demonstrates a pronounced attention to the development of specific skills, particularly marketable tasks and abilities that would add favorably to a female servant's resume. The practical knowledge expected of elite servants in *The Compleat Servant-Maid* is vast and sometimes surprising, and the often abrupt juxtapositions in Woolley's treatise emphasize the fascinating breadth of expertise that she expects of her diligent readers. At the end of a section on keeping household accounts, for instance, Woolley concludes: "Thus have I briefly and plainly shewn you so much of Arithmetick, as is necessary for your keeping account of what you receive and disburse for your Lady, Master, or Mistress. I shall now give you some directions for carving" (C3r). She then proceeds to give advice on preparing and serving various types of fowl, instructing her readers "how to Lift a Swan" and "how to unbrace a Mallard" (C3v, C5r). Whether counting or carving, Woolley's servant readers need to be well-educated practitioners of nearly every form of domestic organization, financial management, and quotidian service such as food preparation.

Woolley is also attentive to the potential economic gains of service, and she repeatedly advocates thrift in her text. She cautions servants to be sure to give "a just and true account of what moneys" they spend on behalf of their masters and mistresses, arguing that this will contribute to earning a "good salary" (D8r, D8v). She also instructs young women to take care to save the money that they earn, telling them to "[l]ay not all your wages upon your back, but lay up something against sickness, and an hundred other casualties" (F8v). In warning young women to look out for their own financial interests and save up money for future "casualities," Woolley recognizes an economic need and a potential for loss at the core of female service— even elite service—that stand in direct contrast to the idealized narrative strands of earlier texts such as *Twelfth Night*.

However, the epistle that introduces Woolley's treatise produces a narrative of service that deviates from the sensible logic that Woolley depends upon throughout the body of her text. The epistle opens with what seems like an appeal to practicality: "The great desire I have for your good, advantage and preferment in the world, is such that I respect it equal with my own. I have therefore with great pains and industry composed this little Book, as a Rich Storehouse for you" (A3r–A3v). But even this promise to lead the way to "advantage and preferment" defers the economic by means of a simile; the advice manual itself, not saved wages, will provide a "Rich Storehouse" for the young female reader. After listing the (quite practical) set of skills that she will address in her book, Woolley concludes her epistle with the following sales pitch:

> So that if you carefully and diligently peruse this Book, and observe the directions therein given, you will soon gain the Title of a Complete Servant-maid, which may be the means of making you a good Mistress: For there is no Sober, Honest, and Discreet man, but will make choice of one, that hath Gained the Reputation of a Good and Complete Servant, for his Wife, rather than one who can do nothing but Trick up her self fine, and like a Bartholomew Baby, is fit for nothing else but to be looked upon.
>
> This Consideration, will I hope, Stir you up to the Attaining of these most Excellent Qualifications, and Accomplishments.   (A5r–A5v)

This passage begins with a clear enough formulation: a young woman can become a "Complete" servant-maid if she follows the directions Woolley offers in her treatise. The logic of the rest of the passage, however, is more obtuse; the leap from "Complete Servant-maid" to "good Mistress" depends not upon the acquisition of specific skills or upon money, but upon reputation. Practical skills seem to matter because they can demonstrate thrift and productivity to a potential husband, not because they can lead to promotion within the service hierarchy or even because they can lead to higher wages that may, in turn, help a woman save up for a dowry. Just as the handwriting sample within the body of her text offers a practical skill for social advancement but positions that skill within a form that advocates social contentment, Woolley's epistle defines the subjectivity of female servants in terms of the mastery of practical skills but locates those skills within the safe trajectory of marriage—the same trajectory found in much earlier texts such as *Twelfth Night*.

Indeed, Woolley makes a similar implication about her own transition from service to marriage in her earlier guidebook, *The Gentlewomans Companion*. In a "short account of the life and abilities of the Authoress of this Book," Woolley tells her readers that it was through her many experiences as a servant in elite households that she "became skilful...and gained so great an esteem among the Nobility and Gentry of two Counties, that I was necessitated to yield to the importunity of one I dearly love, that I might free my self from the tedious caresses of a many more" (B7r). Woolley's own skills lead to social esteem, which in turn leads to an overabundance of potential husbands and the fortunate opportunity to marry for love. As in the epistle to *A Compleat Servant-Maid*, marriage in Woolley's self-narrative serves as an incentive for hard work; it is the ultimate goal that will "stir up" women to become good servants. Like *The Fair Maid of the Exchange*, Woolley acknowledges the economic components of both service and marriage, yet she insists that female servants get married because their labor is seductive, not because it is financially profitable. Practical skills and female desire are channeled into marriage via a route that both relies upon and effaces economic imperatives.

The marriage narrative common to stories about female servants near the beginning of the seventeenth century, then, remains prominent in *The Compleat Servant-Maid*, but it takes on a different social function. By 1677, there was less incentive for female servants to be "stirred up" to great accomplishments, since the social instabilities that characterized the earlier part of the century had given way to more rigid occupational distinctions and fewer opportunities for social mobility via service work. Certainly by the eighteenth century, as Lori Newcomb argues, "A fantasy grounded in real hopes of advancement...became a moral fable enabling female servants to balance their dreams of self-advancement against their knowledge of their vulnerability."[67] As service becomes more of a permanent class position for women, the marriage narrative arguably becomes *more* socially necessary, offering a compelling vision of future happiness at precisely the same time that realistic hopes of upward mobility are disappearing. *The Compleat Servant-Maid* thus carefully arbitrates a new social reality in which concerns about diminished opportunity can be countered through a meticulous discourse of occupational training, tempered by a progressive narrative of romance.

But the epistle to *The Compleat Servant-Maid* also suggests a narrative in which married life is not simply the goal of female service but the continuation of it. In arguing that a "Sober, Honest, and Discreet man" will choose a diligent servant for his wife over a "Bartholomew Baby," Woolley implies that the skills and diligence of the young servant will become useful when she becomes a wife. The epistle thus hints at the continuity between the labor of maidservants and that of wives even as it privileges marriage as the proper "end" of service; Woolley explicitly calls into question the relationship between the termination of service and the beginning of marriage by producing a narrative that resists closure. Her earlier advice to maidservants to save money for potential "casualties" takes on a new and rather ominous meaning if we apply it to the future married life of her readers.

Though Woolley does not explicitly acknowledge the possibility, the continuity of labor between servants and wives was often a function of economic need. Marriage did not necessarily ensure financial stability and married women were often required to supplement "their family incomes by wage work which was for the most part casual, intermittent, and badly paid."[68] Early modern ballads similarly suggest the continuing importance of both male and female labor after marriage. In *The Down-right Wooing of Honest John and Betty*, marriage is possible because of John's inheritance, but postmarital labor is also necessary to stave off poverty. John tells Betty, "We'll work together day and night / and I hope we shall ne'r want money."[69] Like this popular ballad (and like the specters of Mistress Flower and Phillis's anonymous mistress in *Fair Maid*), Woolley's text emphasizes the continuity of female service work across the boundary of marriage, though it stubbornly maintains the validity of its marriage plot.

Though Woolley's choice of genre—the advice book—mandates an attention to practicalities and determines in part the particular narratives of service that she tells, the epistle that frames and advertises a maidservant's responsibilities formally confines those tasks within a structure that advocates a conservative, romantic ideology. By framing her advice book with this particular epistle, Woolley scripts a fantasy that carefully balances the agency of skill against the romantic rhetoric that disingenuously offers hope of advancement. Unlike earlier texts such as *A Sweet Nosgay* and *Twelfth Night*, *The Compleat Servant-Maid* is less invested in providing literary order as a response to social tumult than in offering a fiction of mobility to fill the widening gap between social and economic classes. In so doing, Woolley (like Heywood in *Fair Maid*) insists that the skills women develop while in service will be put to good use within the patriarchal home when these same women become immensely savvy and practical wives. In other words, when a young woman reads in Woolley's book how to dismember a hen or how to wash colored silk, she knows that these are practical skills worth cultivating if she wishes to become a "complete" servant. But she also knows (if she has read carefully) that if she performs these tasks diligently and if a "Sober, Honest, and Discreet man" happens to be watching, she might get the chance to perform them all over again—as a wife.

The texts I have discussed in this chapter suggest that subject positions for female servants emerged over the course of the seventeenth century in conjunction with a discourse of marketable skills. Initially, in texts such as *A Sweet Nosgay* and *Twelfth Night*, this discourse marked the gradual separation between wage-based service and its feudal predecessor. By the time Woolley penned *The Compleat Servant-Maid*, the emphasis on practical ability heralded the development of a tiered domestic labor system that would become more rigid in the eighteenth century. However, representations of women's service also demonstrate striking continuity in the face of much social and economic change. Literary texts throughout the period continue to deploy teleological narratives of marriage that offer fantasies of social order and romantic happiness as reassuring replacements for visions of women's economic independence or social unrest. By creating narratives that end in marriage, these texts assure their readers that women's service is predictable and unthreatening, despite all evidence to the contrary. Tweaked, redeployed, and reformulated, the marriage plot remains socially useful and surprisingly resilient throughout a century of social change.

Writing about historical narrative, Hayden White argues: "The notion that sequences of real events possess the formal attributes of the stories we tell about imaginary events could only have its origin in wishes, daydreams, reveries."[70] Flipping this formulation on its head, we might say that imaginary stories offer formal pleasures rarely available in "sequences of real events," and therein lies their seductive charm. Attending to this process of literary seduction is not only an aesthetic practice but also a social and historical one. The lure of the daydream in narratives about female servants intervenes at discrete moments throughout the late sixteenth and seventeenth centuries to reassure audiences who are concerned about social instability, to champion the training of skillful servants and skillful wives, and to offer servant readers a metaphoric escape, if not a real one. Yet in offering pragmatic, fanciful, or cautionary solutions to social problems, these texts bring into being new forms of subject-hood for female servants, suggesting that the practical demands of a new, commercial culture could not be easily ignored. Relished or not, the figure of the adept and witty female servant takes a firm hold in early modern culture and enjoys a lifespan that stretches well beyond the seventeenth century.

CHAPTER 2

THE SPATIAL SYNTAX OF
MIDWIFERY AND WET-NURSING

In *The Practice of Everyday Life*, Michel de Certeau opens his chapter on "Spatial Stories" by contending that narrative is profoundly connected to space and to the process by which space is socially constructed. He writes: "[E]very day, [stories] traverse and organize places; they select and link them together; they make sentences and itineraries out of them. They are spatial trajectories. In this respect, narrative structures have the status of spatial syntaxes."[1] What I find particularly useful about this description is its clear assertion that narrative has social consequences: stories can actively intervene in the world and shape how people respond to their environment, to their culture, and to other people. Narrative does not simply *describe* space; it produces it and defines its boundaries. For de Certeau, narrative structures and spatial structures have a mutually constitutive relationship. Differentiating "place" from "space" by arguing that the former is determined through "objects that are ultimately reducible to the *being-there* of something dead" and that the latter is determined through operations performed by historical subjects, he argues that stories "carry out a labor that constantly transforms places into spaces or spaces into places. They also organize the play of changing relationships between places and spaces."[2] Narrative is thus an active, transforming process that reshapes social space—which is itself always conditioned by movement and associated with history—and organizes it in order to make sense (and sentences) of the world it purportedly describes.

De Certeau's conceptualization of the spatial syntax of narrative can help us to understand better those narratives that were told about women who worked as midwives and wet nurses in early modern England. Though each of these occupations was unique in many respects, they shared to a large extent the same social space. Both groups of women essentially worked as maternal adjuncts, performing either pre- or postnatal care that necessarily involved a close, physical proximity to the mothers who hired them. And both occupations were historically at their height in seventeenth-century England. Though midwives had been practicing in England for centuries, the widespread cultural authority and occupational legitimacy they enjoyed in the early modern period made this a unique time in their professional history. It was also during this period, however, that midwives began to be regulated more strenuously by church and state officials, and by the end of the seventeenth century, female practitioners gradually began to be displaced by men-midwives and male doctors.[3] This process of displacement was connected to larger changes in medical practices during the period. As Laura Gowing notes, "The very basis of medical knowledge was changing. The expanding role of male physicians, the growth of professional health care, and the gradual eclipse of midwives by men was presaged and reflected in popular and elite health texts."[4] The seventeenth century was thus a striking period of change for midwives, a period in which their medical knowledge and experience was still largely respected but was also undergoing visible signs of erosion.

Wet-nursing followed a similar historical trajectory; indeed, its decline was directly linked to the growing predominance of male midwives at the end of the early modern period. The practice of hiring out infant feeding had become a widespread social institution by the sixteenth century, and it was never more widely practiced in England than during the seventeenth century. During this period, large numbers of middling and upper-class women chose to hire wet nurses rather than nurse their children themselves. Maternal breastfeeding had been advocated for centuries, but these arguments were not successful until the mid-eighteenth century, when, largely due to the publications of several newly notable male midwives, a greater proportion of mothers began to breastfeed their own children.[5] Like midwifery, wet-nursing was both widely practiced and showing signs of strain in early modern England.

Some of these strains were directly related to problems of urban and social space. As we have seen in the introduction and in chapter 1, the seventeenth century witnessed increased social and economic mobility and widespread migration to London, particularly for female workers. Additionally, women were beginning to experience greater geographical mobility within London than they had experienced previously, a spatial fluidity linked both to the explosion of London's population during the period and to the enforced proximity between urban residents that resulted from it. As new residents poured into the city, shared spaces, insufficient partitions, and crowded, subdivided buildings came to characterize much of London's domestic architecture and the experiences of many who lived in it.[6] Midwives and wet nurses would thus have operated within an environment in which boundaries between people, between buildings, and between social categories were increasingly fluid. But these workers also shared a more immediate relationship to social space, since their occupations depended on a degree of proximity to and physical intimacy with mothers, children, and the middling and upper-class households of which they were usually not members. They often found themselves in the position of mediating between different class positions and between the different social spaces that those positions signified. We saw in the previous chapter that female servants often lacked a clear, narrative trajectory in early modern England. In this chapter, I'm interested in questions of space, particularly social concerns about the ambiguous social spaces that midwives and wet nurses occupied within early modern English culture.

The social ambiguity faced by midwives and wet nurses was exacerbated by the fact that maternity was not yet a clearly defined category in seventeenth-century England. As Mary Beth Rose, Janet Adelman, Frances Dolan, and others have argued, motherhood during this period came increasingly to be "construed as a problematic status."[7] The scope of maternal authority was a matter for fierce debate in a wide range of texts, including "medical treatises about reproduction, prescriptive writings on breast-feeding and other maternal conduct, legal constructions of infanticide, and witchcraft discourses and prosecutions."[8] These debates certainly did not disappear by the eighteenth century, but they were largely replaced with new discourses of maternity that stressed affection, parental influence, and the significant role of mothers in nation building. If the eighteenth century witnessed, in Ruth Perry's words, the "invention of motherhood," then the seventeenth century played host to more convoluted and contested discussions about the precise nature of maternal authority and its appropriate scope.[9] Given these highly charged ideological debates about motherhood in the period, it is not surprising that the cultural authority of midwives and wet nurses was often subject to similar scrutiny. How might the agency of these workers be defined when maternal authority itself was questioned, feared, and problematized in early modern discourse? What is the place of these women in the historical narrative that would gradually produce explicit ideologies of "natural" maternity in the eighteenth century?

I argue in this chapter that early modern plays and prescriptive texts that represent midwives and wet nurses often rely on narratives of separation and compartmentalization in order to clarify social relationships and class positions and to enact the spatial syntaxes by which these figures can become culturally legible. Focusing first on the figure of the midwife in Thomas Dekker and John Webster's *Westward Ho* (1607) and then on the wet nurse in William Shakespeare's *Romeo and Juliet* (written in 1595–1596) and Elizabeth Clinton's *The Countesse of Lincolnes Nurserie* (1628), I demonstrate that the cultural authority of these maternal adjuncts is often discursively linked to their geographical mobility and their ability to mediate between social categories, even if those categories are held as mutually exclusive within the texts themselves. But by refusing either to conflate midwives and wet nurses with mothers or to dismiss them completely, these narratives also reinscribe the idea that maternal agency is multiply located. Divisions between women and between forms of maternal labor emerge in these texts with more force than do divisions between men and women. We can thus trace the beginnings of a gradual historical process whereby mothers will come to be separated out and praised for their "natural" childrearing abilities while also recognizing the peculiar early modern discourses that disseminated the work of maternity among several female figures. In shifting attention away from the sexual division of labor and focusing instead on the divisions of labor *among* women that characterized the seventeenth-century reproductive economy, this chapter asks, as Elizabeth Clinton did in 1628, what exactly is the "office of a damme"?

SIXPENNY SINFULNESS IN THE SUBURBS: THE MIDWIFE AND URBAN SPACE

Midwives had a great deal of social authority in early modern England, shaping individual bodies and the narratives of origins that situated those bodies within political and cultural frameworks. They played vital roles in the birth chamber, where they advised expectant mothers about their pregnancies, made preparations for deliveries, and managed women's labor and its aftermath.[10] To perform all of this work successfully, midwives also relied upon a privileged access to the birthroom and to the more intimate spaces of women's bodies. This exclusive access to "women's privities" often produced a degree of societal unease about midwives, as Gail Paster and others have argued.[11] But concerns about midwives and their social authority stemmed not only from the shame that was attached to women's bodies and the birth process, but, on a broader scale, to the geographical mobility of these workers. English midwives "did not restrict their practices to the parish in which they lived, and as a result they worked "over a large geographical area."[12] Midwives were licensed and authoritative workers, and their geographical mobility was a valued and often necessary component of their labor. As David Cressy argues: "Midwives were summoned as servants but performed as officiants. They crossed social boundaries and entered homes of all sorts...The midwife's office allowed her to pass thresholds and open doors."[13] Nevertheless, this official role and the mobility it required always carried with it the potential for misreading, particularly in an urban environment concerned about the sexual and economic mobility that was becoming a common feature of life in early modern London. The midwife's mobility was not in and of itself problematic, but it could quickly become so when it was discursively associated with sexual immorality and economic disorder.

We can see this process at work in the early modern theater, particularly in many of the tragedies and city comedies that were so popular during the period. The midwives in these plays are frequently associated with tropes of secrecy derived from the perceived privacy and seclusion of the birthroom. At the same time, as Caroline Bicks has demonstrated, these figures are portrayed as the powerful producers of narratives of legitimacy and subject formation. In Shakespeare's *Titus Andronicus* (1594), the midwife is the keeper of sexual secrets. As a witness to the black child born to Tamora and Aaron, she possesses dangerous knowledge of miscegenation and its potential to taint the royal bloodline. In order to prevent her from betraying this "guilt of ours," Aaron subsequently orders Chiron and Demetrius to "send the midwife presently to me. / The midwife and the nurse well made away, / Then let the ladies tattle what they please" (4.2.149, 166–168).[14] In dispatching this key witness, Aaron neutralizes her power as a "babbling gossip" who can testify to the child's paternity, thus preventing her secret knowledge of the child's pedigree from becoming a public, culturally authorized narrative of origins. Though the midwife in *Titus* never appears on stage, her disquieting ability to narrate and publicize a shameful secret presages her demise. But the play also construes her authority in terms of her capacity for transversing social space; she poses a danger to Aaron because she can move fluidly between the birthroom and the Roman court. It is through this process of spatial navigation that the "tattle" of the birthroom threatens to become a story with enough authority to throw court politics and Roman society into a "tempest" (4.2.160).

Similar figures—midwives who are able to transmit narratives about the secluded space of the birthroom to the larger world outside—appear in John Webster's *The Duchess of Malfi* (first performed in 1612) and Ben Jonson's *The Magnetic Lady* (first performed in 1632). In order to keep the Duchess's pregnancy secret from Bosola and Ferdinand in Webster's tragedy, Antonio makes sure to secure the "politic safe conveyance for the midwife" as "plotted" by the Duchess herself (2.1.168–169).[15] The old lady who appears on stage in the next scene is most likely this same midwife. Bosola questions her intently about the Duchess's condition and whether or not her "most vulturous eating of the apricocks" that he gave her are in fact "apparent signs of breeding" (2.2.1–3). As in *Titus*, the midwife here is looked to for "signs" and information about the birthroom, to which Bosola does not have direct access. It is precisely this figure's mobility, her ability to enter the birthroom (which Bosola cannot) and leave it again as a public witness to a private event (which the Duchess, at least for the moment, cannot) that legitimizes her labor and her narrative authority.

The midwife is a much more visible and dramatically significant figure in Jonson's *Magnetic Lady*, though she is once again associated with a secret pregnancy. In this case, Placentia, the unmarried niece of wealthy Lady Lodestone, is suddenly found to be pregnant. In the chaos that ensues, a midwife, Mother Chair, is sent for who subsequently concocts a scheme to hide the birth of Placentia's child. Mother Chair unilaterally decides that Placentia will "pretend / T'have had a fit o'the mother" and instructs the other women in the birthroom to "keep these women-matters / Smock-secrets to ourselves, in our own verge. / We shall mar all, if once we ope the mysteries / O'the tiring house, and tell what's done within" (4.7.28–29; 40–43).[16] Though Jonson also satirizes the ineffectual male doctors in the play who are baffled by Placentia's illness and unable to diagnose her condition properly, he draws particular attention to the duplicitous actions of Mother Chair and her ability to transform pregnancy into a "fit o'the mother" through the dissemination of a false narrative, while simultaneously hiding and protecting the "smock-secrets" told behind the closed doors of the birthroom.[17] For Jonson, the agency and potential threat of Mother Chair is related to her protection of female space, her facility as a creator of fanciful but culturally useful narrative, and her social mobility: her capacity for mediating between "what's done within" and the predominately masculine society that has convened at Lady Lodestone's house in London.

In these brief appearances of midwives on the early modern stage, we see that the social authority and, in some cases, the social threat of these figures is construed in terms of their ability to travel and mediate physically between distinct social spaces and groups of people. But we can turn to another Jacobean city comedy—Dekker and Webster's *Westward Ho*—for a more sustained treatment of the midwife and a more complex representation of her navigation of social space. Indeed, space is much more palpably realized in this play than in the other ones I've mentioned, partly due to *Westward Ho*'s intensely urban milieu and Dekker and Webster's fascination with geographical precision. In defining and clarifying the position of the midwife in this play, Dekker and Webster resort to a series of narrative mechanisms that ultimately produce a cautionary tale and a schematic, rigid separation between the citizen wives and the midwife. In the chaotic world of *Westward Ho*, order is largely restored through female self-regulation, but the play suggests that this order can only be maintained through a reiterated insistence on compartmentalization: on the divisions between groups of women.

Webster and Dekker's city comedy traces the activities of three citizen wives, Mistress Honeysuckle, Mistress Wafer, and Mistress Tenterhook, as they develop elaborate schemes in an effort to escape their husbands and homes in London and rendezvous with a group of gallants in the western suburb of Brainford. In the play's subplot, the Italian merchant Justiniano has spread a rumor that he is in dire financial trouble, and he believes that his wife will soon give her sexual services to an old, but wealthy, earl. Justiniano decides to disguise himself as a schoolmaster and assist the wayward wives; by doing so he hopes to force their husbands into the same position that he finds himself. The character that connects these two plots is Birdlime, the midwife who also runs a bawdy house. Birdlime appears throughout the play as the wives' ally and as their go-between for sexual liaisons; she introduces Mistress Justiniano to the earl, and she helps arrange for Mistress Tenterhook's rendezvous with the Earl's high-ranking but impoverished nephew, Monopoly.

The play consistently trades on Birdlime's mobility to knit these various and wide-ranging plots together. As a midwife, she is able to excuse her abrupt departures from the city wives and their gallants by insisting that she is "going to a womans labour" (2.3.128).[18] When one of the gallants, Sir Gosling Glowworm, questions Birdlime's reliability and honesty, Mistress Wafer replies, "No indeed, Sir *Gozlin*, shees a very honest woman, and a Mid-Wife" (2.3.118–120). Though Wafer's response somewhat ambiguously aligns midwifery with honesty, it nevertheless insists on the legitimacy of Birdlime's occupation and her movements within the play. Indeed, in a play fixated on urban travel and geography, Birdlime is by far the most mobile and visible character. She is the first figure to appear and speak on stage, where we see her enticing Mistress Justiniano with clothing and jewels, commodities designed to encourage her to abandon her seemingly impoverished husband and her merchant household and become mistress to the earl. Birdlime's traffic in consumer goods here works to facilitate the mass exodus of city wives from London that triggers the main conflict in the play, instigating dramatic action and establishing her pivotal function as a procurer or go-between for sexual rendezvous.[19] Birdlime moves easily not only between the physical locations within the world of the play but also meta-textually between the city wives plot and the earl/Mistress Justiniano plot. Without Birdlime the play, quite simply, would fall apart.

But while Birdlime's movement within the play is legitimized to the extent that it is coded both as a necessary plot device and as a normative component of her role as a midwife, it is nonetheless clearly threatening to patriarchal domesticity and female chastity. This is most obvious in the play's explicit association of Birdlime with prostitution; she is, after all, not only a midwife but also the owner of a bawdy house. As such, she is the primary catalyst that propels the city wives out of their domestic settings and into the suburbs, a space directly linked in the early modern cultural imagination to illicit sexuality. As a brothelkeeper, Birdlime displays a degree of autonomy and freedom that derives in part from her economic status as an entrepreneur. When Glowworm asks her on the way to Brainford, "how many of my name . . . have paid for your furr'd Gownes, thou Womans broker," she responds, "No Sir, I scorne to bee beholding to any Gloworme that lives uppon Earth for my furre: I can keep my self warme without Glowormes" (5.3.42–46). Birdlime prides herself on her ability to keep herself "warme" through her own financial independence. Throughout the play, this privileged economic position allows her to travel freely around London and its suburbs and control access to female sexuality, forms of social authority that are structurally unavailable to simple prostitutes such as Luce, one of Birdlime's employees.

The economic threat that Birdlime poses is clearly also a sexual threat. Birdlime's position as a bawd links her directly to prostitution, the subject of most official regulations related to sex and public space in London. Like midwifery, prostitution was affected by the fluid geographical boundaries of London. Though city officials had attempted for decades to limit prostitution to the suburbs, particularly Southwark, "by the late sixteenth century no single place could be identified with prostitution...[and] the shadow of illicit sex and prostitution could be seen or imagined everywhere."[20] But even legal and socially legitimate forms of women's work could produce sexual anxieties about women and urban mobility. As Laura Gowing has demonstrated, female street workers in seventeenth-century London—women who worked as fishwives, fruit sellers, or hucksters—were subjected to a range of governmental regulations that associated these women with "lewdness" and disorder. The urban mobility of these women made them particularly subject to circumscription and outright attack. Gowing concludes: "Women's use of the streets, fields and civic spaces of early modern London was neither simple nor free. The rhetoric of enclosure and the identification of female mobility with sexual and economic disorder shaped female identities and women's use of space."[21] The movement of female workers within the city of London and its suburbs, a movement linked to economic wherewithal, was thus often read as a sign of promiscuity and sexual disorder. Similarly, Birdlime's urban mobility aligns her ideologically with the (less prestigious) work of female street laborers, thereby reinforcing the risk of economic and sexual disorder that her occupation as a brothelkeeper has already established. In *Westward Ho*, the legitimate mobility of the midwife is conflated with the dangerous promiscuity of the bawd and the sexually suspect activities of female street workers in order to impugn Birdlime and her movements throughout London. The implicit assumption that women's geographical mobility is a sign of sexual disorder thus becomes an explicit occupational concurrence in the play.

However, at the same time that the play relies on (and criminalizes) Birdlime's mobility, it also positions her more locally, in the literal geography of the play's London setting. From the opening scene—where Birdlime speaks enticingly of Gunpowder Alley and Justiniano heatedly denigrates Graves End, Billingsgate, and Bedlam—to the final farewell to Brainford and the triumphant return to London, this is a play that relishes the intimate spatial details of London and its environs. The language of the play is saturated with geographical specificity: the city wives plan to meet up with the gallants at "the Greyhound in Black-fryers," the Wafers have sent a child to a wet nurse at "More-clacke," and of course ultimately all the major characters find their way to Brainford, a western suburb of London that was notorious in early seventeenth-century literature as a site for lovers' rendezvous and illicit sexual trysts (2.3104; 3.3.35).[22] The sexual activities of the characters as they move from London proper to the seedy underworld of Brainford are plotted and choreographed with spatial precision. Justiniano tells Mistress Honeysuckle that "the Suburbes, and those without the bars, have more privilege then they within the freedome: what need one woman doate upon one Man? Or one man be made like *Orlando* for one woman" (2.1.163–166). That is, it is precisely because the suburbs have been socially construed as spaces that facilitate sexual promiscuity that they can be distinguished from the rest of London. Propelling the shift to the suburbs, Lynstocke invites his fellow gallants and the citizen wives to Brainford: "there you are out of eyes, out of eares, private roomes, sweet Lynnen, winking attendance, and what cheere you will" (2.3.73–75). Lynstocke emphasizes the secrecy and enclosure of the suburbs, the "private roomes" and "winking attendance" that literally make space for illicit sexuality.

At several other points in the play, the characters materialize the shift in setting from London to Brainford through their reiteration of linguistic signifiers of place; phrases such as "West-ward Hoe" and "To Brainford" enable the audience to visualize and trace the geographical movements of the text. The insistence on directional alignment here demonstrates that, in de Certeau's words, "it is the partition of space that structures it." That is, the uneasy relationship between London and its suburbs is forged through a process of spatial differentiation, a process that occurs in conjunction with the stories that are told about those spaces. For de Certeau, spatial stories have "distributive power and performative force" that enable them to construct spaces, not just describe them.[23] In *Westward Ho*, the choreographic narrative of the play enacts a sexualization of space that attempts to restrict Birdlime's work as a bawd and midwife to the demonized location of London's western suburbs in order to moderate and ultimately control her mobility within the text's disparate plot strands and geographic locales.

The male characters in *Westward Ho* are troubled by Birdlime because she directly facilitates illicit female desire and because her physical mobility in the play jeopardizes the reassuring return to reproductive sexuality that the men envision in the play's final scene. In contrast to Birdlime's troubling liminality in the play, and, I would argue, as a partial response to it, Dekker and Webster produce a narrative of spatial separation in which Birdlime's work as a midwife and her (sexually disruptive) work as a brothelkeeper are safely mapped onto fixed geographic settings within the play's world. The textual geography of the play thus safely cordons off Birdlime from London, suggesting in the process that sexual vices, marital infidelity, and female desire can be likewise sequestered from the city. In so doing, this narrative appears to accomplish a simple but necessary task: to section off the illicit female community that the wives have formed with Birdlime in the suburbs, to critique and ultimately condemn that community, and to return the wives intact to London, where they can be safely relocated under the government of their husbands.

The threat that Birdlime represents in the play would thus seem to be female sexual desire and female community outside of marriage, which endanger domestic purity, procreative sexuality, and husbands' control over wives. But at the end of the play, this female community is significantly riven from within. Though they have eagerly taken advantage of Birdlime's assistance throughout the play, in the final scene the city wives join with the men as they attempt to segregate themselves from Birdlime by confining her to the licentious suburbs. After the wives have been reconciled to their husbands with plans to return to London, Justiniano and the others try to dispose of the troublesome Birdlime. Since her labor resists easy categorical definition, Justiniano responds by imposing a clear spatial division: "go, saile with the rest of your baudie-traffikers to the place of sixepenny Sinfulnesse the suburbes" (5.4.248–250). More interesting, however, is the wives' response. Though Mistress Tenterhook exclaims, "Lets hem her out off *Brainford*, if shee get not the faster to *London*," Mistress Wafer quickly rejoins, "O no, for Gods sake, rather hem her out of *London* and let her keep in *Brainford* still" (5.4.268–271). Ultimately, the wives agree with Justiniano that Birdlime must remain outside the city proper, staying in the areas already acknowledged as sites of sexual vice. The city wives clearly distinguish themselves from "sub-burb wenches," the term that Mistress Honeysuckle applies to women who dwell immediately outside of London's walls (5.1.114). With the line, "Quickly shall wee get to Land," the play's final song exacerbates the sense of hasty departure and the need to put space between the newly disciplined wives and the meddling midwife, Birdlime.

However, Birdlime pointedly refuses the geographical separation that Justiniano and the wives propose by reminding them of the mobility that she enjoys as both a bawd and a midwife. She tells Justiniano: "I scorne the Sinfulnesse of any suburbes in Christendom: tis well known I have up-rizers and downe-lyers within the Citty, night by night, like a prophane fellow as thou art...you cannot hem me out of *London*" (5.4.251–253, 272).[24] Despite the warnings from

Justiniano and the city wives, Birdlime forcibly articulates the permeability of London's boundaries, which cannot prevent her from operating "within the Citty." She effectively rewrites the spatial narrative of London, transforming it from the neatly divided metropolis envisioned by the citizens and their wives into a porous city, easily transversed by both women and men.

And yet, the story doesn't end with Birdlime's resistance to the social geography that the wives establish in the final scene. The wives, ultimately reintegrated within London and their merchant households, insist upon an additional, if more subtle separation between themselves and Birdlime. Birdlime's rejection of the spatial limitations imposed on her activities contrasts sharply with the citizen wives' celebrated return to reproductive sexuality at the end of the play. Giving up their escapades in Brainford, the self-disciplined wives return to London in the company of their husbands. In a deceptively offhand remark, Mistress Tenterhook tells the other wives that "the Jest [their attempted Brainford trysts] shal be a stock to maintain us and our pewfellowes in laughing at christnings, cryings out, and upsittings this twelve month" (5.1.171–173). As an act of narrative displacement, this comment safely defers female sexual activity: the translation of illicit action into jesting narrative defuses the danger of the wives' behavior. By rhetorically limiting their storytelling to a future retelling of past events, the wives firmly close off the possibility of present action, namely sexual gratification with the gallants in Brainford. Through self-discipline and imaginative storytelling, the wives store up a "stock" of pleasure that can last the entire year, but this pleasure has been effectively sanitized and deprived of any threatening potential it once held.

Indeed, pleasure has also been reformulated to correlate with reproductive sexuality. Clearly the wives plan on being fully returned to reproductive sexuality within "this twelve month" so they can participate in "[c]hristnings," "cryings out," and "upsittings"—all rituals that accompanied the birth process in seventeenth-century England. The wives thus transform sexual activity into narrative, but they do so by constructing a specific fantasy of female community—the gossips, midwives, nurses, and neighbors that attend the pregnant woman in the birthroom—that will replace the disorderly community of wives, prostitutes, and midwives that they left behind at Brainford. The obvious, if unarticulated, link between these two communities is Birdlime. As the married couples return home so that "every husband play musicke upon the lips of his Wife" (5.4.283), the audience is reminded both of Birdlime the bawd, who organized sexual rendezvous in Brainford, and of Birdlime the midwife, whose services in the birth chamber might very well be needed again soon, perhaps within "this twelve month." The escapades that Birdlime facilitates in the suburbs provide the raw material for future jests and stories. Converted into narrative form, Birdlime's authority as a midwife helps to sustain reproductive labor and the space of the birthroom, but the origins of this narrative remain rooted in the seedy suburb of Brainford. Procreative sexuality, in other words, is constructed out of the narrative remnants of illicit female desire.

We might conclude, then, by claiming that the play envisions a return of the repressed within the future birthrooms of the city wives, a jesting return to illicit pleasure and female community that flies in the face of patriarchal desires for domestic order, just as Birdlime's spatial mobility defies attempts to keep her in her place. But I want to resist this reading, in part because it posits the appealing but ulti-mately reductive fantasy of a cohesive (and ever-so-slightly rebellious) female community at the heart of the early modern birth process. This fantasy, of course, owes much of its force to histories that document the gradual replacement of midwives by male doctors. In construct-ing this historical narrative, however, scholars often tend to describe nostalgically the all-female birthroom communities and the female occupational opportunities that disappeared in tandem with changes in the medical profession. But as Gowing's work on women, touch, and power so brilliantly demonstrates, "[l]ong before men-midwives intervened, women's authority over the body divided women as often as it united them."[25] Her research suggests that the most important divisions within the early modern birthroom were not those created by gender, but those of class and marital status. Mistress Tenterhook pointedly tells the other wives that the stories they will tell in the birthroom will be shared with their "pewfellowes"—not simply a community of women, but women who would have mostly likely shared the same rank, marital status, and age as the city wives.[26] In this envisioned community of women, sutured by fanciful narratives of the past, women are strikingly divided from each other: Birdlime is clearly *not* one of the wives' "pewfellowes," nor is she able to enjoy the same proximity to the city wives in the birthroom that she enjoyed in Brainford.

In its representation of Birdlime, *Westward Ho* offers an extreme solution to the problem of midwives' cultural power and geographical mobility, but one that is nonetheless instructive. What is extreme about this play's treatment of Birdlime is the way in which it establishes an obvious occupational link between midwives and whores, then expels the midwife/whore figure to the urban periphery through a narrative process of geographical separation and differentiation. In part, this move serves a clarifying function: by collapsing together the midwife and the prostitute, the play maps a division of reproductive labor onto the city and thereby resists a conflation of the midwife and the mother. In repositioning these wives as mothers-to-be, Dekker and Webster make use of Birdlime's occupation as a bawd to criminalize her and provide a convenient point of difference between her and the newly self-regulated city wives. Birdlime's agency in the play is largely defined in negative, cautionary terms, and her potentially threatening mobility in and around the city of London is ultimately neutralized.

But it is in Tenterhook's projected narrative of the birthroom that we can glimpse the more complex workings of social space in the play. Though Birdlime provides the material for this narrative, she is excluded from the shared experience of its future telling. This moment in the text exhibits the social operations of space, the way in which narrative can redefine the relationship between subjects and the places they inhabit. As such, it serves as a key site of cultural formation in the play, acting to define, clarify, and reimagine the work of the midwife. In moments such as these we can begin to trace a slow, historical shift in which the labor of midwives, nurses, and servants would be gradually excluded from the definition of motherhood. Though the naturalization of maternity and the privileging of the marital unit would not fully take hold until the eighteenth century, we can see the origins of this process in early seventeenth-century texts, such as *Westward Ho*. But reading synchronically rather than diachronically, we can also see a cultural moment in which maternal authority is *not* centrally located. That is, in so rigidly segregating the midwife from the mothers she worked for, texts such as *Westward Ho* assert that maternity is not self-sustaining but rather symbiotically dependent upon hired labor.

WET-NURSING AND SOCIAL SPACE IN *ROMEO AND JULIET*

Westward Ho offers its audience a cautionary narrative of the midwife whose mobility in and around London threatens to confuse the distinction between licit and illicit sexuality. And yet, midwifery is not represented as inherently problematic in this play or on the early modern stage more generally; the occupational mobility of the midwife only provokes concern when it is aligned with other discourses of disorder, such as female chastity (in *Westward Ho*), miscegenation (in *Titus*), or inheritance (in *The Magentic Lady*). What I find particularly interesting about *Westward Ho* is the expulsion of Birdlime to the urban perimeter through Tenterhook's narrative distancing at the *end* of the play, after female chastity seems to have been safely secured. Insisting on this narrative of separation to the end, Dekker and Webster suggest that proximity is as important as mobility per se as a source of social concern, at least for the citizen wives. That is, when the social space that separates the citizen wives from the midwife starts to erode, the wives quickly reinstate a narrative of differentiation based on class and marital status.

Proximity and the attendant danger of social pollution are even more potent concerns in narratives about wet nurses, who took over the work of infant feeding after the midwife's role in the birth process was completed. Though the employment of midwives and wet nurses as maternal adjuncts remained common into the eighteenth century, the occupation of wet-nursing faced more strident opposition than did midwifery during the 1600s. Wet-nursing was never more popular or more widely practiced in England than it was during the seventeenth century, as the frequent references to wet nurses on the early modern stage attest. Indeed, though the midwife plays a more visible role in *Westward Ho*, the plot structure of the play also depends upon the ability of the citizen wives to purchase the services of a wet nurse. We learn in the first act that Mistress Wafer has an infant child; her husband has forbidden her to hire a wet nurse, preferring that she breastfeed the child herself. Mistress Honeysuckle calls this unfortunate request "the policy of husbands to keepe their Wives in" (1.2.116–117). By the next act, however, the child has been set out of London to a wet nurse. The wives make use of this opportunity to facilitate their escape from Brainford: they devise a "clenly excuse" whereby they will pretend that the Wafer child is sick, requiring the wives to make a visit to the nurse's home outside London. They thus acquire the means to leave London without arousing their husbands' suspicions, dramatically overturning the "policy of husbands to keepe their Wives in" by using it to help them leave both their households and London itself (2.3.79–111).

The debate between Mistress Wafer and her husband about hiring a wet nurse registers the historically contested process of defining the social and occupational position of this figure in early modern England. Though Dekker and Webster do not reveal Master Wafer's specific objections to the practice, his was hardly a lone voice in seventeenth-century English society. The institution of wet-nursing was subject to intense moral and religious debate during this period, and opposition to it came from several fronts: from Protestant theologians, from medical practitioners, and from aristocratic women. The struggle to articulate the social function of wet nurses produced a series of questions: Was it ever acceptable to hire a wet nurse to feed one's child? Was it acceptable for all women to do so, or only women belonging to certain social classes? Could wet-nursing be harmful to the child? To the mother? To the wet nurse? In what ways does the practice of hiring a wet nurse to feed an infant affect the agency ascribed to the biological mother? To her hired help?

Early modern scholars have brought to light many of the historical conditions that provoked these questions. One of the most important things this scholarship has revealed is the significant differentiation in social status between mothers and the wet nurses they hired, a discrepancy that was a primary concern of many early modern writers and moralists. The cost of employing a wet nurse was prohibitively expensive for most families in early modern England. As a result, only mothers from the upper echelons of society—including prosperous members of the merchant classes—could afford to hire out their infant's feeding. And they did so in large numbers: wealthy Englishwomen routinely hired wet nurses throughout the seventeenth century, despite the fact that religious and humanist leaders actively encouraged maternal breast-feeding.[27] Indeed, maternal breast-feeding was so rare among the wealthy that women who chose to do so were viewed as exceptional, even warranting memorials on tombstones that championed their use of "unborrowed milk."[28] But wet nurses themselves came almost exclusively from the lower ranks of English society, and often from impoverished rural areas. This gap in status between mother and wet nurse resulted in a labor hierarchy in which breast milk was commodified and English lineage was, in Wendy Wall's words, "frighteningly perpetuated through the lower-class breast."[29]

Geography, however, might have helped to alleviate some of these concerns about class. While royal families tended to employ live-in nurses, the vast majority of aristocrats, merchants, and other professionals who hired wet nurses sent their children out of the home to live with the nurse and her family. For those living in London, this often meant sending a child up to forty miles away to a wet nurse in the suburbs or countryside for as long as three years. Indeed, Mistress Wafer's plan in *Westward Ho* to substitute a trip to Brainford for a trip to the wet nurse attests to the normalcy of this practice and the rather extensive distances involved. Though this separation could be traumatic for both parents and infants, removing nursing babies from the city offered several distinct advantages to early modern families.

First of all, it could help to assuage parental fears about disease and the generally unhealthy conditions in London, offering protection to children through their isolation from the urban center.[30] It could also free up a small but often urgently needed amount of space within a family's London home. Because of the explosion of London's population during the sixteenth and seventeenth centuries, London's streets, business properties, and residences were extremely overcrowded. Lena Orlin's work on boundary disputes within London demonstrates that problems such as "[s]hared cesspits, chimneys, and gutters; buildings partitioned side to side or up and down; jetties and eavesdroppings and overseeings; blocked entries, restricted access, and property encroachments; neglect, damage, and inconsiderate behavior" would have been common features of daily life in the city.[31] Under such circumstances, bringing a nurse and her family to live with the birth parents, their infant, and any other children and servants would be immensely difficult for urban families, even wealthy ones. The practice of sending children *away* to a wet nurse thus structurally depended upon physical separation and differentiation, conditions that might feel oddly reassuring to parents worried about the social pollution represented by the lower-class nurse.

Returning to the early modern stage, however, we can see that this physical separation, though the norm in early modern England, was not always upheld in fictional representations. By attending to these slippages, we can glimpse the social work that literary narrative performs as it shapes and defines the culture of wet-nursing in which it operates. *Romeo and Juliet* offers an interesting test case, as it represents what is arguably the most famous wet-nursing arrangement in English literature: Juliet's relationship with her Nurse. But it is also a play in which the geographical divide between wet nurse and birth family is nonexistent. As such, it constructs a discourse of wet-nursing that is curiously at odds with social norms and palpably uneasy with the threat to lineage posed by the lower-class nurse.

Shakespeare's Nurse in *Romeo and Juliet* is perhaps most remembered for her long, rambling speech in the play's opening act. The speech follows on the heels of a brief but significant conversation about Juliet's age:

Lady Capulet: Thou knowest my daughter's of a pretty age.
Nurse: Faith, I can tell her age unto an hour.
Lady Capulet: She's not fourteen.
Nurse: I'll lay fourteen of my teeth—
    And yet, to my teen be it spoken, I have but four—

>   She's not fourteen. How long is it now
>   To Lammas-tide?
>   *Lady Capulet*: A fortnight and odd days.   (1.3.10–15)[32]

The Nurse's exchange with Lady Capulet and her attempts to ascertain Juliet's age with precision lead in turn to her extensive description of Juliet's weaning:

>   *Nurse*: Even or odd, of all days in the year,
>   Come Lammas Eve at night shall she be fourteen.
>   Susan and she—God rest all Christian souls—
>   Were of an age. Well, Susan is with God;
>   She was too good for me. But as I said,
>   On Lammas Eve at night shall she be fourteen.
>   That shall she; marry, I remember it well.
>   'Tis since the earthquake now eleven years,
>   And she was wean'd—I never shall forget it—
>   Of all the days of the year upon that day.
>   For I had then laid wormwood to my dug,
>   Sitting in the sun under the dovehouse wall.
>   My lord and you were then at Mantua—
>   Nay I do bear a brain. But as I said,
>   When it did taste the wormwood on the nipple
>   Of my dug and felt it bitter, pretty fool,
>   To see it tetchy and fall out with the dug.
>   Shake! quoth the dovehouse. 'Twas no need, I trow,
>   To bid me trudge.
>   And since that time it is eleven years.
>   For then she could stand high-lone, nay, by th'rood,
>   She could have run and waddled all about;
>   For even the day before she broke her brow,
>   And then my husband—God be with his soul,
>   A was a merry man—took up the child,
>   'Yea', quoth he, 'dost thou fall upon thy face?
>   Thou wilt fall backward when thou hast more wit,
>   Wilt thou not, Jule?' And by my holidame,
>   The pretty wretch left crying and said 'Ay'.
>   To see now how a jest shall come about.
>   I warrant, and I should live a thousand years
>   I never should forget it. 'Wilt thou not, Jule?" quoth he,
>   And, pretty fool, it stinted, and said 'Ay'.
>   *Lady Capulet*: Enough of this, I pray thee, hold thy peace.   (1.3.16–49)

I am hardly the first to draw critical attention to this speech. Scholars have shown a great deal of interest in the Nurse's language and have examined both the relationship between the speech and the

Nurse's character and the function of the Nurse's discourse within the play as a whole.[33] The most important reading of the speech for my purposes is Gail Paster's in *The Body Embarrassed: Drama and the Disciplines of Shame in Early Modern England*. Paster unpacks the complicated economic and psychic relationships between birth parents and what she calls "nurse parents" in Shakespeare's text and focuses on the "meaningfulness of weaning as a powerful, deeply ambivalent signifier of the foundation of desire in shame and loss."[34] Paster is interested in the Nurse's speech because of the material history of wet-nursing that it implies and the psychoanalytical reading it allows; she is less concerned about the narrative structure of the speech. She notes: "The several reasons I have to dwell on this narrative have little to do with its ostensible comic function—to stereotype the Nurse as a tediously garrulous old woman who uses the proverbial nurse's 'privilege to talk.'"[35] But the "ostensible comic function" of the speech and the "garrulity" of the Nurse to which it points cannot be cleanly separated from the discourse of wet-nursing that the Nurse and her speech invoke. The structure and comic tone of the speech, I argue, are intimately connected to her occupational status, as they help to construct a rhetorical buffer between the Nurse and Juliet that offsets their otherwise uneasy proximity. In doing so, this embedded narrative reaffirms social boundaries in the play, mitigating the awkward presence of the Nurse through rhetorical distancing and separation.

Making the connection between the Nurse's language and her labor can help us to answer a relatively simple, though puzzling, question about the play: what exactly is she *doing* in the Capulet household? Clearly she has served as a wet nurse to Juliet up until that momentous occasion when she "put wormwood on [her] nipple" to begin the weaning process. However, though the Nurse is able to time and date Juliet's weaning with precision, the timing of her own work for the Capulets is problematic. In early modern England, wet nurses were usually hired on a temporary contract, which could last anywhere from one to three years. Though occasionally children and families continued to give financial support to former wet nurses, these women were almost never retained in any official capacity, either within the birth family's household or elsewhere.[36] Obviously, a different scenario is at work in the Capulet household. Significantly, Juliet has not been sent away to nurse, a rarity in the period, especially for a wealthy merchant (but nonroyal) family such as the Capulets.[37] In addition, the Nurse remains a fixture in this household economy years after her official duties as a wet nurse are over. Her proximity to Juliet and her parents, which removes the geographical divide that normally separated birth parents from wet nurses, is thus only exacerbated by the fact that the Nurse seems to have dramatically overstayed her welcome in the Capulets' home.

One explanation for the Nurse's continued service with the Capulets is literary precedent. Shakespeare's primary source for *Romeo and Juliet*, Arthur Brooke's *Tragicall Historye of Romeus and Juliet*, not only includes the Nurse as a key figure but also lays the groundwork for much of her characterization as an intrusive go-between. Several other classical and early Renaissance texts featured cunning wet nurses who act as confidant figures, including Ovid's *Metamorphoses*, Virgil's "Ciris," and Spenser's *Faerie Queene*.[38] In other words, the Nurse's role in the plot of Shakespeare's tragedy is part of a long-standing literary tradition that explains, to a certain extent, her sustained presence in the play. And yet, literary convention cannot fully explain Shakespeare's lengthy insistence on her labor as Juliet's wet nurse. There remains a striking disjunction in the play between the Nurse's occupational role and her protracted physical presence in the Capulet household. Given the prominence of wet-nursing in the late sixteenth and seventeenth centuries and the spatial separations that normally attended the practice in this period, Shakespeare's audience would have been poised to find this disjunction more disconcerting than earlier readers and audiences.

The Nurse's first scene with Juliet and Lady Capulet highlights the liminality of her position. Lady Capulet initially asks the Nurse to "give leave awhile" so that she and Juliet may "talk in secret" (1.3.6–7). However, within the space of one line, she changes her mind, telling the Nurse: "come back again, / I have remember'd me, thou's hear our counsel" (6–7). Both Lady Capulet and her daughter attempt to silence the Nurse's ramblings; Lady Capulet exclaims "Enough of this, I pray thee, hold thy peace" and, several lines later, Juliet also asks the Nurse to stop: "And stint thou too, I pray thee, Nurse, say I" (49, 58). The Nurse's language and story are marked as obtrusive and redundant even as she is invited to participate in the conversation. On the one hand, this is a comic gag. On the other hand, this ambivalence in the text reveals one of the primary paradoxes of the Nurse's character: her necessary function within the play's plot is at odds with her occupational function within the Capulet home. How, then, does one construe the social place and appropriate labor of the wet nurse when her work violates standard arrangements of domestic space?

Juliet's Nurse performs a variety of other services for the Capulets in addition to wet-nursing, but all of them depend upon her physical mobility within the household and within the city of Verona. Indeed, the Nurse's limited agency in the text accrues in tandem with her ability to control access to key ideological sites within the world of the play. She has unique access to Juliet—and specifically to Juliet's past—through the history of Juliet's weaning and childhood that she alone can recollect and describe. She controls Romeo's access to Juliet by conveying the all-important rope ladder from the streets of Verona to Juliet's bedchamber. She also has access to a wide range of domestic spaces within the Capulet household. Not only is she privy to Juliet's private conversation with her mother, but she also facilitates her mistress's access to the household pantry. Preparing for Juliet's marriage to Paris later in the play, Lady Capulet instructs the Nurse: "Hold, take these keys and fetch more spices, Nurse" (4.4.1). Put in charge of the keys by her mistress, the Nurse acquires physical access to and control over the Capulet family's food stores. In a wealthy household such as the Capulets', the specialized function of individual rooms often engendered social differentiations; a *place* such as the pantry, linked to the physical labor associated with food preparation, was thus often read as a *space* demarcated by the laboring classes.[39] The Nurse's ability to move easily between the upper- and lower-class spaces within this household renders her service invaluable to the Capulet family, but it also marks her as intrusive and potentially unsettling to domestic order. In contrast to the usual geographic divide between wet nurses and birth families in early modern England, Shakespeare's Nurse is palpably present in the Capulet home. Of course, the world of *Romeo and Juliet* is not an exact reflection of early modern London, nor is it entirely clear how much space is available within the Capulet home (it is large enough to include a walled garden). However, whatever the actual logistics of this household may be, the play is notably saturated with anxiety about the Nurse's proximity to Juliet and the Capulets. By insisting on the Nurse's physical presence within the Capulet home and thus reformulating the spatial logics of early modern wet-nursing, the play draws attention to the social friction and the threat of pollution that disturbed so many families, moralists, and prescriptive writers in the period.

This awkward domestic arrangement thus threatens to remove divisions between upper- and lower-class positions—between parents and servants, between mothers and hired help. But even in large aristocratic homes such as that of the Capulets, where space was becoming increasingly compartmentalized and differentiated according to gender and class, the daily mingling of people from different ranks would have been unavoidable, even expected. The wet nurse posed an additional ideological problem in the period because she was believed

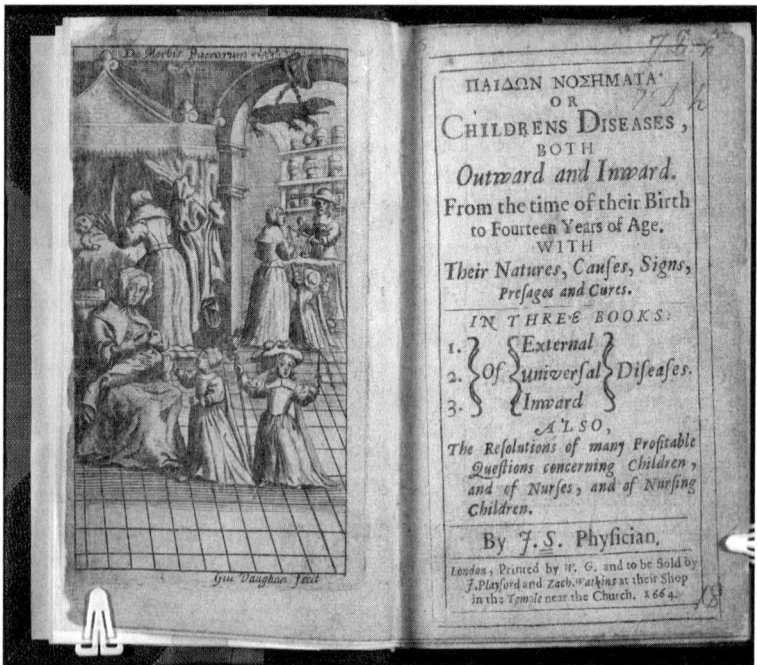

Figure 2.1   Frontispiece and Title Page from J.S. [paidon nosemata], or *Childrens Diseases Both Outward and Inward* (London, 1664).

to have power over the health, constitution, and moral development of the infant she nursed. According to humoral theory, breast milk was a converted form of blood. Most people therefore believed that the wet nurse's qualities, including her religious beliefs, moral character, and even her speech patterns, could be transmitted to the child through her milk.[40] We see, for example, in figure 2.1 that the wet nurse occupies a central position in the frontispiece to J.S.'s *Paidon Nosemata* (1664), a book about children's diseases, visually marking her labor as central to the children's health. Families who hired wet nurses were justifiably concerned with the speech and education of the women they employed to suckle their children, since the transmission of breast milk could directly affect the literal and symbolic health of a dynasty. As Edmund Spenser warned in *A View of the Present State of Ireland* (1596): "The child that sucketh the milk of the nurse must of necessity learn his first speech of her, the which being the first that is inured of his tongue, is ever after the most pleasing unto him insomuch as though he afterwards be taught English, yet the smack of the first will always abide with him and not only of the speech, but also of the manners and conditions" (638).[41] As several scholars have recently argued, early modern writers, including Spenser, who were concerned about the transmission of lower-class behaviors and speech patterns to upper-class children focused intently on the figure of the wet nurse and the potential "class taint" and interruption of genealogical transmission that she introduced to wealthy English families.[42]

The Nurse's economic and educational deficiencies are easily apparent in the language and structure of her speech in Act 1. Her reminiscence is characterized by excessive repetition, syntactic breaks, and digressions ("God rest all Christian souls," "I never shall forget it," "But as I said") as well as by colloquial expressions ("A was a merry man," "by my holidame") indicative of lower-class speech patterns. These recurring idiomatic markers showcase both the Nurse's inferiority in the Capulet household and her intractable presence there: her inability or unwillingness to conform to aristocratic linguistic norms is not hidden but incessantly highlighted.[43] The bawdiness of her story also speaks to the Nurse's earthy sexuality, a trait that Juliet herself displays later in the play during her "Gallop apace, you fiery-footed steeds" monologue. This affinity with the bawdy Nurse signals, in Rachel's Trubowitz's words, Juliet's "loss of hereditary identity" and the degree to which she has been "transformed and remade by the base or noxious qualities of unfamiliar breast milk."[44] Though the Nurse is ultimately too insignificant a figure in the play to bear in full the complex tragic burden of Juliet's death, her presence in this merchant household nevertheless signifies a (potentially tragic) disruption of lineage facilitated by the body of the lower-class female laborer.

The Nurse's anomalous physical presence in the Capulet household, extended well beyond the period of nursing, makes immediate these implicit concerns about her milk and its potential to taint the Capulets' lineage. The play thus ultimately needs to distance the Nurse from Juliet and from the Capulet family in order to mitigate her spatial intrusion and reinstate the normal geographical and class boundaries that wet-nursing presupposes. This physical and symbolic segregation, with the powerful ability to reassure aristocrats who feel uneasy about the work of the wet nurse, is missing from both the domestic space of the Capulet household and from the play's plot, where, at least during the first half of the tragedy, the Nurse plays a vital role as a go-between and as a structural parallel to Friar Lawrence. But separation, I argue, is provided where we might least expect it: in the form and structure of the Nurse's famous speech. Separation, that is, is effected rhetorically, through the spatial syntax of the Nurse's narrative.

As a storyteller, the Nurse takes the audience from the present scene of the play back into a past that is retrievable only through her narrative. Beginning in the present moment, with a projection into the future ("Come Lammas Eve at night shall she be fourteen"), she quickly shifts to a primarily past-tense memorial narrative, signaled by her phrase: "I remember it well." The reconstruction of her deceased husband's words through the use of embedded quotations ("'Yea', quoth he, 'dost thou fall upon thy face?'") further removes her story of Juliet's weaning from the present time and location of the play's action. In its diachronic momentum, the speech deploys time as a mechanism of distancing and separation, much in the same way that some early anthropologic writing locates native peoples within a discourse of a "primitive" past.[45] Though the Nurse is clearly contemporaneous with the Capulets and their domestic world—and perhaps *because* she is—her speech reorganizes the spatial relationship between her and her employers and marks her as anachronistic.

The speech also establishes separation through a series of temporal references that evoke the same distant past embedded in the speech's grammatical structures. First, the references to Lammas-tide and Lammas Eve recollect the festal calendar of the Christian church. Lammas day (traditionally celebrated on August 1) was a harvest festival and a day for paying rents that was frequently noted in the popular almanacs of the period.[46] The mention of the feast day invokes the thematic context of ripening, but the Nurse's turn to an early liturgical calendar also positions both her and her tale within a temporal setting that is significantly distanced from the present world of the play. Though the economic contexts of Lammas day subtly resonate with the Nurse's own economic function within the Capulet household, this connection is imprecise, and its primary effect is to locate the Nurse's labor within a cyclical time scheme that exists beyond (and before) that household. Furthermore, by aligning her with the festal calendar, the references to Lammas day associate the Nurse with a pre-Reformation religious past, marking her as both temporally and religiously outmoded to Shakespeare's audience. The Nurse also alludes to specific natural events in the past, most notably Juliet's weaning and the earthquake that accompanied it, "now eleven years" removed. Her precise remembrance of the time and date of Juliet's weaning, in contrast to Lady Capulet's inexact memory of "a fortnight and odd days," grounds her narrative in a past that is specifically based on her own labor as a wet nurse, who worked "[o]f all the days of the year upon that day" and who "can tell her [Juliet's] age unto an hour." The Nurse also deploys a comparative time scheme ("Susan and she . . . / Were of an age") that situates Juliet's weaning within yet another memorial narrative of death and maternal loss. These formal mechanisms in the speech mark it as anomalous, as a story clearly removed from the play's present action. As such, the speech highlights the belatedness of the Nurse's narrative and the near agelessness of the Nurse herself—she who might "live a thousand years" and yet not forget her tale.

In producing a narrative that safely separates the Nurse from the Capulet family, the play thus relies primarily on a process of rhetorical distancing that is most clearly at work in the Nurse's own lengthy monologue in Act 1. But more tangible forms of differentiation appear later in the play. When the Nurse returns to Juliet to bring news of her forthcoming marriage to Romeo, she once again plays the part of a garrulous, overwrought storyteller who is unable to articulate her message clearly. Her ineffective oral skills drive Juliet to exclaim in frustration, "Here's such a coil. Come, what says Romeo?" (2.5.66), a response that prefigures Juliet's ultimate rejection of the Nurse's advice and company. More seriously, when the Nurse attempts to intervene on behalf of Juliet to curb Capulet's rage at his daughter's refusal to marry Paris, she is harshly silenced:

> *Nurse*: God in heaven bless her.
>   You are to blame, my lord, to rate her so.
> *Capulet*: And why, my Lady Wisdom? Hold your tongue,
>   Good Prudence! Smatter with your gossips, go.
> *Nurse*: I speak no treason.
> *Capulet*: O God 'i' good e'en!
> *Nurse*: May not one speak?
> *Capulet*: Peace, you mumbling fool!
>   Utter your gravity o'er a gossip's bowl,
>   For here we need it not.   (3.5.168–175)

In a move that is both dismissive and vindictive, Capulet attempts to exclude the Nurse's voice from his household by associating her with a (presumably segregated) group of female gossips. Like Tenterhook's projected narrative in *Westward Ho*, Capulet's commands deflect the threat that the Nurse poses to his domestic authority by repositioning her words within a culturally licensed space for female speech. It is Juliet, however, who enacts the most permanent form of separation from the Nurse when she rejects her advice to marry Paris and announces to the audience that "[t]hou and my bosom henceforth shall be twain" (3.5.240). Calling the Nurse "Ancient damnation" (235), Juliet linguistically resituates the family servant within a vilified past, a purposefully diachronic move that enables her own move forward ("henceforth") in the tragic plot.[47] In part, then, Juliet's rejection of the Nurse also enacts a generic differentiation within the play. It is precisely the comic, lower-class Nurse who must be discarded in order for the play to move decisively toward its tragic conclusion. Tragedy, in this instance, hinges to a degree on the elimination of the comic scapegoat.

In the process of telling the story of Juliet's weaning, the Nurse brings into visibility another narrative: a narrative about her own labor in the Capulet household economy and the social protocols for class distinctions and physical distance that it violates. Her tale, and the more forceful rejections that follow it, reaffirm social space and status differentials, mitigating her awkward and protracted presence through rhetorical distancing and separation. Rhetoric in the play thus proves to be a suitable substitute for geography, establishing lines of social demarcation that make up for the absence of clearly defined boundaries. The structures of the Nurse's embedded narrative function as spatial syntaxes in the play, traversing social space and organizing it so that it is intelligible to audiences concerned about social pollution or gratuitous proximity to the lower-class body of the female laborer. Just as Mistress Tenterhook's projected narrative in *Westward Ho* works to exclude the figure of Birdlime from the birthroom, the Nurse's own story works to exclude her from the Capulet family. And we see once again that the text establishes boundaries not only between the upper and lower classes but also between groups of women: between mothers and daughters on the one hand and hired help on the other.

And yet, while *Romeo and Juliet* seems to remove the danger posed by the undue proximity of the lower-class wet nurse, it also associates the Nurse's labor with a degree of authority that is linked to her mobility and to her ability to control access to bodies and origins. As we have seen, the Nurse's function within the plot and her usefulness within the Capulet home are explicitly dependent upon her mobility. In addition, the Nurse retains control over the all-important story of Juliet's origins, origins that are symbolically and humorally linked to the process of breast-feeding. She vocalizes the moment of Juliet's weaning that was notably inaccessible to Lady Capulet, "then at Mantua." In so doing, she produces an alternative history of sorts that manages to bubble through in her lengthy narrative despite Lady

Capulet and Juliet's resistance to it. In a play so consistently focused on the workings of fate and fortune, the Nurse is the only character who gives the audience or reader a sustained sense of the past world beyond and before the play's opening Chorus. And though she is ultimately discarded and silenced by the Capulets, in the world of the early modern theater, that silence can last only until the play's next public performance.

What we see in *Romeo and Juliet*'s representation of wet-nursing, then, is a narrative of spatial separation that is effected through rhetorical structures rather than through concrete references to urban geography. But we also see the wet nurse's authority formulated in terms of a discourse of sanctioned and useful mobility—her ability, for example, to move between city and country, between pantry and bedchamber—and in terms of her access to moments and sites of origins. During a period in England in which wet-nursing was at a historical high, families had to contend with new problems of overcrowding, increased social and geographical mobility, and a bourgeoning proto-capitalist consumer culture in which breast milk was a highly prized commodity. Texts from the period define the labor of wet nurses through narrative processes that center largely on acts of segregation and differentiation, but they also begin to articulate the available subject positions for these workers in line with changing social and economic conditions. One of the things that emerges from this process is that the discursive emphasis on separation leads to a diffusion of maternal authority. Though early modern narratives may carefully distinguish mothers from the women they hire, the result of this process is *not* to solidify the unique role of the mother but paradoxically to insist that these separated figures are symbiotically related. Hinted at in *Westward Ho* and *Romeo and Juliet*, this uneasy relationship between separation and symbiosis is brought into clearer focus in one of the most important prescriptive tracts on breast-feeding in the period, Elizabeth Clinton's *The Countesse of Lincolnes Nurserie*.

The Office of a Damme

Though the wet nurse might ultimately be expendable within the plot of *Romeo and Juliet*, she was an intractable figure in seventeenth-century English culture. The numerous texts advocating maternal breast-feeding during this period attest to the fact that the wet nurse's social position was in need of definition; it had to be discussed and argued about.[48] Of all of these texts, Clinton's didactic treatise, which

vehemently advocates maternal breast-feeding, is perhaps most striking for its development of an uneasy symbiosis between aristocratic
mothers and lower-class wet nurses.[49] *The Nurserie*, a more complex
document than is often acknowledged, vividly articulates the tensions
between maternal labor and hired help; Clinton's focus on the duty
of aristocratic wives to breastfeed their own children paradoxically
mandates an extended discussion of the wet nurses whom these wives
should (in her estimation) refuse to hire. In attempting to navigate
between these two positions, Clinton produces a narrative that com-
partmentalizes them. The logical structures of her text and the way in
which she constructs her readership meticulously enforce social and
religious distinctions, rhetorical divides that, as in *Romeo and Juliet*,
stand in place of social and geographical ones.

Clinton's didacticism requires that she establish at the outset the
validity of her authorship and the legitimacy of her arguments about
breast-feeding. She begins the treatise by advertising her authority
to write and publish her text, an authority purportedly derived from
personal experience hiring wet nurses, since she herself did not nurse
her own children (a decision she claims later to have dearly regretted).
She writes, "Because it hath pleased God to blesse me with many
children, and so caused me to observe many things falling out to
mothers, and to their children; I thought good to open my minde
concerning a speciall matter belonging to all childe-bearing women"
(B1r).[50] Clinton's dissemination of her advice to "all child-bearing
women" reads as both magnanimous and slightly condescending,
since this process necessitates a move from "I" to "all" that is produced
through a discourse of privilege, expertise, and "speciall" knowledge.
She continues to promote the authority and superiority of her narrative throughout the text, most notably through the use of biblical
marginalia. Appearing most frequently in the first half of her treatise,
where she attempts to "shew, that every woman ought to nurse her
owne childe" (B1r), Clinton's marginalia direct the reader to biblical
passages that she has paraphrased or to exemplary biblical figures that
she lauds for maternal breast-feeding. These marginal reinforcements
buttress her own biblical exegesis by alerting the reader to the scriptural basis for her claims. Clinton, for example, supports her position against wet-nursing by citing famous women from the Bible who
suckled their own children. She highlights "the example of *Sarah* the
wife of *Abraham*; For shee both gave her sonne *Isaac* suck, as doing
the dutie commanded of God: And also tooke great comfort, and
delight therein, as in a duty well pleasing to her selfe" (B2r). This exegetical claim is corroborated in the marginal note, which references

the relevant passage from Genesis 21:7. However, the Genesis passage that Clinton cites is notably silent about Sarah's "great comfort, and delight"; these are details that Clinton has taken the liberty to add herself. The marginal note here thus serves a dual purpose: it adds evidentiary support to Clinton's argument, and it simultaneously announces her authorial departure from her biblical source. Clinton, that is, makes her reader perfectly aware that she is creating her own biblical narrative, marshalling the scriptural evidence in order to construct a specific genealogy of maternal breast-feeding.

Clinton's marginalia serve another function too; they create the formal impression of proof even when Clinton's scriptural evidence is weak or nonexistent. The preponderance of biblical notations in the treatise's first pages gives the text the physical appearance of careful documentation. As such, a reader might be less likely to question a portion of Clinton's argument that does *not* receive marginal reinforcement:

> By [God's] word it is proved, first by *Examples*, namely the example of *Eve*. For who suckled her sonnes Cain, Abel, Seth, &c but her selfe? Which shee did not only of meere necessitie, because yet no other woman was created; but especially because shee was their mother, and so sawe it was her duty: and because she had a true naturall affection, which moved her to doe it gladly.   (B2r)

Clinton's argument in this remarkable passage depends solely on speculation and on a spurious, albeit humorous, deployment of circular logic: Eve nursed her children *not* for the obvious reason—that "yet no other woman was created"—but for the reason that best suits Clinton's argument—that she had a "true naturall affection." Though the treatise uses direct biblical citations to augment its credibility, it also, at moments such as this, advertises the ability of Clinton's narrative to stand alone. The didacticism of *The Nurserie*, that is, depends upon the reader's willingness to balance documented evidence and experiential authority with blind faith in the author's exhortations. Clinton authorizes her text and her authorial voice by deploying both a textual system of documentation and an exegetical license that alludes to scriptural authority but proceeds in crafting an independent expository narrative regardless of direct scriptural evidence.

If Clinton's marginalia establish a subtle divide between author and biblical source and between author and reader, the body of the text generates a parallel narrative that segregates the aristocratic women Clinton addresses from the wet nurses they (should not) hire. As we have seen, the institution of wet-nursing mandated a temporary break-down of social and economic boundaries that may have been partially mitigated by geographical separation. In *Romeo and Juliet*, the usual geographical boundaries have been removed and physical separation has to be artificially reinforced. *The Nurserie* is less concerned with geography per se, but it is nevertheless deeply committed to an arrangement of social space in which divisions between women—between mothers and hired help—are meticulously enforced. This division is enacted in the text both through Clinton's invocation of her readership and through her construction of rhetorical boundaries that segregate different categories of women from each other.

In her dedication to her daughter-in-law, Clinton defines her readership along gender lines. She claims that she writes for "such women as will vouchsafe to read this little short treatise" so that they may be "put in minde of a duty, which all mothers are bound to performe" (A2v). But Clinton's imagined audience of female readers is further differentiated in the dedication by Thomas Lodge (T.L.) that follows the opening preface. In his address "To the Courteous, chiefly most Christian, Reader," Lodge insists upon a remarkably precise division in Clinton's readership. At the end of his dedication, Lodge writes: "If Noble, who readest, (likenesse is Mother & Nurse of liking) this comes from Nobility; Approve the rather, and practise. If meaner; blush to deny, what Honour becomes speaker to perswade to, president to lead the way to. And so I either humbly take my leave; or bid farewell" (A4v). Lodge suggests that the different class positions of Clinton's audience dictate distinct logics of reading. For noble readers, like aligns to like; they are to "[a]pprove" and "practise" according to Clinton's advice. "Meaner" readers, on the other hand, must be persuaded and led by Clinton to the correct practice; their relationship to Clinton and to her text cannot simply be a mimetic one, but must be a relationship of educational dependence. This insistence on social division *within* Clinton's female readership is solidified by Lodge's rhetorical act of leave-taking, which he does either "humbly" or by bidding farewell, depending on the status of the individual reader. In thus articulating two distinct author–reader relationships in its prefatory material, *The Nurserie* displays not only an astute awareness of economic and social hierarchy but also a tactical impetus to keep women neatly divided according to social rank.

This narrative momentum in the text is directly related to Clinton's specific concerns about the practice of wet-nursing. Indeed, in his own linguistic separation between mother and nurse ("likenesse is Mother & Nurse of liking"), Lodge suggests the ways in which the text's subject matter necessitates specific strategies of differentiation. In one sense, Lodge's phrase performs Clinton's overall argument: mother and nurse should be interchangeable. But his grammatical articulation of mother and nurse as distinct positions (linked but not entirely conflated by "&") also registers the difficultly involved in bridging the divide between these forms of women's labor, especially given an aristocratic culture in which the hiring of wet nurses was ubiquitous. Clinton's advocacy for maternal breast-feeding depends upon an understanding of work and the ownership of labor power that functions according to the same mimetic model that Lodge sets forth in his dedication. Providing further evidence in favor of her position, Clinton writes:

> Now another *worke* of God, proving this point is the *worke of his provision*, for every kinde to be apt, and able to nourish their own fruit: there is no beast that feeds their young with milke, but the Lord, even from the first ground of the order of nature; *Growe, and multiplie*; hath provided it of milke to suckle their owne young, which every beast takes so naturally unto, as if another beast come toward their young to offer the office of a Damme unto it, they shew according to their fashion, a plaine dislike of it: as if nature did speake in them, and say it is contrary to Gods order in nature, commanding each kinde to increase, and multiplie in their owne bodies, and by their owne breasts, not to bring forth by one Damme, and to bring up by another: but it is his ordinance that every kind should both bring forth, and also nurse its owne fruit.   (C1r)

The careful structure of this passage establishes a boundary between those who adhere to the proper, mimetic process of maternal labor (those who nurse their "owne fruit") and those who violently yoke heterogeneous positions together (those "Dammes" who "bring forth" but do not "bring up"). Clinton's nearly incessant repetition of the word "own" here and throughout the treatise restores to her argument the clear divisions in ownership that the seventeenth-century practice of wet-nursing throws into question. As a form of labor that can be performed for money by a woman completely unrelated to the infant, wet-nursing effectively denies a stable understanding of one's "owne worke" (D2r). Additionally, as we have seen, the potential for class infection introduced by the wet nurse poses a threat to the integrity of aristocratic lineages. Of course, since Clinton's subject *is* wet-nursing, she cannot avoid this problem by eliding the figure of the nurse altogether, but she can insist throughout the treatise on a hermetically sealed, mimetic relationship between mother and child.

The representation of gender and labor in *The Nurserie* is also bifurcated by religious difference. A member of a devout Protestant family, Clinton is invested in creating divisions between women according to her own strict Protestant beliefs in election and predestination.[51] Near the end of her text, she exhorts "all godly women" not to "destroye and drie up those breasts, in which your owne child (and perhaps one of Gods very elect)...might find food of syncere milke." A few lines later, she argues: "I doe knowe that the Lord may deny some women, either to have any milke in their breasts at all, or to have any passage for their milke, or to have any health, or to have a right minde: and so they may be letted from this duty, by *want*, by *sicknesse*, by *lunacy*, &c. But I speake not to these: I speake to you, whose *consciences* witnesse against you, that you cannot justly alleage any of those impediments" (D1r). Clinton here narrows the definition of her upper-class, female audience to include only those women who may be, or may give birth to, the elect. While she acknowledges that mothers may experience difficulty breast-feeding, she insists that her own, godly readers cannot fall back on physical excuses.[52] And since the inability to bear or nurse children was frequently interpreted by Protestants as a sign of God's disfavor, Clinton has an additional motivation for rejecting even the possibility of physical impediments among her readers. Clinton thus avers the godliness of her audience through a circuitous logical route, carefully distinguishing between "these" and "you" in order to segregate her readers from both the ungodly and the physically and mentally unfit.

Clinton's direct address to her readers contrasts sharply with the passage that immediately follows it, in which she describes the occupational hazards involved in hiring wet nurses. She claims to have found "by grievous experience, such dissembling in nurses, pretending sufficiency of milke, when indeed they had too much scarcitie; pretending willingnesse, towardnesse, wakefulnesse, when indeed they have beene most wilfull, most froward, and most slothfull, as I feare the death of one or two of my little Babes came by the defalt of their nurses" (D1v). The physical impediments of the wet nurses whom Clinton has observed—including their sloth and "scarcitie" of milk—suggests that these women are not only economically inferior to Clinton's readers but that they are also ungodly and, therefore, not fit to nurse "perhaps one of Gods very elect." Of course, Clinton's logic here is once again circular in nature: if physical problems mark a woman as religiously unfit for nursing, then it follows that only lower-class women—*not* her aristocratic readers—will have such problems. And yet for Clinton, the belief in election enables her to erect yet another barrier between aristocratic mothers and hired nurses. In doing so, she forcefully staves off the social pollution usually thought to be implicit in the practice of wet-nursing.

At the end of her treatise, Clinton solidifies her argument by emphasizing that maternal breast-feeding is a *"commendable act"* because it is "Gods blessing" (D3r, D2v). She tells her readers: "Thinke againe how your Babe crying for your breast, sucking hartily the milke out of it, and growing by it, is the *Lords owne instruction*, every houre, and every day, that you are suckling it, instructing you to shew that you are his *new borne Babes*, by your earnest desire after his word, & the syncere doctrine thereof" (D2v). Clinton here establishes a parallel between the relationship between mother and child in the act of breast-feeding and the relationship between God and his believers, his "new borne Babes." Clinton thus fashions two independent yet mutually constitutive pedagogical systems that each function mimetically; God instructs his believers in "syncere doctrine" just as mothers provide their "owne instruction" to their children by breast-feeding them. By virtue of this comparison, maternal breast-feeding becomes a sanctified, educational act instead of the unnatural and ungodly act that wet nurses perform "for *lucre* sake" (C4v). Clinton further sanctifies maternal breast-feeding when she tells her audience: "when your child is at your breast, it is a fit occasion to move your heart to pray for a blessing upon that worke; and to give thanks for your child, and for ability & freedome unto that, which many a mother would have done and could not" (D2v–D3r). In her final lines, Clinton rhetorically establishes a sacred space of maternal labor, while again distinguishing her readers from those mothers who "would have done and could not." The treatise thus concludes by designating maternal breast-feeding as both a sanctified and a self-sustaining economic system, a fitting alternative to the polluted economy of wet-nursing.

To a large extent, then, what makes *The Nurserie* so remarkable in the early modern debates about breast-feeding is Clinton's heightened attention to social hierarchy and her reiterated insistence on divisions between women, divisions that are crucial to her polemical attack on wet-nursing. The binaries that Clinton works so hard to articulate— godly versus ungodly, natural versus unnatural, unpaid versus paid, mothers versus nurses—resituate the social practice of wet-nursing within a rational order that eliminates economic, social, and geographical fluidity. The polemical nature of Clinton's treatise produces a text that is far more interested in the precise differentiation of social categories and distinctions between women than either *Westward Ho* or *Romeo and Juliet*. But we can still see a common thread running through these texts: they all produce narratives of separation that articulate the lines of demarcation by which social spaces are constructed and organize the relationships between mothers and hired help that occur within those spaces.

Still, as de Certeau so aptly puts it, "What the map cuts up, the story cuts across." Narration, that is, is made of movements, and it is "only ambivalently that the limit circumscribes in this space."[53] Unlike the static contours of a map, narrative is always in flux and never fully capable of fixing boundaries or ascribing clearly defined limits. Put another way, as ardently as Clinton works to define her readership and to assign clear social, religious, and economic categories to the figures she discusses, her argument constantly runs the risk of occultatio, of rhetorically emphasizing the very topic she wishes to pass over. In order to reject wet-nursing so adamantly, Clinton must repeatedly discuss those women whom she wants to eliminate from discussion. And it is precisely because she cannot completely or cleanly elide wet nurses from her arguments that the treatise can "only ambivalently" circumscribe its subject.

Indeed, the rigid separations that characterize much of the text break down completely at several key points. After berating the "monstrous unnaturalness" of those women who hire wet nurses, Clinton writes:

> And this unthankfulnesse, and unnaturalnesse is often the sinne of the *Higher*, and the *richer sort* then of the meaner, and poorer, except some nice and prowd idle dames, who will imitate their betters, till they make their poore husbands beggars. And this is one hurt which the better ranke doe by their ill example; egge, and imbolden the lower ones to follow them to their losse: were it not better for *Us greater persons* to keepe Gods ordinance, & to shew the meaner their dutie in our good example? I am sure wee have more helpes to performe it, and have fewer probable reasons to alleage against it, then women that live by hard labour, & painfull toile.   (C1v–C2r)

Clinton acknowledges that hiring wet nurses is almost exclusively an upper-class practice, and she chides her aristocratic sisters for failing to provide appropriate pedagogical models for those of lesser rank who might learn by their examples. But Clinton does not limit her discussion to a simple distinction between "higher" and "meaner" women; she also refers to a group of women who are not members of the aristocracy but who nevertheless are able to purchase wet-nursing services, the "nice and prowd idle dames, who will imitate their betters." These women are clearly neither the "higher" nor the "meaner" women that Clinton cites, but rather women of the middling sort who nevertheless have enough money to purchase the service of a wet nurse, women such as Mistress Tenterhook in *Westward Ho*.[54] These "idle dames" disrupt any easy binary between aristocratic women and the lower-class women they hire as wet nurses, but they also disrupt the mimetic potential of Clinton's text. Choosing to "imitate their betters," they perform a type of imitation granted only to fellow noble-women in Lodge's dedication, forcing Clinton to mark their actions as vain and foolish—upward mobility that will ultimately exhaust the resources of the middling families to which they belong. Early modern economic and social divisions were clearly far less distinct than Clinton would have them, and as a result the mimetic argument that she proposes in her treatise is ultimately unable to address in full the social problems that wet-nursing raises. The binary logic that runs throughout the text—especially the dominant binary of mother versus nurse—collapses with the introduction of a third term ("nice and prowd idle dames") and the recognition that mothers themselves are a group internally riven by status differentials.

Clinton's binaries dissolve further when she virulently chastises aristocratic ("higher") mothers for their participation in a culture of wet-nursing. Though the treatise, as we have seen, forthrightly condemns "dissembling in nurses," who breastfeed for "lucre sake," Clinton at times thwarts this overly reductive assignment of blame. Addressing her aristocratic readers, Clinton urges: "Therefore be no longer at the trouble, and at the care to hire others to doe your owne *worke*: bee not so *unnaturall* to thrust away your owne children: be not so *hardy* as to venter a *tender Babe* to a *lessse tender heart*: bee not *accessary* to that disorder of causing a *poorer woman to banish her owne infant*, for the entertaining of a *richer womans child*, as it were, bidding her *unlove her owne to love yours*" (D1v–D2r). Referring specifically to the fact that wet nurses would usually not have continued to breastfeed their own babies due to a concern about the adequacy of their milk supply, Clinton derides upper-class women for being "accessary" to the estrangement of poorer wet nurses from their own children.[55] In doing so, she acknowledges, as she did earlier when she denounced the "sinne of the *Higher*, and the *richer sort*," the social inequality that structures the relationship between wet nurse and mother. But the oscillation in the treatise between the disparagements of "dissembling" nurses and the attack on rich women who refuse to do their "owne worke" disallows a clear causality or an easy dispensation of blame. In other words, the tangled and at times contradictory logic of Clinton's argument ultimately succeeds not in carefully delineating discrete class positions or divisions between women, but in revealing the degree to which the institution of wet-nursing makes any such delineation impossible. Wet nurses and the women who hire them are equally implicated in the occupational system that Clinton censures so harshly.

The rhetorical structures of *The Nurserie* thus work to compensate for the fluid social and economic boundaries that attended early modern wet-nursing practices. In part, Clinton finds her solution in a sanctified space of maternal labor that functions according to a mimetic relationship between mother and child and between God and the individual believer. Relying on a pedagogical model throughout the treatise, Clinton instructs her readers according to arguments based upon entrenched beliefs in social hierarchies and fears of social pollution. The result, however, is a text that makes visible not the social abjection of the wet nurse so much as the symbiotic relationships between women who occupy different positions within wet-nursing's labor hierarchy. In her attempt to reject the practice of wet-nursing, to enforce strict hierarchies among women, and to solidify the figure of the (aristocratic) birth mother, Clinton produces a narrative in which wet nurses are differentiated from their social betters but are never completely removed from the scene or deprived of agency. Clinton succeeds only ambivalently in circumscribing her subject.

Early modern texts that represent the work of midwives and wet nurses, such as those I've discussed here, demonstrate that the subjectivity of these figures was culturally defined in terms of their mobility both within London and between different social groups, in addition to their privileged access to bodies and the spaces socially demarcated as sites of reproduction. Moving between country and city, between impoverished rural spaces and wealthy merchant households, and between the birthchamber and the world outside, these figures acquire occupational identities and positions of social authority that in many ways set them apart from the other female laborers that this book considers. Perhaps it is for this reason that writers argue so forcefully about these workers in print and strive so diligently to delineate clear-cut definitions of the spaces, boundaries, and social arrangements that their work makes culturally visible. Prompted by increased social and geographical mobility, the fluidity of urban boundaries, and the social pollution threatened by the lower-class female laborer who cares for middling and upper-class infants, writers of the period—both prescriptive and dramatic—turn frequently to narratives that emphasize separation and compartmentalization. This recurring narrative is not simply a sign of prevailing cultural anxieties, though that is one of the ways in which it can be read. More significantly, this narrative is a culturally useful story: it constructs a reassuring system of boundaries and hierarchies during a historical period in which wet-nursing and midwifery were widely practiced yet beset by newly intensified concerns over urban space, social stratification, and maternal responsibility.

In these narratives, midwives and wet nurses are distanced from the mothers who hire them either through rhetorical strategies that demarcate social space—as in *Romeo and Juliet* and *The Nurserie*—or through the textual manipulation of geographical space—as in *Westward Ho*. This process of differentiation works to clarify and define the nature of the relationships between mothers and the women they hire by separating them neatly from each other and by assigning each a role of either privilege or deference. But by multiplying the locations of maternal labor—by insisting that this work is and often must be performed by several different women—these narratives diffuse maternal authority rather than solidify it. What these texts reveal, then, is that prior to the more explicit articulation of maternal ideology that would take hold in the eighteenth century, early modern writers formulated multiple sites of maternal authority. Though mothers, midwives, and wet nurses were often in conflict in seventeenth-century England, they were also discursively constructed in terms of an uneasy symbiosis. On the one hand, the conflicts between women and hired help that are so apparent in *Westward Ho* and *The Nurserie* prefigure the more substantial social divisions and shifts in maternal ideology that would obtain in the next century, leading to a gradual replacement of midwives by men-midwives and medical doctors and a gradual transition (both in theory and practice) to maternal breast-feeding. But on the other hand, this narrativized dissemination of maternal authority served a pragmatic social function: intentional or not, it vindicated the labor practices of a wide range of families, particularly aristocrats, who, despite late seventeenth-century concerns about the medical authority of midwives and the warnings of Clinton and numerous others about the benefits of maternal breast-feeding, continued to hire midwives and wet nurses in large numbers throughout the period. Indeed, because narratives that carefully differentiated these maternal adjuncts from the mothers who hired them necessarily had to discuss and assign social categories to these workers, the prevalence of these stories may have paradoxically helped to ensure that midwives and wet nurses would remain on the scene in England well into the eighteenth century. Once again, the trope of occultatio rears its head. In producing "sentences and itineraries" to make sense of women's reproductive work, early modern narratives succeeded to a degree in mapping and organizing the social space of this labor, but they could neither dictate the precise endpoints of these discursive roadmaps nor fully suppress the subject positions that they enabled.

CHAPTER 3

———✴◉✴———

DIVINE DRUDGERY: THE SPIRITUAL
LOGIC OF HOUSEWORK

In 1616 the Hanmer family of Wales began to compile an intriguing assortment of domestic documents that now reside in the Folger Shakespeare Library in Washington, D.C. Folger MS V.a. 347, best described as a manuscript commonplace and receipt book, seems to have served a wide variety of practical and spiritual purposes for the Hanmer family. The manuscript is labeled "A Sermon booke" on the flyleaf and begins, appropriately enough, with twenty-two pages of sermon notes, concluding with notes from a sermon on Romans 7:21. A mere turn of the page, however, brings the reader to a very different set of notes: a recipe entitled "to pot hare" (fo. 23r), one of several recipes that fill the manuscript's next five pages. This juxtaposition of sermon notes, recipes, and other personal records continues throughout the manuscript.[1] The Folger collection also includes a late seventeenth-century manuscript (MS V.a. 468) owned by Elizabeth Fowler that shares many of the characteristics of the Hanmer document. This book begins with numerous pages of recipes, with titles such as "to pot venison" (fo. 1r), "To make Goosbury Creame" (fo. 7r), and "To Stew Mutton" (fo. 22r). Later in the manuscript, however, we find sermon notes in different italic hands, a few medicinal recipes, and, on the final page, a devotional poem.

A modern reader of these documents might well wonder what recipes for gooseberry cream and notations on a sermon could possibly have in common; these are not items likely to be anthologized together in the twenty-first-century home. But early modern families such as the Hanmers and the Fowlers appear to have had little trouble accepting these seemingly odd textual arrangements. The somewhat surprising juxtapositions that characterize these eclectic compilations provide subtle clues about how early modern families understood not only the books on their shelves but also the day-to-day labors that constituted the broader category of housework.[2] By demonstrating that materials as apparently discrete as sermons and recipes for stewed mutton could be conceptualized within the same textual space, the Hanmer and Fowler manuscripts imply that household chores and religious practices could be imagined as complementary and interrelated activities in the early modern home. The physical organization of these documents enacts and testifies to a relationship between the activities of housework and the practice of personal piety.

The Hanmer and Fowler texts connect two aspects of early modern domesticity—religion and household labor—that modern scholars have tended to separate. In recent years, literary scholars such as Wendy Wall, Lena Orlin, and Natasha Korda, among others, have rightly devoted considerable attention to the economic and social aspects of housewifery, resulting in several important studies of early modern domestic economy.[3] As we saw in chapter 1, Korda in particular has demonstrated that the housewife's role was shifting quite dramatically during the early modern period as England developed a mercantile, commodity-based economic system. This historical shift, she argues, created a period of tension between two divergent ideological constructions of the sexual division of labor within the home: "During the long period of transition from feudal to nascent capitalist modes of production, the residual ideal of the self-sufficient housewife who produces what she consumes competed with the emergent ideal of the passive and obedient keeper who mothers the goods her husband provides."[4] The emerging figure of the obedient yet commercially savvy housewife signaled not only a transformation in England's economy but also a fundamental change in women's labor.

These economic shifts, however, coincided with profound changes in the daily religious practices of early modern Englishwomen—a connection that has been largely overlooked by contemporary scholarship.[5] By the early seventeenth century, the Reformation's heightened emphasis on women's roles within the family coupled with the Protestant understanding of the household as an extension of the Church altered the balance of power within the English home. Women were increasingly expected to wield a greater spiritual and physical influence over the space of the household and over its subordinate children and servants. At the same time, by significantly reducing the number of official roles open to devout women (particularly those available through Catholic convents) and eliminating many opportunities for public religious expression, the Reformation dramatically increased the importance of women's private religious practices.[6] As Christine Peters has argued, "the association between women and piety was more strongly articulated during this period," so much so that by the mid-seventeenth century, "elite epitaphs suggest that religiosity had developed to an unprecedented extent as the defining feature of a virtuous and praiseworthy female life."[7] Ministers, theologians, and writers of conduct books encouraged women to practice daily devotions in their own homes and to develop a regime of piety characterized by rigorous introspection and self-scrutiny. Though the pious regime emphasized private practice over public religious participation, it nevertheless offered a new set of opportunities for many early modern women by enabling them to pursue culturally and religiously sanctioned modes of self-expression and independent thought.[8]

Early modern housewives thus performed the daily tasks of cooking, cleaning, and managing servants within a much larger religious and ideological context. For Protestants eager to ensure the order and proper functioning of the household, these chores could not stand alone: they had to be practiced as part of a pious regime. But this emerging interest in the importance of personal piety to daily housewifery also raised urgent new questions about the housewife's reliability, morality, and introspection. Women were lynchpins of domestic order, but this order was precariously reliant on female interiority and self-scrutiny—activities that were fundamental to Protestant piety but by definition hidden from the purview of others. If household order depends in part upon women's internal processes of introspection, then how can that order ever be assured, monitored, or controlled? How can the good (or bad) housewife even be recognized if the housewife herself is the only one who can ensure her own compliance with devotional practices? This tension between interiority and its representation was at the heart of the post-Reformation household, and it compounded an already vexed set of questions about women's proper role in the early modern home.

In this chapter, I argue that early modern texts that represent the figure of the housewife—including domestic dramas for the public stage and Protestant women's private diaries—create narratives that enact and make visible an essential relationship between housework and personal piety. By insisting on this interrelationship these early seventeenth-century texts produce compelling fictions about the

Protestant household in which women's labor is neatly aligned with religious ideologies about domestic order.[9] In addition, since the link between housework and piety necessarily depends on the invisible processes of women's introspection and self-scrutiny, these narratives frequently display an evidentiary quality. That is, dramatists such as Thomas Heywood and diarists such as Margaret Hoby and Anne Clifford create narratives that solidify the link between the housewife's labor and her practice of piety by demonstrating the otherwise hidden aspects of devotion and introspection. Such stories, I suggest, are largely compensatory in nature; the images of the virtuous housewife that they project help assuage fundamental concerns not only about women's domestic labor but also about the inscrutability of the housewife's inner life.

Of course, these narratives of pious housewifery are rarely free of internal contradictions. At times, particularly in the drama, these stories tell us more about the epistemological uncertainties that threaten to undermine the neat alignment of domestic duties and spirituality than they do about domestic order. And yet, in struggling to articulate the scope of women's domestic labor during a period in which both housework and the position of women within the household were being actively redefined and reimagined, writers from the period make room for new formulations of housewifely authority. They construe the housewife's subjectivity in accordance with her ability to manage diligently not only her domestic duties, but also her own soul. In so doing, these narratives both speak to the specific domestic tensions that animated the early seventeenth-century household and anticipate the conflation of domesticity, femininity, and piety that would come to be a hallmark of eighteenth-century domestic ideology, thus participating in a slow and irregular process whereby housework would become a uniquely feminized form of labor.

SERMONS AND STEWED MUTTON: PIOUS HOUSEWIFERY IN LADY HOBY'S DIARY

Contemporary texts that prescribe the duties of housewifery suggest that women's spiritual devotion was as important to household order as were household chores such as cooking, cleaning, and supervising servants and guests. The frequent injunctions of conduct books and marriage manuals that direct women to make their families a "little Church" depend upon a commonplace analogy that was taken very seriously in the first half of the seventeenth century, especially by Protestant ministers and authors.[10] In order to make the home a "little

Church," women needed to maintain a clean and fully functioning home by cooking meals, scrubbing floors, and managing servants and tenants.[11] (Though both men and women were responsible for maintaining orderly and productive homes, contemporary domestic manuals clearly articulate a sexual division of household labor, a divide that would become more rigid in the eighteenth century. Whereas the husband was expected to "travell abroad to seek living," the wife was told to "keep the house"; the husband was to "dispatch all things without doore" while the wife was to "oversee and give order for all things within.")[12] However, women also needed to ensure order within their own souls, an order created through the personal piety that was associated with female religiosity in seventeenth-century England. Women's spirituality was thus deeply intertwined with their domestic duty to provide order within the household.

Of course, Protestant conduct books such as those written by William Gouge and Robert Cleaver prescribe ideal practice and affirm a desire for balance and household order that may or may not match up with the lived experience of any early modern family. But we can see quite vividly in the diary writings of early seventeenth-century women that the interrelation between housework and piety helps to shape the *stories* they tell about their own domestic lives and labors, even if those narratives fail to mirror actual practice. Though individual diaries take various forms, household labor is the thematic cornerstone of a vast majority of them. Devotional diaries in particular often offer a very detailed and complex picture of the housewife's domestic routine, and even those diaries kept by elite women are frequently filled with descriptions of daily housework.[13]

Structurally, diaries from this period tend to fall into two broad categories: the daily record of events organized by date that we have come to associate with the word "diary"; and the spiritual journal, which originated in the specific guidelines of puritan preachers.[14] Keeping a spiritual journal was particularly common among devout, and mainly Protestant, women in early seventeenth-century England. Advice books appeared regularly that taught women what types of devotion should be practiced each day, and many of them advocated diary writing as an integral component of personal piety. The main focus of these prescriptive works—including Richard Rogers's *Seven Treatises* (1603), aimed at both male and female readers; John Featley's *A Fountaine of Teares* (1646), directed specifically toward women; and John Beadle's *The Journal or Diary of a Thankful Christian* (1656), a manual for Protestant diary-keepers— was on self-examination and careful scrutiny of the day's activities.[15]

Beadle's tract explicitly encouraged diary-keepers to record ordinary as well as extraordinary events; the diary, for Beadle, should be used as a "Register-Book" or daily account book of one's soul (B1r–B1v).[16] The spiritual journal thus served as a physical trace of self-scrutiny; by keeping a diary faithfully, early modern women could demonstrate that their daily tasks were orderly and spiritually fulfilled.

The manuscript diary of Lady Margaret Hoby offers a particularly rich and fascinating narrative of the conjunction between personal spirituality and a housewife's daily chores. Hoby, the only daughter of a wealthy landowner, kept a personal diary that covers the years 1599–1603, during which she was married to Sir Thomas Posthumous Hoby, an outspoken puritan well known for fighting recusancy in the north of Yorkshire.[17] Lady Hoby's diary is in many ways a hybrid of the daily record and the spiritual journal, since she records and dates her daily events while also documenting the processes of self-examination that were fundamental to Protestant practice. The diary's entries—brief, but saturated accounts of Hoby's domestic activities—consistently tout her allegiance to Protestantism and to the puritan tenets of predestination and justification by faith.[18] As such, this text serves a spiritual and extremely personal role for Hoby. While clearly not intended for any sort of public readership, the text is nevertheless constructed with such meticulous care—both in terms of its rhetorical structure and the practice of self-examination that it embodies—that it seems designed for a particular, and particularly intimate, audience. Individual entries record and provide evidence of Hoby's faith both for herself and for God; these are the only truly relevant audiences for Hoby, given the self-scrutinizing motives that lie behind the genre of the spiritual journal.

The entries also repeatedly juxtapose religious devotion and household tasks in a manner that suggests an intimate relationship between these discrete domestic activities. For instance, on November 24, 1599, Lady Hoby writes: "After privat praers I did eate my breakfast and then wret of my sarmon book then I walked reed of the bible praied and so went to dinner after dinner I tooke order for thinges about the house paied billes medetated and praied and so went to the Lector then to supper after I walked and talked with Mr. Rhodes reed of the Bible and after praied and then went to bed."[19] Hoby's litany of her daily tasks includes common components of early seventeenth-century housewifery: she must carefully arrange "thinges about the house," place orders for necessary household goods, and maintain economic stability by paying the household "billes." But alongside the description of her physical chores, Hoby records her daily religious duties, which range from private meditation and prayer to reading the Bible to speaking with her chaplain, Mr. Rhodes. Hoby grants these seemingly dissimilar activities equal weight in her text, suggesting that she uses her diary as a spiritual tool or "Register-Book" to account for both her religious practice and her more concrete, household commitments.

The equal importance of economic duties and spiritual meditation is apparent throughout the diary. Even those passages in which Hoby describes the aspects of her housewifery that must be performed outside her home (such as purchasing household items and offering medical care to neighbors) reiterate the twinned interests of piety and labor. On May 12, 1600, Hoby writes: "After praier I did eate and then went to the church after I Came hom I praied and then went to dinner after I went in to the faire and bought divers things then I went to the church againe and after I had talked a whill with my Cossins I went to supper after I walked abroad and then cam home and went to publick praers and after that to bed." A month later, Hoby indicates that she "talked with a goldsmith and bought some thing of him after I went about the house and then wrett in my sarmon book tell [*sic*] I went to privat examenation and praier" (June 13, 1600). Hoby describes offering medical care to a poor neighbor in a similar vein; she "looked upon a poore mans Legg" after Church on Sunday, September 16, 1599 and "saw a mans Legg dressed" the following day "[a]fter privat praier." In carefully narrating this wide variety of tasks, Hoby provides evidence of the orderly success of her household, a success that simultaneously involves buying provisions, caring for the sick, and practicing pious devotion and self-examination.

The content of Hoby's diary entries consistently reinscribes a discourse of pious housewifery, in which spiritual practice and household chores are equally valued and mutually dependent. But the style and organization of this content tell a yet more interesting story: a story that begins with documentation and reflection, but adds to it a rhetorical weight that transforms quotidian description into a spiritually efficacious narrative. The diary entries in Hoby's manuscript possess an energy and a sense of forward momentum that might not be immediately discernible to readers of either of the two modern printed editions of the text. Both Dorothy M. Meads, who edited the first printed edition of the diary in 1930, and Joanna Moody, editor of the 1998 edition, interrupt Hoby's prose with modern punctuation, separating Hoby's undifferentiated clauses and assigning them representative values.[20] The phrase "after to supper then to work and hard [heard] readings of the bible" becomes in Moody's edition, "after, to supper, then to work, and hard readinge of the bible"—a small change, but one that no longer allows for the possibility that working and hearing a reading from the Bible were *simultaneous* rather than consecutive activities for Hoby.[21] In providing commas and colons that encourage readers to pause, modern editors significantly alter and redirect Hoby's prose, diffusing the urgency of individual entries by segmenting them into discrete units.

However, it is all too easy to criticize editors for the necessary alterations they make to texts for the benefit of modern readers— particularly student readers. In the case of the Hoby diary at least, punctuation is only part of the issue. There is an essential grammar to Hoby's diary that is not dependent upon punctuation alone but is created through stylistic and syntactic balance. Hoby's devotional practice and household chores are contextually linked in the diary, but these activities are also conjoined through the text's syntactic structure. Hoby frequently uses coordinating rather than subordinating clauses to connect discrete activities, resulting in a grammatical equilibrium that suggests that piety is both a context for and a crucial component of her household labor. The regular cadences and characteristic polysyndeton of the entries, particularly in the first hundred pages of the manuscript, seem designed to advertise Hoby's orderly household and her particular success in scrutinizing her daily thoughts and labors.

In an entry written on December 1, 1599, Hoby writes: "After privat praers I did eate my breakfast then I wrough [*sic*] and reed of the bible tell dinner time after I wrought and did my deutie in the house tell alMost 6 a clock and then I praied privatly and examened my self then I went to supper after I discharged houshold billes and after praied then reed a whill of perkins and so went to bed:". Hoby's choice of reading material (the Bible and the writings of puritan preacher and theologian William Perkins) advertises her spiritual devotions and her specific interests in Protestant theology. But the grammatical structure of Hoby's prose yokes spiritual and practical household tasks together and offers proof of their orderly balance in Hoby's godly household. Parallel structure combined with the ambiguous use of the word "wrought" emphasizes the equal importance of spiritual devotion ("I wrough and reed of the bible") and household chores ("I wrought and did my deutie in the house"). The word "wrought" is frequently synonymous in the period with needlework, but Hoby's repetition of the word in this passage suggests a broader possibility of meaning. The *Oxford English Dictionary* records contemporary definitions of "wrought" that are quite general ("created, shaped, molded"[22]) and almost endlessly adaptable. Hoby's "wrought" could signify her Bible reading, her "deutie" in the house, or some other physical task in addition to needlework. Regardless of its precise meaning in each instance, the repetition of the word "wrought" in the diary entry works rhetorically—almost as a form of zeugma—to link the acts of reading the Bible and doing one's duty in the house, thereby creating the impression of a tidy balance between religious devotion and household tasks.

If we return briefly to the entry for May 12, 1600, we can see that pious housewifery and its implications for daily life were deeply ingrained in Hoby's textual practice. In the manuscript, the word "praier" is struck out immediately before the word "dinner" in the phrase: "I Came hom I praied and then went to ~~praier~~ dinner." There is, admittedly, some humor in this tiny slip: the word "praier" occurs so many times in the diary that it is hardly surprising that Hoby might initially interchange praying and eating. And yet, the visible correction turns this entry into a palimpsest, revealing trace evidence of the grammatical and contextual interchangeability of prayer and dinner. It is always risky to attempt to describe the unconscious workings of a text per se or to posit a direct connection between self-writings and personal practice. We should also not make too much of such a small textual idiosyncrasy. Nevertheless, the praier/dinner substitution seems to me to reveal in a subtle but striking way the degree to which Hoby internalized her pious regime and integrated it almost seamlessly with her daily housework. Though it is not, strictly speaking, part of the syntactic structure of Hoby's sentence or even perhaps a conscious act of the writer, the correction of "praier" produces a subtle record of the writing process that both proves and celebrates Hoby's pious housewifery. In Hoby's prose, the action of "dinner" retains an embedded connection to the action of "prayer."

The sense of balance that characterizes Hoby's prose style does more than simply mirror the content of her diary entries. Rather, the style and form of the diary transform her content and put it to work for her. The individual details of the diary ultimately matter because Hoby has constructed them to matter; she situates her daily activities within a rhetorical framework that specifically draws attention to her consummate behavior as a pious and orderly housewife. Though seventeenth-century personal diaries are not usually discussed in the context of classical or Renaissance rhetorical models, much of Hoby's stylistic approach in her diary resembles the strategies characteristic of demonstrative or epideictic rhetoric. In *The Arte of Rhetorique* (1553), Thomas Wilson defines this style as one in which a speaker or writer "standeth either in praise or dispraise of some one man, or of some one thing, or of some one deede doen" (B2v).[23] Epideictic rhetoric is usually associated in the period with poetic genres, such as the hymn, the ode, and the elegy, but the tradition of demonstrative literature was broad enough to include a wide range of objects of praise or censure—everything from countries to animals to people and their deeds. Indeed, in Katherine Philips's poem "In memory of that excellent person Mrs. Mary Lloyd of Bodidrist" (1667), we see that epideictic rhetoric and pious housewifery could be explicitly linked. Praising Mrs. Bodidrist, Philips writes:

> She was so pious, that when she did Dye,
> She scarce chang'd Place, I'me sure not company.
> Her zeale was primitive, and practick too;
> She did believe, and pray, and read, and doe.   (45–48)[24]

Philips's poem of praise, like Hoby's diary, relies upon precise grammatical balance (most notable here in the parallelism and polysyndeton of lines 47–48) in order to demonstrate the pious housewifery of its female subject. And though Philips's poem is a more traditional example of demonstrative rhetoric than the Hoby diary, the category of epideictic narrative (which I will use somewhat loosely here to describe a rhetorical style of persuasion that depends upon the praise of an individual person and his or her actions) helps to illuminate the similar strategies at work in Hoby's personal writings.

In Hoby's diary, Hoby herself is both the author and the object of a subtle narrative of praise. By offering up the details of her daily labor in a form that emphasizes balance and order, Hoby offers evidence, both to herself and to God, of her pious housewifery and rigorous self-scrutiny. There is, in short, a story that runs through these sometimes fragmented or seemingly random entries: a story that makes visible the spiritual and domestic successes of an early modern housewife. Far from a banal narrative, the narrative of the good housewife in Hoby's diary is a consuming and essential one that animates the pages of the diary and gives them a compelling purpose. Indeed, it is in part through the act of recording and creating these images in her diary that Lady Hoby fulfills the requirements of her faith; her spiritual journal provides a medium in which both the invisible processes of introspection and the physical acts of housewifery can take new, material forms.

The importance of this epideictic rhetoric to the diary is most readily apparent when the predictability of the text disappears. Though the vast majority of the diary construes Hoby as a rigorously pious and organized housewife, it also records moments of spiritual crisis in which Hoby criticizes herself for behavior that she deems negligent. At several points in her diary, she makes note of her idleness and her failure to maintain her diary properly. She berates herself for "speakinge and thinking of many Idle matres" (August 19, 1599) or for "omittinge thorowe neccligence some exercise" (May 4, 1601). Like the ambiguous word "wrought," the phrases "Idle matres" and "some exercise" could refer to either housewifery or piety, but Hoby implies that a failure in either arena threatens the order of her household.

In the last two years of her diary, Hoby's entries become much shorter than in previous years and her language loses its characteristic balance. The physical appearance of the manuscript changes dramatically as well: ink stains and crossed-out phrases become more frequent, Hoby begins to leave large blank spaces between many entries, and the time span between individual entries grows wider. Many of the discrete entries in this part of the diary consist of only brief, fragmentary phrases such as "day very stormie and snowie wether" (April 5–7, 1604) or "day Came my Cossine Arthur Dakin Came, and The Lords day" (May 19, 1604). As these sentence fragments indicate, the syntactic order that Hoby usually achieves in the earlier parts of her text is not simply a standard feature of the diary genre; Hoby must work diligently to create and maintain this formal balance. The disorderly language of many of the later entries thus indicates a slip in Hoby's diligence—a slip that she is, however, keen to acknowledge and rectify. On April 1, 1605, she writes:

> The first day Mr Rhodes preached in the Morninge Mr Hunter his father in law and he after the sarmon tooke possision of Underill his house to Mr Hobys Use and mine at Night I thought to writt my daies Journee as before becaus in the readinge over some of my former spent time I finde some profitt might be made of that Course from which thorow two much neccligence I had a Longe time dissisted but they are unworthye of godes benefittes and especiall favours that Can finde no time to make a thankfull recorde of them

Hoby reads the failure in her record-keeping, and the "neccligence" in her self-scrutiny that it implies, as a failure in her practice of pious housewifery. She berates herself for failing to "make a thankfull recorde" of her daily tasks and assigns this failure a direct, spiritual consequence: the disorder of her diary-keeping will bar her from "godes benefittes and especiall favours."

Each of these moments of self-flagellation registers a trace of turmoil in Hoby's devotional exercises. And yet the formal and ideological design of the spiritual journal and the tenets of her Protestant faith insist that Hoby confess her sins and record her moments of failure. By choosing to record these slips in her spiritual journal, Hoby offsets their potential to disrupt her domestic practice; essentially, she turns transgression into confession. What appears disorderly to Hoby (if not, perhaps, to us as modern observers) becomes in the diary an integral component of her efforts to preserve the piety and order of her home. Self-chastisement is as rhetorically effective in this context as praise, since it proves her diligence and self-scrutiny while simultaneously highlighting the textual and domestic order that Hoby is able to maintain elsewhere in the diary. Her spiritual regime seems to fall into temporary disarray, yet she is able to salvage it by recording it, scrutinizing it, and commenting on it. Hoby is her own best reader, in large part because she is her own most rigorous critic.

The "neccligence" that Hoby so carefully documents and the physical changes to the manuscript that accompany it indicate the extraordinary amount of effort needed to sustain both textual and household stability through self-examination, record-keeping, and physical labor. In the text, as in the household, order must be created, maintained, and continually scrutinized. This careful balance between personal piety and domestic labor is a rhetorical construct, produced through a demonstrative narrative in which Hoby's domestic achievements and her adeptness at self-regulation are displayed and justified. In creating this narrative, the diary figures this early modern housewife's subjectivity in terms of her successful management of her domestic duties and her own soul. Agency for Hoby, in other words, is a function of obedience, self-regulation, and both spiritual and household order. We might even say that in the context of the diary, Hoby acquires her most compelling authority when she records her failure to "make a thankfull recorde," since in these moments she is able to announce and acknowledge not only the details of her daily routines but more importantly the process of spiritual introspection that she has admirably cultivated. The narrative of pious housewifery that Hoby establishes in her diary enables her to make the invisible visible and to demonstrate (to herself and to God) that the hidden workings of her spiritual life are as orderly and as properly domesticated as are the "things about the house," the "billes," and the servants that she labors to maintain.

VIRTUOUS RESISTANCE: ANNE CLIFFORD AND ANNE HARDING

Hoby's primary focus in her diary is on internal conflict: she is ultimately less concerned about affairs of state than about the affairs of her own soul. Though the intended audience for the diary is impossible to define precisely, we can assume that Hoby's text was not explicitly intended for readers other than herself. Hoby, that is, may have been her own best reader, but she was also her own primary audience. By contrast, the personal diaries of Lady Anne Clifford (1589–1676) maintain throughout a striking awareness of their public audience and future readership.[25] This broader social and textual context gives Clifford's diaries a rather different burden of proof than Hoby's text, especially since Clifford's diaries respond directly to the familial conflict in which she was embroiled for much of her life. As such, Clifford's diaries offer a more deliberate narrative of pious housewifery, one that publicly demonstrates and advertises Clifford's piety and her skills of domestic management.

But the explicit awareness of a public audience is not the only thing that differentiates Clifford's diary from Hoby's. We can begin to see in Clifford's text some of the contradictions implicit in narratives of pious housewifery, contradictions that will be developed even further in the domestic drama of the period. Like Hoby, Clifford produces a story of housewifery in which personal piety and domestic labor are essentially and safely aligned. This reiterated link between housework and devotion creates the appearance of orderliness and produces a textual trace of spiritual diligence, reassuring fictions that eliminate the possibility that the housewife may shirk either her spiritual exercises or her daily chores. But for Clifford, this narrative—and the adherence to Protestant guidelines on devotion and household order that it implies—is not its own reward. Rather, she creates and deploys a story of her own pious housewifery in order to justify a very tangible act of familial *disobedience*, namely, her fight to inherit and ultimately manage her father's estates. Narratives about the spiritual household thus paradoxically help to sustain competing narratives of dissent and resistance.

Unlike the diary of Lady Hoby, the diaries of Lady Anne Clifford seem at first glance to have little relevance to a discussion of the spiritual aspects of domestic labor. Clifford's diaries have received a great deal of critical attention in recent years—significantly more than the Hoby diary—but much of this scholarship has emphasized the secular nature of Clifford's personal accounts. Helen Wilcox, for example, distinguishes between the Clifford and Hoby diaries explicitly on the basis of their religious motivations. Writing about the Hoby diary, she argues that "the initial impetus to write was devotional and the framework for repeated self-analysis took the form of prayer or confession." However, Wilcox introduces the Clifford diaries by claiming that "[a] more secular desire to keep some kind of record of her own achievements and relationships would seem to be the chief motivation of Lady Anne Clifford, who kept diaries intermittently from 1603...until her death in 1676."[26] Certainly Clifford's diaries do not adhere to the strict model of puritan self-scrutiny that writers such as Hoby follow so precisely. But neither, I would argue, are they so easily categorized as "secular" documents. Though her diaries are not primarily focused on the fine points of Protestant spirituality, Clifford nevertheless uses her diaries to provide a textual record of the spiritual labor that she performs to maintain her household and family estates.

Clifford's diaries often demonstrate a rhetorical similarity to the Hoby diary. Like Hoby, Clifford reveals the importance of spiritual devotion to her housewifery through the odd juxtapositions characteristic of her diary entries and through the balanced grammatical structure of her sentences. In February of 1619, for example, Clifford records two consecutive entries that highlight her household activities: "The 8th. Lady Wootton sent Mr Page to see me, and that day I made Pancakes with my women in the Great Chamber. The 10th. Wat Coniston began to read St Austin [Augustine] *Of The City of God* to me, & I received a Letter from Mr Davis with another enclosed in it of Ralph Coniston, whereby I perceived things went in Westmoreland as I would have them" (68).[27] The consecutive positioning of these entries and the use of coordinating rather than subordinating conjunctions throughout (as we saw in Hoby's diary) emphasizes that spirituality—the reading of the religious text *The City of God*—was one in a series of interrelated household concerns that included preparing food with her servants and attending to the state of her legal dispute over her ancestral lands in Westmoreland. The well-ordered state of Clifford's home, in other words, is visible in the orderly balance of her syntax. But Clifford's sentence structure also implies a causal relationship between her religious and legal actions; her reading of Augustine seems both to precede and to provoke the letter from Mr. Davis, with its favorable tidings about her claims in Westmoreland. By claiming that pious devotion was a crucial part of her daily housewifery, Clifford rhetorically asserts the orderliness and spirituality of her home.

However, Clifford's diaries are more than private confessional documents. They are also family chronicles that serve a public function as
a history of the Clifford dynasty. This project had a particular urgency
for Anne Clifford because for most of her adult life she was engaged
in a protracted legal dispute concerning ancestral lands that had been
willed by her father, George Clifford, the third Earl of Cumberland, to
his brother Francis Clifford. Anne and her mother, Margaret Clifford,
challenged Francis's claims to the lands on the basis of an entail made
by King Edward II to Clifford's heirs regardless of gender. Both of
Anne Clifford's husbands—Robert Sackville, Earl of Dorset, and Philip
Herbert, Earl of Pembroke and Montgomery—urged her to give up
her claims for the lands and attempted to use the lands as leverage to
further their own financial and dynastic agendas.[28] Though Clifford's
claims to her father's lands were certainly legitimate, they were viewed
as disruptive and disobedient by her contemporaries, since the claims
"openly defied conventional rules of primogeniture, female coverture
and social decorum, and they did so chronically and conspicuously."[29]
Clifford finally received the lands in 1643, when Francis died without
a male heir, but the disputed inheritance provided the impetus for
much of her writing. As Barbara Lewalski has demonstrated, "Anne
and her mother compiled massive tomes of records and family papers
(called "The Chronicles" in implicit analogy to chronicle histories of
the life and times of princes), in part from pride in the family's illus-
trious history but chiefly to reinforce Anne's own legal claims as sole
heir."[30] Clifford thus explicitly envisioned a public role for her diary as
a constituent part of her hotly contested legal disputes.

The image of the pious household that Clifford projects throughout her diary thus differs slightly in its rhetorical function from
Hoby's record of self-examination. Clifford's demonstrative narrative
gives her a moral legitimacy that allows her to challenge the legal
authority of her husband and uncle with a degree of impunity and
leave a textual record of her proper household management to her
descendants. In so doing, she provides a self-justificatory account of
her abilities as a household manager that bears witness to the validity
of her claims to her father's inheritance. I suggest that the moments of
spiritual reflection and pious housewifery that have been largely overlooked in accounts of Clifford's diaries constitute an integral part of
her family chronicle and ultimately work to legitimize her challenge
to her father's will.

At times in the diary, Clifford lays claim to moral authority by
presenting herself as a patient, virtuous wife, a trope that she borrows from the literary tradition of secular martyrs and from John

Foxe's models of female Protestant martyrs in *Acts and Monuments*.[31] On April 5, 1617, Clifford writes: "my Lord went up to my closet & said how little money I had left contrary to all they had told him. Sometimes I had fair words from him & sometimes foul, but I took all patiently, & did strive to give him as much content & assurance of my love as I could possibly, yet told him that I would never part with Westmoreland upon any condition whatever" (53). Clifford here contextualizes her legal dispute with her husband and her challenge to his authority by rhetorically establishing herself as a model housewife and embodiment of Christian virtue. She calls attention to her patience and wifely assurances in order to set up the "yet"—the conjunction that changes the implication of the entire passage and encodes the tension between Clifford's pious household labor and her disobedience to her husband. Clifford is a devout and loving housewife, but she refuses to accede to her husband's demands to relinquish her property claims. By repeatedly trumpeting the exemplary nature of her pious housewifery, the text of the diary resolves the seeming contradiction between familial dissent and household order, thereby rendering Clifford's spousal disobedience palatable to potential readers and future generations of Cliffords.

Clifford continued to justify her property and inheritance rights long after she gained control of her ancestral lands in 1643. Following the death of her second husband, Philip Herbert, Clifford became the sole manager of the Westmoreland estates, where she began a second diary that recorded her renewed attention to her household and the legacies she would leave to posterity.[32] In the Kendall Diary, Clifford describes her newly transformed managerial duties, which included supervising a large number of servants and tenants. Her description of these new roles continues to emphasize the spiritual and economic order of her household that she depicts in the earlier diary. In January of 1676, Clifford writes:

> And this day in the afternoon did George Good[gion] pay mee the Kitchen stuff money and Mr Hasell received it off him in the Painted Room…The 9th day, being Sunday, yet I went not out of my Chamber all this day…but my 2 gentlewomen and 3 of my Laundry maids and most of my menservants went to the Church of Ninekirks where Mr Grasty our parson preached a good Sermon to them and the Congregation.   (234)

Clifford attends to the "Kitchen stuff money" that will buy household provisions, but also to her own devotional needs and those of her servants. Being too ill to attend church herself, Clifford offers her servants to the reader as a viable substitute—as a "them" which suitably replaces the absent "I." Clifford marks her concern at her own inability to attend Sunday services, but she also carefully notes the diligence of her servants in their fulfillment of religious duties. As the mistress of those servants, Clifford reaps the benefits of their spiritual devotion; their presence at church gives Clifford's own devotion a physical form, even though she herself is absent. The diary, that is, records not a lack of devotion but its exact opposite: a substitution of servant for mistress that signals Clifford's rigorous attention to the religious life of her servants and her proper performance of her duties as a mistress. By transforming the inactive "I" into the pious "them," Clifford's text showcases the orderliness of her household and offers evidence to posterity that she is a truly deserving heir to her father's estates.

Clifford further improved upon the lands she inherited by instigating large-scale building projects that provided necessary upkeep for the estate and monumentalized her place in the Clifford family history, and she is keen to celebrate these achievements in her diaries.[33] On January 12, 1664, Clifford writes that she purchased "Landes to the value of £11 per annum for which I payed two hundred and twentie poundes, which Landes I gave for the maintenance of a parson qualified to read praiers & the Homilies of the Church of England & to teach the Children of the Dale to write and read English in Mallerstang Chappell for ever" (169). Clifford draws attention to the explicit relationship between her managerial role on her estate and her religious devotion; the purchasing and distributing of lands serves a tangible religious purpose by demonstrating her allegiance to the Church of England and leaving a legacy of that allegiance for posterity. This passage also exploits the account-book qualities of Protestant diary writing, linking Clifford's household management (her keeping of accounting records) with her pious practices (her keeping of a spiritual "Register-Book" in the form of a diary). Piety, that is, is an important component of Clifford's managerial roles, but it is also a rhetorical construct, serving an epideictic function that amplifies her domestic projects and singular achievements. The textual legacy of spiritual housewifery that Clifford leaves to posterity via her diaries underscores the legitimacy of her legal claims by providing evidence of the successful transformation of the Westmoreland estate from a site of familial rancor to the epitome of household order.

The moral force of Clifford's pious housewifery yields direct textual benefits: it enables her to challenge her father's and husband's wishes and champion her own rights of inheritance. The powerful narrative of personal devotion and orderly housewifery that characterizes the diary helps to authorize Clifford's participation in the more public disputes in which she was embroiled. Like the "them" that substitutes for the absent "I," the diary texts offer their readers a discursive vision of an orderly home as a substitute for a disorderly legal situation. Clifford is able to draw on a rich literary and religious tradition as she constructs this narrative, borrowing extensively throughout the diary from literary tropes, such as the paradigm of the female martyr, and from specific textual sources, such as the Bible and *The City of God*.[34] But in writing her own narrative of pious housewifery, Clifford also seems to have taken advantage of a literary connection that was much closer to home. In 1630, after her second marriage to Philip Herbert, Clifford stayed at Wilton, the famous Pembroke estate and home to the Sidney family. From a few of her letters that survive, we can gather that she met and became friends with one of her distant kinsmen by marriage: the devotional poet George Herbert.[35] Although this friendship only lasted three years, until the poet's death in 1633, other evidence suggests that Clifford became very familiar with Herbert's poetry. The famous triptych of Clifford and her family, which Clifford commissioned and saw completed by 1646, depicts Clifford at different stages of her life with approximately forty-four books in the background (figure 3.1). Wilcox has noted that a book of Herbert's poetry lies on the shelf above the mature Lady Clifford in the third panel of the portrait. She goes on to argue that though Clifford may have chosen to include this particular book in the painting either as a status symbol or because of her previous personal connection with Herbert, other motivations are equally possible:

> While the books in the panel depicting the young Lady Anne are rather too neat to imply regular consultation, those shown behind the older portrait are refreshingly messy, resembling the true jumble of a much-used collection—and this is where *The Temple* is found, suggesting that she almost certainly did read it. Lady Anne may have read Herbert's poems as private devotions, or had them read aloud to her by her chaplain or companion; her diary indicates that both modes of "reading" were her custom.[36]

Not only does the triptych depict Clifford as an avid reader of Herbert, but it also suggests the intriguing possibility that this reading may have informed and shaped her spirituality. Reading *The Temple* (1633) as a form of "private devotions," Clifford would have immersed herself in

Figure 3.1 The Great Picture, Attributed to Jan van Belcamp (1646).

Source: Reproduced by Courtesy of Abbot Hall Art Gallery, Kendal, Cumbria, England.

Herbert's images of household labor and spiritual examination. Read side-by-side, the writings of Clifford and Herbert demonstrate a similarly inflected understanding of the religious contexts of housework in seventeenth-century England.

Throughout his poetry, Herbert creates images of domesticity and housework that are inseparable from pious devotion. In "The Family," Herbert emphasizes the importance of order within the home:

> But, Lord, the house and family are thine,
>   Though some of them repine.
> Turn out these wranglers, which defile thy seat:
>   For where thou dwellest all is neat.
> First Peace and Silence all disputes control,
>   Then Order plays the soul;
> And giving all things their set forms and hours,
>   Makes of wild woods sweet walks and bowers.   (5–12)[37]

For Herbert, the household must be ordered and "neat" according to "set forms and hours" because it is the house of the Lord. Domestic order, in other words, is intricately tied to one's submission to divine authority and to a regimen of time not unlike that produced by the diary genre. Herbert's stanza structure and rhyme scheme reinforce this idea since they, like the house and family that he describes, are meticulously "neat" and designed according to "set forms."

In other poems Herbert highlights the human labor that goes into creating this type of order. Near the end of "The Church Porch," Herbert tells his reader:

> Sum up at night, what thou hast done by day;
> And in the morning, what thou hast to do.
> Dress and undress thy soul: mark the decay
> And growth of it: if with thy watch, that too
> Be down, then wind up both; since we shall be
> Most surely judged, make thy accounts agree.   (451–456)[38]

Herbert's advice to keep spiritual "accounts" of one's physical activities and chores as well as the "decay / And growth" of one's soul reinforces recommendations given by Protestant conduct-book writers, such as Beadle.[39] Herbert, like Beadle, emphasizes the textual form of self-examination: one should "sum up" and "mark" one's internal thoughts and physical actions. Moreover, both spiritual examination and daily tasks contribute to the upkeep of one's "accounts." Recording "what thou hast done by day" is as important as the self-examination of the soul, while the soul—metaphorically figured as a clothed body—must be carefully dressed and undressed so that it can be inspected and maintained as part of a daily routine. Like Clifford, Herbert vividly articulates both the economic and spiritual dimensions of personal accounting, the daily processes by which the soul is laid open to judgment.

Throughout *The Temple*, Herbert stresses the importance of work and self-discipline to stave off idleness. The first person narrator in "Discipline" tells God that he can "[t]hrow away thy rod" because he, the sinner, has internalized the "full consent" of God's wishes (1, 8).[40] In "Business" Herbert asks his reader: "Canst be idle? canst thou play, / Foolish soul who sinned today?" and goes on to urge a life of hard work (1–2).[41] These poems and others suggest that Herbert was in tune with Protestant theologians of the period who insisted on the necessity of work not only to prevent idleness but also to ensure the proper upkeep of the spiritual home. But Herbert makes a more explicit connection between proper piety and proper household management in "The Elixir":

> Teach me, my God and King,
> In all things thee to see,
> And what I do in anything,
> To do it as for thee:
> ....
> A servant with this clause
> Makes drudgery divine:
> Who sweeps a room, as for thy laws,
> Makes that and th'action fine.   (1–4, 16–20)[42]

Even sweeping a room can be a devotional exercise if it is understood that God is in "all things" and that every individual action should have a spiritual motive. Though Herbert specifically writes about a "servant," the understanding that God should be present in even the most mundane domestic chores is equally applicable to wives and mistresses.[43] Perhaps most importantly, Herbert emphasizes not the chore itself but how it is done and understood; sweeping a room is only "divine" when it is done in accordance with God's laws. The poem suggests that housework itself can be a devotional exercise, given the appropriate spiritual framework.

In the context of Herbert's devotional poetry, Clifford's description of her exemplary pious housewifery serves to make "fine" her disruptive actions against her uncle and two husbands. Because these actions were done according to "God's laws" and with the blessing of "Succeeding Providence,"[44] Clifford can lay claim to a moral righteousness that justifies her challenge to her father's will. That is, the text privileges a form of female authority obtained through household labor and righteous conformity to pious practices that offsets the public disruption caused by Clifford's legal claims. Clifford's personal chronicles have a more pronounced sense of political and dynastic history than the Hoby diary, and Clifford goes to great effort to monumentalize her position as a daughter, mother, and prosperous landowner. She is acutely aware of her audience and the potential implications of her narrative—a narrative that is carefully constructed to project a sense of balance, order, and moral rectitude. This narrative forges a discursive link between piety and housewifery, enabling the internal aspects of Clifford's pious domesticity to take a textual form that will outlast her and provide evidence of her household order to future generations and readers of her Chronicles.

Clifford's compelling self-representation contributes to the ongoing process of discursively defining the good housewife in post-Reformation terms by suggesting that the pious performance of domestic labor constitutes a crucial and legitimate source of wifely authority that can occasionally trump the wishes of a father or husband. But by suggesting that a housewife may be both spiritually regulated and diligent in her daily labors yet still disobedient, Clifford's diaries reveal that the concept of pious housewifery is more fraught than it may initially seem to be, even in texts such as Clifford's that draw clear connections between good housewifery and religious devotion. For Clifford, as for Hoby, the spiritual requirements of seventeenth-century housewifery demanded heightened vigilance and self-awareness but offered in return additional opportunities for pious reflection, domestic agency, and even (in Clifford's case) a small measure of virtuous resistance.

Clifford's version of the insubordinate housewife is in many ways a subtle one. Disobedience in her diaries is a relative category, defined in specific terms and balanced by a narrative of spiritual and domestic rigor. But in early modern domestic dramas, the figure of the disobedient housewife is virtually omnipresent and often explicitly linked to startling depictions of female vice. On a weekly or even daily basis, audiences could be entertained by theatrical images of duplicitous wives, adulteresses, and murderesses—figures who brought excitement to the stage through the template of domestic conflict. Conflict, of course, is fundamental to drama, but early modern audiences seemed particularly eager to see (and willing to pay for) domestic conflict writ large. The domestic plays that became so popular in

the early decades of the seventeenth century were particularly interested in staging the quarrels and contradictions of the household,
in vividly enacting domestic tensions and the consequences—both
comic and tragic—that they could produce.[45] Though differing radically in structure and tone from women's private journals, these plays
often share a surprising connection to the writings of diarists such
as Clifford and Hoby: a narrative emphasis on the interrelationship
between piety and housework. But in the drama, these narratives
reveal as much about the ambiguities of the housewife's duties and
allegiances as they do about the confluence of labor and personal
devotion. Dramatic texts are particularly adept at exploring these
kinds of ambiguities; writers such as Heywood can capitalize on the
uniquely physical and visual resources of the stage to create vivid por-
trayals of the interconnectedness between the housewife's internal
devotions and her external actions.[46] As such, domestic dramas that
represent the pious housewife rely less often on the syntactic precision and epideictic rhetoric characteristic of diaries such as Hoby's
and Clifford's and more frequently on the visual syntaxes afforded by
early modern stagecraft.

Despite these significant differences in generic convention and formal technique, early modern domestic dramas and women's private
diaries reiterate remarkably similar narratives about the housewife and
the scope of her domestic labor, narratives that establish a direct connection between housewifery and personal piety. Thomas Heywood
and William Rowley's *Fortune By Land and Sea* (printed in 1655,
though probably written around 1607) is a particularly striking text
to pair with Clifford's diary, since it shares with that text a pointed
interest in dramatizing the delicate balancing act between the spiritual household and wifely disobedience. In *Fortune*, Heywood and
Rowley explore the contradictions inherent in pious housewifery,
though they ultimately insist upon the legitimacy and virtue of their
domestic heroine. Like Clifford's diary, what makes Heywood and
Rowley's play so fascinating is the notable way in which it outlines
the parameters of virtuous resistance, ultimately demonstrating that
the good housewife and the disobedient housewife can be one and
the same.

Heywood and Rowley's little-known play tells the story of young
Frank Forest, a gentleman's son who kills his brother's murderer in a
duel, flees England, and ends up earning his fortune at sea by fighting
off the infamous pirates Purser and Clinton and saving the wealth of
an English merchant.[47] The catalyst in Forest's escape from England
to the sea is Anne Harding, the new wife of the aged Mr. Harding.[48]

Old Harding disapproves of his son Philip's marriage to Forest's sister Susan, disowns them, and forces them to work as servants in his home. Anne, however, is charitable toward Philip and Susan and makes sure that their work load is not too heavy:

> to see them thus afflicted
> It grates my very heart-strings every hour:
> For though before their Fathers rathless eye,
> And their remorsless brothers, I seem stern,
> Yet privately they taste of my best bounty,
> And other of my servants are by me
> Hired to overcome their chiefest drudgery.   (2.2)

Like many plays of the period, *Fortune* is not theologically specific in its religious language.[49] The play praises Anne for her rather vague embodiment of Christian virtue—her "bounty" toward her stepchildren and the pious attitude toward the disadvantaged that this implies—rather than for any specific religious practices. However, as recent scholarship on the early modern theater demonstrates, even "secular" drama of the period consistently engages with questions of religion, including the religious practices of piety, interiority, and self-examination that would seem to resist theatrical representation. Paul Whitfield White, for example, cites Christopher Marlowe's *Doctor Faustus* as a "penetrating exercise in religious self-scrutiny," but he also demonstrates that drama continued to depict religious practices and ideas "through to the closing of the theaters in 1642"— years after state censorship supposedly "prohibited the overt treatment of religion on the stage."[50]

What we see in plays such as *Fortune* is the vivid externalization of personal piety and self-scrutiny and a dramatic conjunction between these internal processes and the physical performance of household tasks. Anne's soliloquized reflection allows her to qualify (and perhaps justify) her public sternness by assuring the audience of her private "bounty," but it also provides an opportunity for her pious thoughts and intentions to be externalized. A similar technique is at work in Thomas Dekker, Henry Chettle, and William Haughton's *The Pleasant Comodie of Patient Grissill* (1603), a retelling of the Griselda story from the *Decameron*. This play dramatizes the piety and virtue of its heroine explicitly through her carefully executed housewifery. Grissill makes baskets in order to provide needed income for her impoverished family, but she does so "within" so as not to "draw mens eyes" (1.2.28, 34, 26).[51] She is instructed to "run and kindle fire" and to "[f]etch water from the spring" in a pitcher (1.2.157, 153), a prop that reappears throughout the play to emblematize not only Grissill's lowly birth and the virtue of patience that she demonstrates so admirably during all of her trials, but also her successful completion of her household chores.[52] The play also reveals Grissill's internal virtues as a housewife through the series of trials that the Marquis plans for her after their marriage. In each of these tests, domestic labor provides a theatrical supplement for Grissill's personal piety: she obediently follows her husband's orders when she is asked to perform humiliating acts of household service (such as picking up the Marquis's glove from the floor, kneeling and tying Furio's shoes, and responding immediately to a request to fetch a cup of wine), and she passes the final test by carrying both wood and coals into the court. It is ultimately through this enactment of household drudgery that she is reconciled with her husband and publicly pronounced a truly constant and "most vertuous tree" (5.2.201).

Like *The Pleasant Comodie of Patient Grissill, Fortune By Land and Sea* dramatizes wifely labor as a visual extension of its heroine's internal virtue. In Anne Harding's case, this virtue is inseparable from an astute awareness of household labor hierarchies. Part of Anne's charitable "bounty" is her realization that Philip and Susan should not be performing the "chiefest drudgery" in the Harding household. As a gentleman's wife in charge of the management of servants, Anne makes certain that "other" servants are paid to do the "chiefest drudgery" that Philip and Susan should be exempted from by birthright. Anne's charity, in other words, is directly tied to her sense of the proper hierarchical arrangement of labor in her home. Though this soliloquy demonstrates Anne's properly pious disposition (clearly missing from Old Harding and his other sons), it reveals that household order is as dependent on the maintenance of status differentials as it is on the practices of Christian charity.

Anne must be equally careful in evaluating the actions of the renegade Forest when she offers him some of her charitable "bounty." After the duel, Forest flees his pursuers and finds himself in Anne's garden. He appeals to Anne's piety, asking her to pity him as she is "a Christian, / And therefore one that should be charitable" (2.2). Anne agrees to hide Forest, but only after rigorously questioning him about his offense:

Anne: What's your offence
   That such suspitious fear, and timerous doubts
   Waits on your guilty steps?

Young Forest: I have kild a man,
    But fairly as I am a Gentleman,
    Without all base advantage in even tryal
    Of both our desperate fortunes.
Anne: Fairly?
Young Forest: And though I say it, valiantly.
Anne: And hand to hand?
Young Forest: In single opposition.
Anne: In a good quarrel?
Young Forest: Else let the hope I have in you of safety
    Turn to my base confusion. (2.2)

In order to discern the righteousness of Forest's cause and, therefore, of her own act of hospitality, Anne questions him in a scrutinizing manner reminiscent of the procedures for self-examination advocated by Featley and other writers of Protestant devotional manuals. These manuals instruct readers to account for and examine their time and daily activities scrupulously for signs (or "assurance") of election.[53] In *The Fountaine of Teares*, a text aimed at female readers, Featley includes a series of questions that women should ask themselves at night in order to determine how they have "spent the day" (D9r). The questions read as a dialogue between the individual woman and her conscience:

1. At what time, in the morning, did I arise from my bed?
2. What first did I?
3. How devoutly prayed I?
4. What Scripture read I?
  ....
9. How lawfull was my Imployment?
10. How diligently did I follow it?
11. To what end, and purpose did I it?
12. What thoughts entertained I?
13. What companie kept I?
  ....
What new sinne this day hath beene added to mine account?
What ould offence hath beene new sinned over? (D9v–D10r)

Featley's questions emphasize the rigorous self-scrutiny that female believers must practice in order to examine their consciences properly. Anne's stichomythic questioning of Forest in *Fortune* is stylistically similar to Featley's list, but it also shares its focus on the lawfulness of one's actions and the importance of listing any "new sinnes" added to one's "account." In part, the play uses this catechistical dialogue to smooth over the fact that its hero is a murderer; Heywood and Rowley's narrative stresses that this crime took place "in a good quarrel" and is, therefore, justified. But the scene between Anne and Forest, which converts internal rigor into engaging dialogue, thus externalizing the process of self-examination, also encodes Anne's properly discriminating practice of charity. It is essential to the integrity of her household that she offer hospitality to a deserving man rather than to a base criminal, and, in order to tell the difference, Anne must evaluate Forest's actions and motives as she would her own. She says as much to herself after Forest's pursuers have gone: "if this should be some bloody murderer, / Great were my guilt to shrowd him from the Law" (2.2). Charity demands that she help those in need, but the mandates of the spiritual household require that she help *only* those who are both in need and deserving of her hospitality.

Anne ultimately decides that she will help Forest "as Heaven shall direct" since it is "charity to succor the distrest" (2.2). Taking her cue from heaven, Anne substitutes the religious logic of charity for her doubts about Forest's innocence. She insists that

> Heaven hath sent
> This gentleman because hee's penitent,
> To me for succor, therefore till the violence
> Of all his search be past, Ile shrowd him here,
> And bring you meat and wine to comfort you.   (2.2)

For Anne, her act of hospitality is not just the mark of a good hostess but also the mark of a good Christian. She accepts Forest into her home because "hee's penitent" and she offers to provide a "shrowd" of protection for him that includes the physical necessities of food and drink. And as the bearer of "meat and wine," Anne symbolically invites her guest to share in the gift of holy communion. Her housewifery, in other words, is not simply pious; it is almost sacramental.

Unlike Grissill, however, whose Christian virtues and model housewifery are never in doubt, Anne's pious acts of hospitality exist uneasily alongside her blatant disregard of her husband's wishes. We have already seen that the play codes Anne's furtive support of Philip and Susan as charitable "bounty" rather than harping on her circumvention of her husband's orders (which the play figures as overly harsh). But Heywood and Rowley also emphasize the tendentious nature of Anne's virtue when they reveal precisely *where* Anne chooses to offer Forest hospitality. Forest's hiding place is revealed when Anne is unable to prevent his sister Susan, instructed to "scatter this Wheat and Barley 'mongst the hens," from finding him in the chicken coop (3.1). By turning her chicken coop into a guest house, Anne exposes the fact that her hospitality is every bit as furtive as Forest's escape from the law; instead of inviting him into her household proper, she secretes him away in a place where poultry, not guests, are usually "serve[d]" (3.1).[54]

Furthermore, the chicken coop itself is not an arbitrary location, but a site over which Anne, as mistress of the household, has managerial control. Though the end results of Anne's actions (charity, hospitality) are beyond reproach, her modus operandi consists of manipulating her managerial powers in order to deceive her husband. Anne's careful interrogation of Forest gives her the justification to circumvent her husband's wishes; her personal piety trumps her husband's authority. Even though the play clearly validates Anne's actions and reveals that it is her husband, not Anne, who practices bad household government, it simultaneously implies that disobedience is not erased by spiritual housewifery but can in fact be justified and even sustained by it.[55] The marriage of Forest and Anne at the end of the play, which restores right order in the household, does not fully resolve the contradictions of Anne's housework. Rather, the play reveals the tension between the obedience Anne owes her husband and her duty as a Christian housewife through the disjunction between dramatic action (Anne's hospitable and pious act of bringing meat and wine to Forest) and its figurative location on stage (the furtive chicken coop).

Heywood and Rowley's *Fortune By Land and Sea*, like the diaries of Anne Clifford, operates according to a narrative in which the verifiable virtue and spiritual authority of the housewife counterbalance a degree of spousal discord. Transgression against fathers and husbands is allowed, in other words, because it is shielded by a discourse of moral authority. The housewife's subjectivity emerges in these texts in relation to her pious deployment of household duties—regardless of whether those duties are recorded personally or dramatized publicly. In this cultural formulation of housewifely authority, we see hints of an emerging domestic ideology that would become more entrenched by the eighteenth century. As Patricia Crawford has argued, the decades following the Civil Wars and Interregnum were characterized by a "broad general movement away from emotional and intense belief" in conjunction with a separation between belief and reason along gendered and class lines. "Religion, based on emotion," she argues, "was desirable for women as well as for men of lower status." By the early 1700s, the feminization of religion also implied its domestication, and religious practice became more exclusively associated with the virtuous housewife, who was expected to instruct her children in "personal morality."[56]

We can catch an early glimpse of this virtuous housewife in the stories of Clifford and Anne Harding, stories that link women's household labor to their devotional practice and thereby create a compelling source of female domestic authority. These stories participate in an ongoing and uneven historical process by which the figure of the pious and diligent housewife gradually assumes more and more cultural capital. But these narratives of pious housewifery also intervene more immediately in early seventeenth-century English culture by imagining the parameters of the housewife's agency during a period in which the gendered implications of housework in the post-Reformation home were far more uncertain than they would become a century later. Housewives such as Anne Clifford or Anne Harding must actively choose between the acts of charity, hospitality, self-examination, spousal obedience, and the orderly performance of domestic tasks as they piece together their daily rounds. Virtuous resistance becomes an almost inevitable result of this balancing act, since pious housewifery and wifely submission—though interconnected—may not always be mutually constitutive. And while internal diligence and household order can be advertised and celebrated to a degree in fictional narratives, the threat of the disconnect between a woman's inner thoughts and her outward actions haunts the margins of these texts, reemerging with more force in Heywood's most famous domestic tragedy, *A Woman Killed with Kindness* (1607).

THE FAULT WRIT IN HER BROW

In *Fortune By Land and Sea*, Heywood and Rowley create the resonant image of Anne Harding, the good (albeit disobedient) wife who manages servants, guests, and chickens with aplomb. But in *A Woman Killed with Kindness*, Heywood dramatizes the household activities of a very different Anne whose spectacular failure of pious housewifery produces domestic unrest and the ultimate dissolution of an entire household.[57] *A Woman Killed* is arguably the clearest example of a text that transforms the historical tension between the post-Reformation housewife's inner piety and her outward labors into dramatic narrative. In this text, however, the implications of spiritual housework are reversed: *A Woman Killed* vividly demonstrates that impiety is directly connected to bad housewifery. Because of this shift in emphasis, Heywood's domestic tragedy reveals the fault lines in the narrative of pious housewifery that I have been tracing in this chapter. More so than the other texts I have considered, *A Woman Killed* clearly articulates the dangers that lurk behind its heroine's housewifery, even suggesting at times that the narrative link between piety and housework may be a precarious one. In the process, the play exposes an epistemological gap that threatens to undermine the clarity of seventeenth-century ideologies of domestic order.

The opening of *A Woman Killed with Kindness*, which takes place immediately following the wedding ceremony of John and Anne Frankford, promises domestic harmony rather than turmoil. We see the nuptial celebrations, and we hear the praise lavished upon Anne as she takes up her new role as Frankford's wife. Sir Charles Mountford tells Frankford that he is a "happy man" because his wife is "so qualified, and with such ornaments / Both of the mind and body"; her attributes include her noble birth, her education, and her agility in speech and music (1.13–20).[58] Anne's brother, Sir Francis Acton, adds that she is "a perfect wife already, meek and patient" (1.37). The catalog of Anne's virtues reads like a passage from any of a number of popular early modern marriage manuals. Gouge's extremely popular treatise, *Of Domesticall Duties* (1622), for example, specifically exhorts wives to follow St. Peter's exhortation to possess "sobrietie, mildness, courtesie, and modestie" in their "conversation before their husbands" (T3r). Anne's meekness, patience, education, beauty, and eloquence thus set her up to be a Christian heroine similar to Grissill or Anne Harding. However, in *A Woman Killed* this promise of the virtuous housewife is never realized; the spousal harmony of the opening scene quickly gives way to a stunning display of Anne's domestic and spiritual disorder.

Of course, it is not necessarily easy to determine if a housewife such as Anne has succeeded or failed in her practice of pious housewifery, since, as we have seen, the interconnectedness of personal devotion and household labor in the Protestant home necessarily depends upon a rigorous process of self-examination. Indeed, Gouge himself anticipates the problems of visibility and accurate discernment that inevitably complicate the virtue of housewives such as Anne Frankford. Gouge begins his section on "wive-like sobriety" by admitting the potential discrepancy between inward virtue and outward appearance: "A wives outward reverence towards her husband is a manifestation of her inward due respect of him. Now then seeing the intent of the heart, and inward disposition cannot be discerned by man simply in it selfe, that the husband may know his wives good affection towards him, it is behouvefull that she manifest the same by her outward reverence" (T3r). Gouge's shift in emphasis from husbandly discernment to wifely manifestation nicely captures one of the central dilemmas of the post-Reformation household: a wife's "inward disposition" is key to her obedience and to household order, but it is impossible for a husband to read his wife's true affection "in it selfe." Gouge's unease about this possibility is palpable; his forthright statement about wives' outward manifestation of their inward reverence rapidly devolves into a plea in which he urges wives to provide their husbands with epistemological surety. There is no way around female responsibility and agency in this argument; it may be "behouvefull" for a wife to manifest her "intent of the heart" through "outward reverence," but there is no guarantee that she will do so. A husband's ability to decode his wife's actions correctly—and in doing so to maintain domestic order—is perilously dependent upon a seamless connection between those actions and their inner referent.

Much of *A Woman Killed with Kindness* depends upon the fantasy of such a seamless connection, though it does so to showcase Anne's failure as a pious housewife rather than her "outward reverence." The central action of the play is Anne's adultery with John Frankford's houseguest and friend, Wendoll. Frankford welcomes Wendoll into his home, but subsequently instructs Anne to manage domestic affairs and offer hospitality in her husband's absence. Leaving the house in Wendoll and Anne's control, he instructs his wife to "use him with all thy loving'st courtesy." She responds by saying: "As far as modesty may well extend / It is my duty to receive your friend" (4.80–82). Anne is expected to perform the role of the gracious host, but this duty is both mandatory and laced with danger. Hospitality is an essential part of Anne's housewifery, as it is for Anne in *Fortune*. However, Anne Frankford's careful qualification of her duty ("As far as modesty may well extend") suggests that the boundary between improper and proper hospitality must be rigorously policed. Tendentiously limited by its conditional clause, Anne's acceptance of responsibility contains within it a syntactic hint of the threat to household order that lies behind Anne's "duty." The performance of hospitality is not in and of itself a guarantee of household order; only if that work is performed with Christian modesty will right order be maintained.

We see in the very next meeting between Anne and Wendoll that right order will not be maintained for long. In fact, it is Anne's spectacular mismanagement of her duties of hospitality that leads her astray. When Wendoll tells Anne of his love for her, she is torn between the "passion" and "pity" that she feels toward him and her concerns about betraying her husband's trust (6.137). The role of hostess enables her to bridge this divide by positioning her to substitute Wendoll for her husband. Anne thus invites Wendoll to "be a present Frankford in his absence" (6.78). Certainly, as Orlin has argued, Frankford "is implicated in and must accept responsibility for his own undoing" because he accepts Wendoll into his home; he has essentially created the double bind in which Anne finds herself.[59] However, Anne is equally responsible for performing her hospitality only "as far as modesty may well extend." The problem lies not in Anne's hospitality per se or in her pity for Wendoll, but in her inability to control and limit the bounds of her household tasks. Anne takes the logic of the hospitality analogy too far; she literally allows Wendoll to "be a present Frankford" in her home and in her bed. By doing so, Anne further demonstrates that her housework—in this case her duty to provide hospitality to guests—is not integrally connected to the processes of self-examination and personal piety that ensure moral behavior. Unlike the exemplary behavior of Anne Harding, Anne Frankford's outward actions suggest an inner turmoil. Her adultery with Wendoll, the catalyst of tragedy in the play, constitutes a specific failure of spiritual housewifery; adultery is both a sin and an egregious distortion of her domestic duties as a wife.

Anne's adultery sets in motion a series of interrelated, chaotic moments in the Frankford household that dramatize her spiritual confusion and its disastrous effects on domestic order. At the moment when she agrees to Wendoll's advances, Anne exclaims: "What shall I say? / My soul is wandering and hath lost her way" (6.149–150). A few lines later she describes the state of her soul in a monologue characterized by fear and confusion:

> I ne'er offended yet.
> My fault, I fear, will in my brow be writ.
> Women that fall not quite bereft of grace
> Have their offences noted in their face.
> I blush and am ashamed. O master Wendoll,
> Pray God, I be not born to curse your tongue
> That hath enchanted me. This maze I am in
> I fear will prove the labyrinth of sin　(153–160).

Anne's speech shifts uneasily between present and future tenses as the conditional "yet" of her uncommitted crime haunts and confuses her. No longer the linguistically agile wife praised in the play's first scene, Anne gives voice to a newly developed religious uncertainty characterized by "maze[s]" and "labyrinth[s] of sin." The images of the wandering soul, the maze, and the labyrinth were characteristic of puritan rhetoric about personal salvation.[60] Heywood thus represents Anne's hesitation in specifically religious terms that mark her failure of self-examination. In a passage that speaks directly to the presumed continuity between inner "faults" and outward expressions "writ" in one's brows, Anne's halting expression of interiority bears witness to a disorderly state of mind and an inability to comprehend her house-wifery within a theological framework. Rather than being a testament to her internal order or to her catechistic precision, as are Anne's solil-oquies in *Fortune*, Anne Frankford's labyrinth monologue displays only confusion and a lack of spiritual diligence. This failure on Anne's part significantly damages the integrity of the Frankford household, since it not only threatens her own state of salvation but also compro-mises her husband's control over his home and his wife's sexuality.

After Anne commences her affair with Wendoll, we see that she is no longer able to manage her servants or routine household tasks effectively. In scene two of *A Woman Killed*, Frankford's servants Nick and Jenkin participate in celebratory dancing that mimics the wedding festivities that precede it. The play represents the servants' mimicry as properly ordered and subordinate; the plot/subplot rela-tionship between the first two scenes figures proper hierarchy as a function of the play's formal structure. However, during the rest of the play, Nick and Jenkin are far more integrated into the Frankford home and the actions that occur there. Indeed, when Anne is unable to exercise proper spiritual and domestic diligence, the play turns that task over to Nick: when he suspects (following Anne's labyrinth speech) that she and Wendoll are up to "tricks" that he "like[s] not," he resolves that he will "henceforth turn a spy, / And watch them in their close conveyances" (6.168, 174–175). A comic character from the subplot is thus forced to insinuate himself into the main plot to insure household order, a formal shift that translates Anne's failure to police herself into a visible warning of disorder yet to come. Additionally, since Anne has failed markedly in her development of a sufficiently watchful and rigorous conscience, Nick must fulfill these duties for her, serving as an external "spy" to Anne's soul. These alterations in plot structure are telling, as they signal the increasingly disorderly activities within the Frankford household that dramatically expose the disastrous effects of Anne's domestic improprieties. Interestingly, though Anne fails miserably to uphold domestic order, Heywood's play doggedly insists that inner virtue (or its lack) can be detected in "outward reverence," as Gouge maintains in *Of Domesticall Duties*. In this case, Heywood creates a narrative that vividly articulates both the precarious piety and negligent housewifery of his heroine.

The formal divisions in the play that segregate masters and servants thus dissolve in response to Anne's dramatic failure as a pious housewife. This structural confusion is exacerbated by the fact that basic social hierarchies within the Frankford home also seem to disintegrate along with Anne's chastity. For example, after Frankford has plotted with Nick to learn the truth about his wife's relationship with Wendoll, we see Anne arranging a dinner for her husband and lover. From the beginning of the scene, there is a sense of disorder in the mealtime preparations:

> *Anne*: Sirrah, 'tis six o'clock already struck.
>   Go bid them spread the cloth and serve in supper.
> *Jenkin*: It shall be done forsooth, mistress. Where is Spiggot the butler
>   to give us our salt and trenchers?   (11.10–13)

Whereas in an earlier scene, Jenkin and the servingmen arrive "in order" to prepare the dinner table (8.1), the dinner preparations here seem both poorly timed and poorly organized; Anne frets that "'tis six o'clock already" while Jenkin searches for another servant, Spiggot, to bring essentials to the table. When Frankford arrives for dinner, he asks his wife, "Where be those lazy knaves to serve in supper?" (11.43). Though Frankford casts his aspersions at the servants and not directly as his wife, his comments about the disorderly meal suggest problems with Anne's domestic management. The "lazy knaves" should be under Anne's control; the mishandling of "salt and trenchers" indicates that Anne's failure of domestic responsibility has permeated even the minutest components of the household.

Later in the scene, Cranwell, another friend and dinner guest of Frankford, leaves the dinner to go to his chamber, saying, "I am on the sudden grown exceeding ill, / And would be spared from supper" (11.96–97). Cranwell's departure is, of course, a convenient plot device to leave Anne and Wendoll alone together, but his illness also indicates just how disorderly this dinner is. Cranwell's implicit suggestion that the food has made him ill provides further condemnation of Anne's housewifery. Instead of providing nourishment for her family and guests—or offering a sacramental gesture of "meat and wine" as Anne Harding does in *Fortune*—Anne Frankford's dinner table affords only illness and disarray. Perhaps most significantly, Anne has violated one of the key domestic sites (the table) where early modern husbands and wives were supposed to develop and strengthen their marital relationship. This betrayal *a mensa* is a fitting complement to her ongoing betrayal *a thoro*—since the bed was generally understood as the other primary locus of marital accord within the home.[61] As in *Fortune*, dramatic action conflates good housewifery and spiritual devotion by signaling and supplementing the unrepresentable. In this case, the disorderly dinner offers visual evidence of Anne's adultery and the failure of her pious self-examination; Spiggot's forgetting of the salt and trenchers serves as a physical reminder that Anne's soul has "lost her way."

When Anne and Wendoll are left alone following the meal, Anne draws an explicit connection between the dinner and the state of her soul. Wendoll tells Anne that they should "sup within" in the bedchamber, transforming the meal from a semipublic celebration of hospitality and nourishment into a private and illicit affair. Anne responds by saying, "O what a clog unto the soul is sin," an exclamation that articulates not only the link between the illicit dinner and her own spiritual crimes but also the crucial need for spiritual examination in order to remove both sin and the domestic disorder it produces (11.103). Of course it is not in Wendoll's interest to aid Anne in her examination of conscience; instead, he rebukes her remorse by comparing her to "a puritan," suggesting that her self-scrutiny is extreme and unnecessary. But clearly the formal drive of the play proves Wendoll wrong; it is the failure of pious introspection, not an overly zealous pursuit of it, that results in the "clog" upon Anne's soul, the chaos in her household, and, ultimately, her death.

The play's representation of Anne's spiritual and domestic disorder culminates in Frankford's direct confrontation of her after finding her in bed with Wendoll. Anne acknowledges that she is a shame to womanhood and an "abject" sinner (13.97, 105). Even more dramatically, all of the household servants approach Anne and chastise her:

> *All*: O mistress, mistress, what have you done, mistress?
> *Nick*: 'Sblood, what a caterwauling keep you here.
> *Jenkin*: O lord, mistress, how comes this to pass? My master is run away in his shirt, and never so much as called me to bring his clothes after him.
> *Anne*: See what guilt is: here stand I in this place,
> Ashamed to look my servants in the face.   (13.146–152)

Anne's adultery has caused a reversal in the proper household hierarchy; her servants accuse her of actions that she has been unable to acknowledge and evaluate herself, rendering her "ashamed" to look at them.[62] Even Jenkin's consternation that his "master is run away in his shirt" signals the breakdown in domestic order and master–servant relations; the "master" Jenkin refers to here is Wendoll, not Frankford, and this divided duty (exacerbated by Anne's sexual betrayal) confounds relationships of service and proper subordination. Through the narrative of Anne's adultery, Heywood dramatizes the dissolution of the household, a dissolution that is a direct result of Anne's inability to perform her domestic and spiritual work, including the chastity that she owes her husband, in a proper manner. Unlike the ideal housewife envisioned by Gouge, Anne Frankford mangles her duties of hospitality and household management and leaves little trace of the Christian heroine and conduct-book wife praised in the play's first scene.

That is, of course, until the final two scenes of the play when Anne, on her deathbed, emotively repents her sinful life. After her expulsion from Frankford's home, Anne decides to starve herself to death as a means of atonement for her crimes. She speaks in eloquent, measured phrases:

> So, now unto my coach, then to my home,
> So to my deathbed, for from this sad hour
> I never will nor eat, nor drink, nor taste
> Of any cates that may preserve my life.
> I never will nor smile, nor sleep, nor rest,
> But when my tears have washed my black soul white,
> Sweet Saviour, to Thy hands I yield my sprite.   (16.101–107)

The use of isocolons and anaphora create a sense of order and balance in this passage, a marked departure from Anne's tangled soliloquies earlier in the play. Anne's verbal agility and precision return with her repentance, attesting to her newfound spiritual clarity and internal order. Anne's reordered speech thus complements her ascetic fasting—an act of excessive gastronomical control that stands in direct contrast to the disorderly dinner earlier in the play. Even though they come too late to save her life, this outward order and self-deprivation serve as proof of Anne's reformed soul.

However, though Anne dies pardoned by her husband and reconfirmed as a wife and mother, her deathbed performance maintains an uneasy balance between her interiority and its outward expression. When Sir Charles, Sir Frances, and others come to attend her as she dies, Anne asks them: "Blush I not, brother Acton? Blush I not, Sir Charles? / Can you not read my fault writ in my cheek? / Is not my crime there? Tell me, gentlemen." Sir Charles responds by saying, "Alas, good mistress, sickness hath not left you / Blood in your face enough to make you blush" (17.55–59). Earlier, as we have seen, Anne does "blush" and is "ashamed" of her betrayal of her husband; her inward offense is clearly "noted" in her face. But in the final scene of the play, the good death that Anne aspires to is momentarily thwarted by the disconnect between her inward remorse and its external expression. This is precisely the type of failure that Gouge worries about in *Of Domesticall Duties*. Though it is "behouvefull" that Anne manifest the intent of her heart in her outward actions, her body betrays her at the end, allowing her inner virtue only pained and difficult expression in the play's final scene. Indeed, the same wasted body that proves Anne's repentance to the audience simultaneously disallows it by erasing the "fault" from her cheek. The collapse of spiritual and household order that *A Woman Killed* dramatizes is thus mitigated but not erased by its deathbed finale, which can only hesitantly imagine the reemergence of the good wife at the moment of her death. The play ends with a striking visual reminder that the internal mechanisms of pious devotion may very well *not* be readable to external observers. Anne's adultery pales in comparison to the more insidious threat that lurks under the surface of the play: namely the worrisome possibility that the housewife's virtue or vice may be impossible to detect with absolute certainty.

The underlying fear that a housewife's external actions—including her domestic labor—do not accurately represent her inward disposition and piety is more forcefully realized in Heywood's play than it is in the other texts that I have discussed in this chapter. But *A Woman Killed* shares with *Fortune* and the diaries of Hoby and Clifford an interest in connecting housewifery directly to discourses of personal piety. As women acquired new forms of responsibility for the economic and religious well-being of their households in the seventeenth century, stories such as Anne Frankford's begin to figure the housewife's subjectivity in terms of her ability to manage both her domestic and her spiritual duties successfully. Female agency in these narratives thus becomes linked to self-scrutiny, interiority, and rigorous management of the home and the soul. To put it simply: piety was work, and work could be piety if it were performed with a properly spiritual mindset. Household order depended upon both. And yet, the fact remains that the continuity between female interiority and outward actions was particularly difficult to secure, since it depended upon the certain knowledge of uncertain things, namely, a housewife's motives, desires, and prayers.

In creating narratives of pious housewifery, early modern texts produce a specific fantasy of the Protestant household—a fantasy in which wifely obedience, diligence, and virtue are documented and knowable. Deploying evidentiary narrative structures, texts such as Lady Hoby's diary and *Fortune By Land and Sea* verify their heroines' internal pious regimes and domestic management, thereby offering the semblance of epistemological surety and domestic order to readers or audiences who may be justifiably concerned about the inscrutability of the housewife's conscience and the potential for disorder within the post-Reformation household. In part, these narratives presage the conflation of femininity, piety, and housework that would become more explicit in eighteenth-century domestic ideology—a historical development that I will explore further in the next chapter. But these stories also attempt to solve cultural problems that would become less relevant in the later period, when tensions between male and female roles *within* the household, for example, would be subordinated by the doctrine of separate spheres. As the housewife's duties become part of a more well-defined sexual division of labor in the eighteenth century, the epistemological gap between introspective piety and its outward manifestation in orderly housewifery no longer elicits such immediate concern.

Translating women's housework into consumable literary commodities, early seventeenth-century texts offer a voyeuristic glimpse into the housewife's soul, supplying her otherwise inaccessible motives and creating, in essence, a compelling chronology of individual action that helps to mitigate the post-Reformation tension between interiority and its representation. Even when it is figured negatively, as it is in *A Woman Killed*, this literary voyeurism—an insistence that a woman's thoughts can be exposed and knowable—sidesteps the epistemological problem that often complicated attempts to define the "good" or the "bad" housewife and the appropriate scope of her domestic labor. But of course, as we see perhaps most vividly in *A Woman Killed*, these compensatory narratives, and the supposed epistemological certainty about the housewife's personal morality that they establish, are precarious at best. For, as Gouge and Heywood remind us, it is always possible that some part of a housewife's thoughts will remain inaccessible to the watchful eyes of her husband. Though the narratives I have considered here attempt to forestall this discrepancy, they nevertheless attest to housewifery's dangerous potency as a form of women's work that was essential to domestic order yet disturbingly dependent upon the proper ordering of a woman's soul—a space that could be defined and managed in literary narratives far more easily than it could be in the early modern home.

CHAPTER 4

———⟡———

HOUSEHOLD PEDAGOGIES:
FEMALE EDUCATORS AND
THE LANGUAGE OF LEGACY

"To Penshurst," (1616) Ben Jonson's paean to English aristocratic country life, famously concludes not with its resonant images of "purpled pheasant[s]" and "bright eels" that willingly offer themselves up for human consumption, but with a scene of women's work (28, 37).[1] By the end of the poem, Jonson has shifted his focus from the lush grounds of the estate to the inner workings of the Penshurst household, run by Barbara Gamage, wife of Robert Sidney. The poet recalls a time when King James and his son, Prince Henry, were entertained at the estate while on a hunting expedition:

> What (great, I will not say, but) sudden cheer
> Didst thou then make them! And what praise was heaped
> On thy good lady then! Who therein reaped
> The just reward of her high huswifery;
> To have her linen, plate and all things nigh,
> When she was far; and not a room but dressed,
> As if it had expected such a guest!
> These, Penshurst, are thy praise, and yet not all.
> Thy lady's noble, fruitful, chaste withal.
> His children thy great lord may call his own,
> A fortune in this age but rarely known.
> They are and have been taught religion; thence
> Their gentler spirits have sucked innocence.
> Each morn and even they are taught to pray

> With the whole household, and may, every day,
> Read, in their virtuous parents' noble parts,
> The mysteries of manners, arms and arts.   (82–97)

Jonson moves subtly from the undifferentiated "sudden cheer" offered to the King and Prince Henry to the individual "just reward" due to the lady of the house. Barbara Gamage's "high huswifery" is exemplary; her household is the model of order and preparedness, with "linen, plate, and all things" awaiting her guests without any sense of haste or fuss.

This orderly housewifery is neatly bound up with domestic piety in the poem, a common narrative trope, as we saw in the previous chapter. Jonson is quick to indicate that the Sidney children have been "taught religion" as part of their idyllic, aristocratic upbringing. But if Jonson explicitly singles out Barbara Gamage's housewifery as worthy of praise, he is decidedly less clear about the extent of her work in educating her children in "mysteries of manners, arms and arts." These concluding lines make copious use of verbs that obscure agency; the Sidney heirs "have been taught" and "are taught" with no clear indication of precisely who is doing the teaching. Indeed, Jonson moves away from the specific praise of Barbara Gamage almost as quietly as he segued into it; the "noble, fruitful, chaste" lady has been replaced by "virtuous parents" who together educate their children in religious matters, social arts, and practical skills. In "To Penshurst," the only clear link between the lady of the house and the education of her children is her chastity. The legitimacy of the Sidney heirs ensures the successful reproduction of the Sidney family lineage into the next generation, and their virtuous behavior—gleaned from parental education—offers further evidence of that legitimacy. In the shift from "good lady" to "virtuous parents," Barbara Gamage's particular role in educating her children is rhetorically erased, or rather rhetorically subsumed under the umbrella of parental pedagogy.

Jonson's representation of maternal education at Penshurst is indebted to a broader post-Reformation discourse about women's educational duties in the early English home. Education in seventeenth-century England certainly involved formal schooling, which began in the home, usually under a mother's supervision, and continued until children were seven years old, at which time (at least in wealthier families) they would be sent away to a tutor.[2] But "education" was also a more expansive category in the period, encompassing not only "systematic instruction, schooling or training" but also more generally the "bringing up" of children in terms of "social station" and the "kind of manners" to be acquired.[3] Early modern education was thus an extended process of socialization that would encourage sons and daughters to grow up to be morally upstanding, spiritually devout, and culturally informed men and women.[4] This pedagogical process could include a range of instructional activities that we may no longer think of as specifically educational, including instruction on how to choose a good wife or husband or how to treat servants, guidelines for private prayer and meditation, or more general advice on how to live a good life or how to excel at the practical skills of "arms and arts." We can glimpse in "To Penshurst" some of these educational practices, what I refer to in this chapter as "household pedagogies"— the often informal work of social instruction that helped to reproduce the social structures of the early modern family.

"Penshurst," as we have seen, also forges an ideological link between education and lineage; the "gentler spirits" of the Sidney children prove both their legitimacy and their proper socialization. This connection is hardly accidental. The humanist principles of education most popular during the period emphasized imitative learning techniques, whereby pupils learned morality and character development by modeling their behavior on that of parents and schoolmasters.[5] Early modern religious education involved a wide range of pedagogical methods, including catechism and various listening and memory aids, but the primary emphasis was on the use of exemplars. In his treatise, *The Scholemaster* (1570), intended for an elite male audience, Roger Ascham insists that examples are the best kind of teaching; for Ascham, a single example is more valuable than a whole host of "preceptes written in bookes" (G4v).[6] Writing specifically about religious education within the household, Thomas Elyot argues that by "beholding their fathers' lives as it were in a mirror, the children may eschew all foul or unseemly act or word" (F4r), and Robert Cleaver advises parents in general that "verball instruction, without example of good deeds, is a dead doctrine" (R3r–R3v).[7] In Jonson's poem, the Sidney children learn "manners, arms and arts" by reading these skills directly in their parents "noble parts"; they successfully copy the model of parental virtue that is presented to them. Mimetic education thus helps to ensure a direct transmission of practical skills and ethical and spiritual values from one generation to the next. The social instruction of children during the period, then, was directly linked to England's patrilineal inheritance system, which similarly emphasized the direct, uninterrupted transmission of land and property to children, preferably sons.[8]

If this emphasis on mimesis in seventeenth-century English education helped to reinforce the interests of a patrilineal system of property transmission, then one important question remains unanswered: what exactly was the educative function of women within this system? Or, to put it another way, why is the Sidney household whipped into shape by a "good lady" while the Sidney children are whipped into shape by "virtuous parents"? As we saw in chapters 2 and 3, the post-Reformation period in England played host to questions about the role of women within the increasingly significant domain of the household and to fierce debates about the nature and scope of maternal authority. Where household pedagogy was concerned, the common law doctrine of coverture directly affected ways of thinking about female agency. Becoming a "feme covert" in marriage, a woman gave up her legal identity, including her right to contract and sue, and relinquished the property she brought to the marriage as part of her dowry or portion.[9] Texts of the period imagined parental education in similar terms, suggesting that the wife was "covered" by her husband in marriage and her agency transplanted by his. Whereas, as we saw in the previous chapter, an emerging gendered division of labor served to distinguish women's household labors from men's, this division was not clearly articulated for parental education: moral instruction was usually assumed to be a task shared between husband and wife. Though William Gouge's *Of Domesticall Duties* (1622), for example, contains separate sections detailing the duties of wives and husbands, it devotes only one section to the joint duties of parents. Apparently, for Gouge at least, mothers and fathers do not have the individual and distinctly gendered responsibilities that wives and husbands do. Similarly, writers including Thomas Becon and William Perkins offer generalized advice to parents on how best to educate their children, but they do not clearly or consistently differentiate between male and female roles.[10] Given the legal and ideological strictures of coverture, it was often difficult to determine under what circumstances *maternal* authority—as opposed to parental authority—was justifiable or necessary. Jonson solves this problem with a disappearing act; Barbara Gamage's educational agency at Penshurst is neatly eclipsed by the catchall category of "virtuous parents."

In one sense, then, the doctrine of coverture meant that women's educational duties were effectively unrepresentable. Or, perhaps more precisely, a woman's participation in the social education of her children could only exist to the extent that it coincided with the direct transmission of her husband's values, mimicking the patrilineal inheritance system to which it was so closely aligned. This is exactly what seems to happen in "To Penshurst." And yet, as numerous scholars have documented, the doctrine of coverture was to a great extent a legal fiction, often untenable in actual practice.[11] During the late six-teenth and seventeenth centuries, "Chancery remedied some of the disabilities of coverture by enforcing prenuptial contracts or trusts that created married women's separate property."[12] This meant that "different types of pre-nuptial settlements to preserve the wife's prop-erty interests were implemented by all levels of society."[13] In addition, in accordance with the rise of consumer culture during the period, women took on new roles in "managing the household economy . . . its stuff and provisions" despite legal strictures on women's property and inheritance rights.[14] Though still under heavy legal restrictions, wives were thus not only expected to take on greater responsibilities in the post-Reformation household but were also able to control property under certain circumstances and play an active, if sometimes indirect, role in familial inheritance practices.

The idea that wives would simply transmit their husband's values each and every time they instructed their children in religious, moral, or social behavior was similarly a practical impossibility. As we saw in the previous chapter, Reformation culture celebrated not only mar-riage but the spiritual equality of wives. As "religious observance and religious education increasingly took place within the confines of the family," women likewise acquired additional responsibilities to pro-vide religious instruction for their children.[15] Early modern women were thus expected and enjoined to play key roles in the economic, spiritual, and educational lives of their families. Women's position vis-à-vis both inheritance and coverture was thus more complicated in the period than texts such as "To Penshurst" might imply. The real problem was not so much *whether* women should help to educate their children but *how* and *under what circumstances* that education should take place. The Reformation may have increased the status and responsibility of wives and mothers, but it did not definitively establish the parameters for female pedagogy or clearly differentiate a wife's instructional role from that of her husband.

I argue that the doctrine of coverture, the same theory that effec-tively obscured female agency in early modern culture, provides the terms for representing women's pedagogical roles (and their implicit contradictions) in literature of the period. Barbara Gamage's house-wifery and educative functions are effectively co-opted for patrilineal imperatives in "To Penshurst," but what we know from other sources about her life at the estate suggests that she frequently acted indepen-dently, both in managing the estate and in raising her children while her husband, Robert, was fighting in Europe. In a letter addressed to Robert Sidney, for example, his servant Rowland Whyte singles out

Barbara Gamage for ensuring that her children are "well taught, and brought up in learning, and qualities, fitt for theire birth and condicion" despite her husband's absence.[16] Robert Sidney's departure from Penshurst is arguably the enabling condition for his wife's domestic authority, and yet the extent of her involvement and influence at the estate is clearly not compatible with any simple, straightforward reading of coverture as an erasure of female autonomy. Barbara Gamage is but one example of this cultural paradox; early modern society provided numerous models of women's educative roles that were not simply equivalent to the roles of "virtuous parents." For a patriarchal society concerned about its social reproduction, this was a potentially unsettling situation, since the gap between the theory and practice of coverture allowed for a degree of female independence in educative matters that could not be easily predicted or regulated. These disconcerting possibilities are not visible in "To Penshurst." As a panegyric with an explicit focus on rural, aristocratic ideals, Jonson's genial representation of household pedagogy is necessarily limited in both scope and nuance. Other kinds of texts from the period, however, tell a different story. Stage plays and mothers' legacy books, for instance, more frequently reveal rather than obscure the ideological slippages that were possible within pedagogical practices. In doing so, these texts narrate coverture and female pedagogy in ways that both illuminate and often disturb the mimetic principles implicitly underlying these categories.

As I demonstrate in this chapter, stories about female educators attempt to offset the potential for female autonomy within the discourse of coverture by linking women's pedagogy to inheritance via narratives that focus on seamless transition and transference. They thus emphasize the process of direct generational transmission as key to both humanist pedagogy and patrilineal inheritance practices. These narratives derive their basic structure from the representational terms provided by coverture: women's educational work in these texts is temporally limited by a distinct beginning (which usually involves the absence of a father or husband), a generally short duration, and a finite conclusion—often the woman's death. As in coverture, a wife's agency seems only to exist where her husband's ends. Looking at dramatic texts such as William Shakespeare's *All's Well That Ends Well* (written in 1602–1603) and the mothers' legacy books of Dorothy Leigh, Elizabeth Jocelin, and Elizabeth Grymeston, I argue that the curtailed narratives of female pedagogy that they depict offer partial and equivocal solutions to the household dilemmas posed by coverture. During a period in which maternal authority in the household was increasingly expected yet imprecisely defined, these stories create a refreshingly clear timeline of female pedagogy that limits it in both scope and duration. Like the stories about female servants we saw in chapter 1, these are reassuring narratives to those concerned about the extent of women's domestic authority: they allow for female agency within the household but place primary emphasis on the transference of education *to* children and *away from* mothers.

However, these texts can never completely close the fissure that separates the theory and practice of coverture or eliminate the potential for female autonomy that emerges from that divide. Even as these texts project the appearance of simplicity and order, they are grappling with the fundamental problem of coverture, namely, that the theoretical restraints imposed on female agency are consistently thwarted by both the practical and ideological demands of post-Reformation English culture. Despite the compressed nature of their narrative timelines, then, stories about female educators suggest that women's ability to bequeath advice and instruction—like their ability to control and bequeath property—will not always simply mimic patriarchal prerogatives but will sometimes take the form of more complex and flexible narrative relationships between mother and child. It is in these narrative deviations—produced by the irreconcilable contradictions of coverture as a lived cultural system—that we can detect the possibility of more sustained subject positions for women as household educators.

By the eighteenth century, widespread cultural changes would clarify the connection between women and domestic education. As I discussed in the previous chapter, religious practice as a whole would become more feminized over the course of the seventeenth century, and women and men would be more neatly associated with separate ideological spheres. Moral instruction too would become almost exclusively associated with women and the household by the early 1700s. As Patricia Crawford has demonstrated, "Virtuous middle-class women became [in eighteenth-century England] the good conscience of the family. Religion was for the household, where women taught their children personal morality. In the public sphere, educated men deemed secular values and virtues more appropriate."[17] What, one might ask, has to happen in seventeenth-century English culture to occasion a shift from the "virtuous parents" of Penshurst to the celebration of explicitly maternal education in the eighteenth century? By locating the available subject positions for female educators in earlier, seventeenth-century narratives, I both demonstrate the ways in which that literature struggles with the implications of coverture for parental education that were particularly resonant in early modern England and suggest the subtle ways in which that literature unintentionally foreshadows the separate-sphere ideology of the eighteenth century that will feminize both moral education and the household.

PRINCES AND POT QUARRELS: WOMEN, PEDAGOGY, AND INHERITANCE ON STAGE

The early modern stage offers several examples of women who attempt, with varied degrees of success, to provide a social education for their children and dependents. Plays from the period often represent the duty to provide such an education as a story of inheritance in which moral values—like physical goods—may be bequeathed and passed down in a direct line from parents to child. These texts emphasize the importance of maternal education, but they do so indirectly by associating women's educative function with tropes of substitution. Women's household pedagogy, that is, becomes visible on stage only as a replacement for paternal education. This is a fundamentally con-servative narrative pattern, in that it deals with the problem of cover-ture by suppressing most of its contradictions and difficulties.

Margaret in Shakespeare's *3 Henry VI* (written in 1590–1591) is a prime example of a woman who gains pedagogical authority over her son in direct proportion to her husband's abdication of it. The play makes the link between socialization and inheritance explicit from its opening scene, when Henry announces his decision to "unnaturally... disinherit" his son, Prince Edward (1.1.193).[18] Margaret is swift to chastise her husband for his decision:

> Ah, wretched man, would I had died a maid
> And never seen thee, never borne thee son,
> Seeing thou hast prov'd so unnatural a father!
> Hath he deserv'd to lose his birthright thus?
> Hadst thou but lov'd him half so well as I,
> Or felt that pain which I did for him once,
> Or nourish'd him as I did with my blood,
> Thou wouldst have left thy dearest heart-blood there
> Rather than have made that savage duke thine heir,
> And disinherited thine only son.   (1.1.216–225)

As Katherine Schwarz has cogently argued, this passage creates a "tautological relationship between maternity and good sovereignty" that specifically "excludes the king."[19] But it is also through her vehe-ment condemnation of her husband's actions that Margaret establishes herself as a fitting pedagogical substitute for Henry, one who will restore the birthright Edward has lost due to his "wretched" and "unnatural" father.

Margaret's influence over her son's development into an impressive king and warrior—the very things his father is not—becomes more apparent in later acts. In response to young Edward's forceful denial of Warwick's right to the throne, Richard tells the Prince: "Whoever got thee, there thy mother stands, / For well I wot, thou hast thy mother's tongue" (2.2.133–134). Both a critique of Margaret's brazen outspokenness and a compliment to Edward's rhetorical skill, Richard's comment pointedly insists that it is Margaret, not Henry, who ensures the connection between generation ("whoever got thee") and inheritance. When Margaret goes to the French court to plea for military support, she explains that the king has become a "banish'd man," thus prompting her to seek "just and lawful aid" on behalf of "this my son, Prince Edward, Henry's heir" (3.3.25, 32, 31). The king's political irrelevance necessitates Margaret's aggressive actions in defense of her son's political future. If Edward is to succeed as "Henry's heir," it will only be through his mother's doing.

Indeed, while still at the French court, Margaret negotiates a politically advantageous marriage for Edward, promising him to Warwick's eldest daughter. She thus fulfills a parental duty that was explicitly tied with proper socialization in the period. Early modern conduct books and advice manuals make it clear that the successful arrangement of suitable marriages was one of the primary responsibilities of parents, a vital component of the household pedagogy that would produce properly socialized children. In 1582, Thomas Bentley's *The Sixt Lampe of Virginite; Conteining a Mirror for Maidens and Matrons* in *The Monument of Matrones* advised those parents with sons to "instructe them, bryng them up in nourture and learnyng," and he instructed all parents that they "ought to have great care in the marrying and bestowing of [their] children" (C3r). Several decades later, in his treatise *Ten Sermons tending chiefely to the fitting of men for the worthy receiving of the Lords Supper* (1609), John Dod argued that parents must not only instruct their children but bestow them "timely, and religiously in marriage" (B3v).[20] The contract Margaret negotiates between her son and Warwick's daughter (whom she describes as "fair and virtuous") promises not only a good marriage but also good diplomatic relations. In showing "great care" for the bestowing of her son in marriage, Margaret ensures that her son will have a successful transition to the throne and that we will be supported by strong dynastic alliances.

By the end of the play, it is clear to everyone on both sides of the civil conflict that Margaret's influence has been primarily responsible for transforming Edward into a courageous and worthy prince. Before the final battle, Oxford praises both Margaret and her son for their "so high a courage," concluding, "O brave young prince! Thy famous grandfather / doth live again in thee. Long mayst thou live / to bear his image and renew his glories!" (5.4.50, 52–54). Again, Edward's courage and bravery are virtuous qualities that he has acquired through patrilineal inheritance. But if Edward's "famous grandfather" lives again in him, it is due to the "woman of...valiant spirit" who, in Edward's own words, would "infuse" even a coward's breast "with magnanimity" (5.4.39, 41). Kingly virtue, that is, has skipped a generation, but it has done so only through Margaret's forceful intervention. In the words of Jean Howard and Phyllis Rackin, "Edward claims the throne in this father's name, but he does so in his mother's spirit."[21]

Of course, 3 *Henry VI* does not end with Edward (or rather, with Margaret's Edward) on the throne, renewing his grandfather's glories. The final movement of the play—Edward's death and Margaret's ignoble departure—neatly frames Margaret's acts of maternal pedagogy by endowing it with a sense of finality. In doing so, I argue, the play offers up a relatively common narrative about female educators in the period. Social education—an explicitly generational transition involving the transferal of moral principles—is a form of work granted to women only under very specific narrative circumstances. Margaret, that is, can play a primary role in her son's education when she substitutes for her all-but-absent husband. As Mary Beth Rose has argued about Shakespearean drama more generally, "mothers are empowered when fathers fail," an insight that helps to explain Margaret's circumscribed agency in this scene.[22] Perhaps even more significant is the truncated timeline to which this mother's educational labors adhere. Margaret is extraordinarily successful at socializing her son to be what his father should be but is not. However, her military defeat and the premature death of her son endow her actions with only temporary authority. Maternal education is not sanctioned indefinitely, but only as long as its enabling conditions—in this case the absence of a strong king and father figure—are in place.

Though famously branded an "Amazonian trull" (1.4.114), Margaret is in many ways a very conservative figure, since she uses her political authority in the service of a decidedly patriarchal ideal: a strong monarchy secured through patrilineal inheritance. As Schwarz notes, "Margaret constructs her Amazonian performance in the

service of a masculinist and chauvinist attempt to preserve patrilineality in its established form."[23] The play's forceful representation of
maternal education is thus tempered by its political context, but also
by its narrative conditions, namely an ideologically absent husband
and a clear ending that repositions Margaret within normative gender
and political hierarchies. Those concerned about the specter of the
"Amazonian" rebel that Margaret seems to project can be comforted
at least by the play's ending, in which her authority is curtailed and
she is re-subordinated to a new monarchy. And yet, as Schwarz so
aptly puts it: "Her agency becomes most dangerous when it is turned
to patriarchy's own ends, and in a sense this is always the flaw in the
system: it is difficult to give women significance without at least lending them power."[24] This is the central dilemma posed by coverture.
Specifically in terms of parental education, women's significance in
patrilineal transmission must be carefully balanced with the power
that they can gain from that process. In *3 Henry VI*, the solution
to this problem comes through the temporality implied by the act
of "lending" power. Though the perpetuation of patrilineal inheritance by mothers is never "risk-free,"[25] Shakespeare's play nevertheless insists that maternal education can flourish only as a temporary
and narratively limited substitute for parental pedagogy.

The concept of "lending" temporary authority to female educators
reappears in Henry Porter's little-known play, *The Two Angry Women
of Abington* (1599). This late Elizabethan comedy represents a very
different scenario of maternal pedagogy than the one dramatized in
3 Henry VI. In Porter's text, a quarrel between two mothers leads
them not only to a lengthy family feud but to the complete neglect of
the social education of their children.[26] Nevertheless, similar narrative patterns are at work in both plays: education is discursively connected to inheritance, and women's role in the process, governed by
the dictates of coverture, produces a very conspicuous story of substitution. What is perhaps most striking about *Two Angry Women*,
however, is the fact that fathers in the play are not pointedly absent,
like King Henry, but are very much present on stage and in the ensu-
ing chain of events. Indeed, it is the fathers in Porter's play who must
take over the duty of socializing their children that their wives have
disregarded.

Two Angry Women dramatizes a prolonged feud between two
neighboring, middling-sort women, Mistress Goursey and Mistress
Barnes. The feud begins with a game of tables that quickly devolves
into a heated quarrel in which "neighbour-amity" and "good faith" are
replaced by a "pot-quarrel" that consists of "woman's jangling" (1.1).[27]

Though the wives' quarrel initially seems to threaten only their own reputations, the play soon shifts focus to the potential damage that their actions cause to the next generation. Once it is clear to Master Barnes that his wife will not give up her "pot-quarrel" with Mistress Goursey, he takes on the role of social educator that Mistress Barnes seems unable to fulfill. It is Master Barnes, not his wife, who first turns his attention to his daughter and questions her about her willingness to marry. He begins to express concerns about Mall's virtue, assuming that she will inherit the same "spirit as her mother," which would make her a "plague unto her husband." He plans to arrange for her marriage to the Goursey's son to test her moral constitution, "how she would demean herself" (2.1). Mall's marriage thus becomes a scientific experiment of sorts by which Barnes can prove or disprove the transference of vice from one generation to the next. Of course, the heightened attention to lineage and inheritance that the marriage negotiations entail exposes the work that has been left undone by Mistress Barnes through her neglect of Mall's social education.

There are two interesting consequences of Master's Barnes convoluted plan for his daughter. First, despite the fact that Mall's marriage to Frank Goursey would be an upwardly mobile one (we learn that his "lands are great") and thus an advantageous prospect for this middling family, Mistress Barnes rejects the marriage outright, insisting that her daughter is "too young to marry" (2.1). Her stubbornness in this matter is illogical and disruptive and a direct violation of her educational duties to secure a good marriage for her child, as Margaret does confidently for Prince Edward. As such, Mistress Barnes poses a threat to the financial and social well-being of her daughter and to the continuance of the Barnes family lineage. Second, the refusal of both mothers to approve the marriage results in a scene in which Frank and Mall give their consent *per verba de praesenti* (by words of the present). Though in doing so, Mall and Frank manage to outsmart their mothers and marry despite the feud, this solution is socially and religiously unsatisfactory. Though legally binding, marriages contracted *per verba de praesenti* were morally undesirable.[28] In *Ten Sermons tending chiefely to the fitting of men for the worthy receiving of the Lords Supper*, for example, Dod lists one of the sins against the seventh commandment as "[u]nholy mariages, in regard of religion, age, neerenes of blood, want of parents consent, &c" (B4v). Frank and Mall's marriage is thus not only clandestine but also religiously suspect. By neglecting a vital part of their educational duties, Mistresses Barnes and Goursey have burdened their children with a highly vexed entrée into marriage.

Not surprisingly perhaps, Mistresses Barnes and Goursey eventually agree to reconcile, deciding not to persist in the "crossing of true love" (5.1). But in the midst of its tangled story of female feud, this odd and mostly forgotten play produces a narrative of women's educational work that, like Margaret's socialization of Edward, connects this labor directly to patrilineal inheritance patterns. The proper socialization of Mall depends both on the qualities she has inherited from her mother and on her success in entering into a promising marriage that will secure the Goursey inheritance well into the future. We see as well that the parental work of educating children, which was largely assumed to be a shared duty in early modern England, is once again staged as a solitary task, though here it is the father who must go it alone and substitute for the absent mother. As educators, mothers and fathers cannot seem to share the same representational space, a textual residue of the problems for marital agency produced by coverture.

As was true of Margaret in *3 Henry VI*, the wives' educational labors in *Two Angry Women* are transitory and narrowly defined. Once the quarrel between the wives leads to their failure as educators, their time is up, and they are largely eliminated from the play's focus until the final scene. The extraneous nature of maternal pedagogy in the play is articulated through a formal shift in plot structure. The quarrelling wives plot quickly takes second billing to a new comic plot in which the marriage of the younger generation becomes the driving force of the narrative and the wives' quarrel becomes a mere blocking agent, an annoying obstacle that stands in the way of that marriage. In thus structurally demoting the wives' quarrel, Porter creates an extremely circumscribed narrative of women's pedagogical agency, insisting that these wives fail to socialize their children properly because they are too caught up in their own petty quarrel to secure suitable marriages for them. The play also limits the educational role of these women (however tenuous that role is to begin with) to a narrow timeframe, after which the wives are replaced by their husbands and their quarrel is replaced by the play's romantic plotline. While not erased, women's pedagogical authority is limited in efficacy and materialized only through a carefully controlled and shortly lived narrative trajectory.

At the same time, however, *Two Angry Women* articulates the importance of women's responsibility to socialize their children by insisting that the failure of such maternal duty leads to dire, if comic, consequences. In other words, despite the restrictions on agency presupposed by coverture, even the discursively circumscribed educational activities of Mistresses Barnes and Goursey acquire an independent significance that is not simply equivalent to their husband's desires or the broader goals of "parental" pedagogy. Both *3 Henry VI* and *Two Angry Women* solve the problem of household pedagogy under coverture through conservative narratives that emphasize the idealized workings of patrilineal inheritance and the limited duration of maternal authority. But if agency is only lent to these female characters so that they can ensure (or attempt to ensure) the smooth transition between one generation and the next, we can nonetheless glimpse the unsettling potential for female autonomy in the pot quarrels of Mistresses Barnes and Goursey and, more obviously, in the Amazonian rhetoric of Margaret. The representational possibilities for women's educational labors afforded by the discourse of coverture may be strictly limited, but they are possibilities all the same. Though tentative and constraining, these texts begin to imagine an ideological space for female educators embedded within the very discursive system that seems to exclude them.

GENRE AND THE FORMS OF EDUCATION IN MOTHERS' LEGACY BOOKS

Mothers' legacy books, popular prose texts consisting of women's printed advice to their children, offer a very different point of entry into these ideological spaces. Though mothers' legacies had been written and circulated in England since the 800s, they achieved their greatest popularity during the first half of the seventeenth century.[29] These texts are unique in that they display early modern women deploying the rhetoric and authority of the deathbed to represent their own work as educators. Perhaps most strikingly, these books exist as decidedly public entities despite the ostensibly personal and familial nature of their subject matter. Many of these texts had impressive print runs and wide readerships. Dorothy Leigh's *The Mothers Blessing* (1616) was the best-known text in the genre and became one of the century's bestsellers, running to twenty-three editions between 1616 and 1674. Elizabeth Jocelin's *The Mothers Legacie, To her unborne Childe* (1624) went through seven editions between 1624 and 1640, and Elizabeth Grymeston's *Miscelanea, Meditations, Memoratives* (1604) had seen four editions by 1618.[30] As texts published for popular audiences, these books served a dual purpose: they offered written instruction in spiritual, personal, and (on occasion) political matters tailored specifically to the authors' children, and they also offered more generalized moral guidance to a wider audience during a period of political and religious upheaval.[31] But this dual purpose also made them ideally poised to negotiate the thorny issues related to women's educational responsibilities under coverture. Balanced between familial duty and the commercial marketplace, between circumscribed household authority and more extensive forms of social influence, these books augment and reformulate the limited narratives of female education that we saw in *3 Henry VI* and *Two Angry Women*. Though they still retain many of the characteristic narrative patterns of those dramatic texts, the mothers' legacy books as a genre deploy formal structures that bring into visibility broader and more flexible models of household pedagogy.

One of the most notable features of this genre is the common rhetorical stance assumed by its authors, in which the (real or imagined) imminent death of the writer legitimizes her authorial voice. Writing as if from their deathbeds, these women can lay claim to the temporary authority granted specifically to dying women during the period. Guides to the *ars moriendi* (the art of dying well) exhorted all Christians to look not only to the well-being of their own souls but also to the spiritual and physical health of their children and dependants. In *A salve for a sicke man* (1595), for example, William Perkins advises householders to "set their families in order before they die," to "dispose of lands and goods... well and wisely" and to charge their children to "learn, beleeve, and obey the true Religion," since the householder has responsibility for the "soules of such as be under his government" (F2r, F3v).[32] Women on their deathbeds were expected to fulfill all of these general parental responsibilities, but they also had the opportunity to voice their individual prayers, blessings, and bequeathals to a semipublic gathering of friends and family who would respectfully listen to their advice and requests.[33]

We can see the careful attention paid to dying women in texts such as Philip Stubbes's *A Christal Glas for Christian women* (1592), in which he recounts the godly death of his wife Katherine, including her detailed confession of faith. Stubbes describes his wife's particular care for the well-being of her infant child:

> And so calling for her child, which the Nurse brought unto her, she tooke it in her armes, and kissing it, said: God blesse thee my sweete babe, and make thee an heire of the kingdome of heaven: and kissing it againe, delivered it to the nurse, with these wordes to her husband standing by. Beloved husband, I bequeath this my child unto you, hee is no longer mine, hee is the Lordes and yours... And I pray you sweet husband bring up this childe in good letters. In learning

and discipline, and above all things, see that he be brought up and instructed in the exercise of true religion.   (A4v)[34]

In Stubbes's narrative, Katherine follows the advice of writers such as Perkins to the letter, setting her family in order before she dies. Through the syntax of substitution (her child is now the "Lordes and yours" instead of "mine"), Stubbes depicts the godliness of his wife and her successful delegation to her husband of her own responsibilities to educate her son in "learning," "discipline," and "the exercise of true religion."[35] Katherine thus seamlessly transfers her instruction to her child through a process that both expresses (temporary) maternal authority and transfers it ("bequeath[s]" it) to her husband.

The histrionic scenario that Stubbes depicts for his readers emphasizes the deathbed as a limited but sanctioned space for verbal female authority. The mothers' legacy books, which resemble Stubbes's narrative in their overall design, operate according to a very similar trope. As many critics have argued, the legacies offered women a public voice through print publication, but a voice that was contingent upon their ultimate silence in death.[36] In terms of its representation of education, Stubbes's depiction of his wife's final hours also recalls the narrative of female educators that we saw in *3 Henry VI* and *Two Angry Women*. Katherine's exemplary maternal pedagogy is figured in terms of patrilineal inheritance; it is transferred to her husband, not shared with him; and it is markedly short in duration, being followed immediately by her death. We can see a similar narrative trajectory at work in the mothers' legacies. Indeed, by utilizing the rhetorical stance of the deathbed, these authors specifically invoke a timeline that sanctions their educational discourses, but only for a limited period with a clear and projected endpoint.

This temporal restriction on maternal agency is most clearly visible in Leigh's *Mothers Blessing*. Born to a wealthy gentry family with strong, godly Protestant leanings, Leigh dedicates her treatise to her "beloved sonnes, George, John, and William Leigh," and devotes the contents of the text to their religious and moral instruction.[37] She advises her children to practice "continuall meditation" and to be always "provided to dye" (B8r–B8v), and she advocates daily private prayer and scripture reading (D8r–D8v, F1r–F1v). She also instructs her sons in somewhat more practical matters, such as how best to choose a good wife (C10r–C12r) and how to manage servants (D2v–D4r). For Leigh, as for other seventeenth-century authors of mothers' legacies, her pedagogical duties to her children include both spiritual guidance and thorough indoctrination in early modern social practices.

One factor, however, complicates her narrative of household pedagogy. Leigh was a widow, a point that she makes quite clear in the preface addressed to her children, in which she explicitly positions herself as a substitute for her absent husband:

> My Children, God having taken your Father out of this vale of tears, to his everlasting mercy in Christ, my selfe not onely knowing what a care hee had in his life time, that you should be brought up godily, but also at his death being charged in his will by the love and duty which I bare him, to see you well instructed and brought up in knowledge, I could not chuse but seeke (according as I was by duty bound) to fulfill his will in all things... (A6r–A6v)

The legacy Leigh will leave her sons is already a second-generation one; she has herself been left a legacy in her husband's will, a command to bring up her children "godily" and "in knowledge." As a substitute for her husband, Leigh assumes the authority of the dead father whose "will" for his children's education posthumously enables the production of her text, though she herself gets to determine its precise scope and contents. Still, the parental responsibility to provide religious instruction for children is again represented as a divided duty. God's decision to take Leigh's husband "out of this vale of tears" is the conditional premise that authorizes Leigh's text and allows her to fulfill her wifely duties "in all things." Moreover, Leigh figures herself as a mother about to die, a rhetorical construct that further defines and limits the scope of her maternal authority, even as a substitute for her husband. As she tells her sons: "And seeing my selfe going out of the world, and you but coming in, I know not how to performe this duty so well, as to leave you these few lines" (A6v–A7r). Positioning herself and her sons on opposite ends of a human timeline, Leigh justifies her textual production by emphasizing her own temporal marginality. Even Leigh's syntax suggests a seamless transference between one generation and the next: by deploying the present progressive ("my selfe going out...and you but coming in"), this passage stresses movement, transition, and the giving way of a present life (Leigh's) to future ones (her sons'). Leigh's representation of education in *The Mothers Blessing* thus seems to support quite directly the standard critical argument about mothers' legacies as a genre, that the immanent death of the author is the primary justification for her text. It also bears striking similarities to the restricted narratives of household pedagogy that we saw in *3 Henry VI* and *Two Angry Women*, in which women's educative authority is imagined in terms of patrilineal inheritance and temporally limited in extent.

But the mothers' legacies are far more than collections of ventril-oquized patriarchal mandates about the proper socialization of children. These are texts that exude individual personality, making it difficult to confine them solely to a conservative ideology buttressed by a strict definition of coverture. Though at times the content of the legacies seems utterly conventional, the formal structures of these books are surprisingly varied and experimental. Mothers' legacy books were not precisely defined in terms of their structural design or generic components, and as a result these texts often make innovative use of a range of literary models. The formal design of the mothers' legacies, I argue, directly affects the type of written guidance their authors could leave for the benefit of their surviving children and the forms of maternal education they could represent. My analysis thus shifts focus away from the authorizing principles of these texts to their deployment of form and generic structure, a topic that has been largely neglected by critics of the legacies. The generic fluidity and potential for formal creativity within the legacy genre produces unique opportunities for self-authorization and the representation of more flexible narratives of women's household pedagogy. Generic hybridity is not simply a feature of these texts; it is a structure that allows these authors to redefine both the mimetic, father-centered model of education that restricts the duration of female participation and the patrilineal model of inheritance to which that pedagogical paradigm is so closely tied.

In *The Mothers Blessing*, for example, Leigh makes use of a wide range of structural forms to shape the advice she leaves for her children's edification. She follows her dedicatory epistles with a "versi-fied parable" in ballad measure that praises the "labourous Bee" and condemns the idle one that "seekes too soone for rest" (A8r–A8v). The forty-five short chapters that constitute the main text of the *Blessing* often adopt the didactic tone of sermons, and her advice like-wise stresses prayer, self-discipline, and the avoidance of idleness.[38] The sermon-like quality of much of Leigh's text enables her to present herself to her children and readers as a religious instructor: "Me thinks if I were a man and a preacher of Gods word, as (I hope) some of you shall be, and I pray God for Christs sake, you may, I surely perswade my selfe, that through Gods grace I should bring many to pray rightly, which now pray unadvisedly or not at all" (G3r–G3v). Conditional though it is, Leigh's phrasing authorizes her voice as a maternal instructor, advising her readers on the best way to live a moral life. By infusing her manual with the tonal quality of spiritual instruction, Leigh gives added weight to her own pedagogy.

The formal flexibility of Jocelin's treatise is even more notable. Like Leigh, Jocelin (1596–1622) was born into a godly Protestant family, and she fills her text with religious directives based on scriptural exegesis.[39] Commenting on Ecclesiastes 12.1, for example, she advises her readers: "Remember thy Creator in the dayes of thy youth," a lesson, she claims, that is "fit...for a childe" (C3v).[40] She also sets out a schedule of prayer for her children, encouraging them to "meditate on the mercies of God" everyday (C5v) and warning them against social vices such as idleness and "new fangled fashions, and apish behaviour" (D1v). In addition, Jocelin borrows directly from the structure and language of marriage manuals—such as Gouge's *Of Domesticall Duties*—and of conduct books for women, most notably Juan Luis Vives's *A Very frutefull and pleasant boke called the Instruction of a Christen Woman* (1529). She advises her daughters not only to learn to read the Bible but also to learn to do "good housewifery," to write, and to practice doing "good workes"—noting, much in the manner of Vives, that "other learning a woman needs not" (B3v).[41] Weaving together these textual threads, Jocelin produces both an educational template for her readers and a textual record of her own learning and moral principles.

One of the most intriguing features of Jocelin's texts is her occasional penchant for set prayers. At first glance, these prayers might seem to be an inconsequential or even banal aspect of Jocelin's book, but since Jocelin was a godly Protestant, her very decision to include set prayers (more common to Anglican and Catholic practices of piety) is notable.[42] And the prayers themselves articulate a remarkable degree of maternal authority, thus belying their apparently rote or static quality. The majority of her *Legacie* presents general advice for daily living and education and gives guidelines—but not exact language—for daily prayer. But in a few instances, Jocelin offers up a script for her readers to follow, at least until they can find words "as may better expresse thine own soule" (C8r). In Chapter 2 of the treatise, she instructs her children to "begin to give God thankes, and to desire the continuance of his mercy towards thee" using these words:

> Oh eternall God gracious from the beginning, and mercifull to the latter ending of the world, I give thee humble thankes, that according to thine abundant goodnesse, thou hast graciously defended mee this night from all dangers that might have happened unto mee. I beseech thee continue this thy favourable goodnesse toward mee, and so grant mee thy grace, that in all my thoughts, words, and actions I may seeke thy glory, and evermore so live in thy feare, that I may die in thy favour, for thy Sonne my onely Saviours sake. *Amen.* (C8r–C8v)[43]

Jocelin does not simply urge daily prayer; she provides precise words by which to pray. In doing so, she directly intervenes into the religious education of her children, using the embedded prayers to control the precise scope and content of her children's religious upbringing. Jocelin does not act solely as a transmitter or facilitator, passing off these prayers, like the *Legacie* itself, as an inheritable artifact. Instead she positions her prayers as a starter kit of sorts, a catechism by which her children will learn over time to "expresse" their own souls. Her children are expected to act as revising readers, adopting Jocelin's prayers as they become more adept at expressing their own spirituality. She thus creates a model of education that is fluid and adaptable in nature: Jocelin herself provides the script, but her children will revise and remake that script as necessary in the future.

But it would be misleading to conclude that Jocelin represents education as congenial and progressive, with her children incrementally adding value to her own maternal pedagogy. I pause here primarily because this formulation tends to romanticize the mother–child relationship that Jocelin depicts, and it risks a reductive binary formulation in which women's participation in the dissemination of more conservative, patriarchal values get categorized exclusively in negative terms, whereas their role in expounding more individual and flexible modes of instruction is unequivocally celebrated. In these texts, flexibility and individuality are not inherently transgressive or utopian qualities. Even though Jocelin conceives of a flexible pedagogy in which her children can add to and transform her own advice, she does not envision a family without hierarchy. She never relinquishes her own parental authority. Folded into the body of her legacy, Jocelin's set prayers work to ensure the moral virtue of her children, but they also insist upon her own lasting influence as a female educator. By providing a spiritual script within her legacy, Jocelin insists that her words be recorded, marked, and taken to heart. And through this process, she effectively keeps her children properly subservient, enjoining them to obey her maternal dictates for their spiritual well-being.

We can see in Jocelin's *Legacie* that the range of possibilities afforded by the fluid structure of the legacy genre enables her to construct a complex narrative about her intervention in her children's education. But perhaps the most fascinating example of this generic hybridity and the opportunities it affords for the authors of mothers' legacies is Grymeston's *Miscelanea, Meditations, Memoratives*. Grymeston's suggestive title highlights the range of textual forms that compose her legacy. As an advertisement of its contents, this title page draws attention to the fluid formal structure—the "miscelanea"—of her book: following the epistle, the body of the text consists of a diverse mixture of poetry, aphorisms, and religious teachings from Latin, Greek, Italian, and biblical sources.[44] In the dedicatory epistle to her son, Bernye, Grymeston openly acknowledges that her text borrows freely from the words of others: "And the spiders webbe is neither the better because woven out of his owne brest, nor the bees hony the worse for that gathered out of many flowers; neither could I ever brooke to set down that haltingly in my broken stile, which I found better expressed by a graver author" (A3v).[45] Grymeston depicts a choice between two natural models for authorial labor: the spider who weaves a web out of "his owne brest" and the bee who produces honey "out of many flowers." Like Isabella Whitney in *A Sweet Nosgay*, Grymeston chooses the process of anthologizing, of gathering the words of others and compiling them alongside her own. Her chosen metaphor subtly codes the labor of the anthologizer as sweet and pleasing ("the bees hony") in contrast to the potentially deceptive work of the single author ("the spiders webbe," designed to trap and ensnare), thereby undermining the implicit dichotomy that deems solo authorship "better" and the collaborative process of anthologizing "worse." Rejecting arguments that privilege textual uniformity, Grymeston celebrates the mixed forms and multiple sources of her *Miscelanea*. Even more so than Jocelin's *Legacie* or Leigh's *Blessing*, Grymeston's legacy is an avowedly hybrid construction.

Indeed, Grymeston ends her epistle by drawing attention to the limitations of individual generic forms. She apologizes for her epistle's abrupt ending, saying: "I could be content to dwell with thee in this argument: but I must confine my selfe to the limits of an epistle... To which rule I doe the more willingly submit my selfe, for that the discourses following are motives to the same effect" (A4v). Grymeston is clearly aware of both the restrictions and the possibilities of genre. Her epistle can only do so much in the way of educating Bernye "out of her owne experience" (A3r), but she can make use of the various "discourses" that comprise the rest of the *Miscelanea* to establish more fully the means and motives by which her son can lead a good life. Megan Matchinske has pointed out that it is only in Grymeston's epistle that we find her explicitly offering domestic advice.[46] While this is certainly true, I suggest that Grymeston continues to fulfill her pedagogical objectives throughout the remainder of her text by deploying and manipulating a wide range of literary forms and styles. Her epistle may be limited in scope, but the varied discourses that follow, facilitated by the diverse textual forms through which they are imagined, can be marshaled to produce the same edifying effects.

In the dedicatory epistle, Grymeston presents Bernye with an educational legacy that is not static, but susceptible to adaptation over time:

> as I am now a dead woman among the living, so stand I doubtfull of thy fathers life;…yet for that I see that…I leave thee this portable *veni mecum* for thy Counseller, in which thou maist see the true portrature of thy mother's minde, and finde something either to resolve thee in thy doubts, or comfort thee in thy distresse; hoping, that being my last speeches, they will be better kept in the conference of thy memorie; which I desire thou wilt make a Register of heavenly meditations. (A3r–A3v)

Grymeston wishes for her "last speeches" to provide future comfort for her son—indeed hoping that Bernye will internalize the "heavenly meditations" offered in her text, making them part of his own memory.[47] But if Grymeston justifies her writing in the conventional way (by citing her impending death), the epistle also assumes a provocative reciprocity between her son's memory and her own text. By reading his mother's *Miscelanea*, Bernye can transform a physical text into a metaphorical one, creating for himself a "Register of heavenly meditations" in his memory. However, the epistle never suggests that this register will fully replace the portable *veni mecum* which Grymeston hopes will counsel Bernye. Instead, text becomes memory, which metaphorically becomes text again. As a Catholic, Grymeston may have found this fluid narrative of education particularly appealing, since it enables her to articulate two separate yet mutually exclusive sites in which knowledge can be retained. By legitimizing both text and memory, Grymeston can (at least rhetorically) safeguard her legacy against either the mind that may forget or, more urgently, the censorship and confiscation threatened by Protestant authorities.[48]

The various chapters that comprise the *Miscelanea* continue not only to mix textual forms but also to maintain a reciprocal relationship between mother and son. Like both Leigh and Jocelin, Grymeston includes the standard educational and moral dictums, advising Bernye to "Marrie in thine owne ranke" (A3v) and "Be not at any time idle" (H3r). She also, like Jocelin, (though less surprisingly, given her Catholicism) provides set prayers to be recited, including an "Evening Meditation" that takes the form of "Odes in imitation of the seven penitentiall Psalms, in seven severall kinde of verse" (F1r). But one of the oddest and, for my purposes, most intriguing, of all of the chapters in the *Miscelanea* is Chapter 12 (figure 4.1). In this extremely short entry, Grymeston records:

> A Madrigall made by Berny Grymeston upon the conceit of his
> mothers play to the former ditties.
> How many pipes, as many sounds
> Do still impart to your sonnes hart
> As many deadly wounds.
> How many strokes, as many stounds,
> Ech stroke a dart, ech stound a smart,
> Poore Captive me confounds.
> And yet how oft the strokes of sounding keyes hath slaine,
> As oft the looks of your kind eies restores my life againe.   (E4v)

The headnote to this unusual chapter juxtaposes the madrigal "made" by Bernye on the one hand and Grymeston's "conceit" and her act of anthologizing the madrigal on the other. Grymeston bequeaths her son this compilation in order to fulfill her duty to educate him "out of her own experience" (A3r), but this madrigal vexes both the definition of that experience (what counts as "her own" here?) and of the meaning of inheritance itself. By the time we get to the final line of the madrigal, it is no longer clear who the "my" is whose life will be restored. Certainly the "my" refers to Bernye, as speaker and creator of the madrigal, who wishes that his beloved will return his love and thereby "restore" him. But the poem is also Grymeston's conceit, and hers to record in print. As such, it is equally *her* life that is restored when readers peruse her words and follow her advice. Like the trajectory leading from text to memory back to text set forth in the epistle, the madrigal makes visible a trajectory leading from mother to son to mother that is repeatable ad infinitum. Grymeston may be the maternal authority figure who can bequeath both advice and text to her son, but Bernye is also the coauthor of his own legacy. Significantly, this diachronic collaboration extends Grymeston's authority through her son rather than weakening it. The embedded genre of the madrigal facilitates a narrative of Grymeston's educational labors that emphasizes the creativity and longevity of maternal pedagogy as well as the striking reciprocity that it can engender, even within a patrilineal system of inheritance that theoretically eclipses female agency via coverture and privileges direct transmission over more elusive patterns of give-and-take.

The generic hybridity of mothers' legacies such as Grymeston's thus highlights temporal fluidity and exchange in a way that subtly challenges strictly lineal models of education. As a consequence,

CHAP. XII.

A Madrigall made by *Berny Grymeſton* vpon
the conceit of his mothers play to
the former ditties.

Ow many pipes, as many ſounds
Do ſtill impart to your ſonnes hart
As many deadly wounds.
How many ſtrokes, as many ſtounds,
Ech ſtroke a dart, ech ſtound a ſmart,
Poore Captiue me confounds.
And yet how oft the ſtrokes of ſounding keyes hath ſlaine,
As oft the looks of your kind eies reſtores my life againe.

Figure 4.1 Elizabeth Grymeston, *Micelanea, Meditations, Memoratives* (London, 1604), E4v.

attending to the formal flexibility of these texts can suggest a new way of reading their legal status as material traces of coverture. Returning briefly to Jocelin's *Legacie*, we can see that the discourse of coverture explicitly determines that text's imaginative scope, providing the terms by which Jocelin can narrate her household pedagogy. In his Approbation, Thomas Goad introduces Jocelin's treatise by invoking the contradictions of coverture:

> Our lawes disable those, that are under *Covertbaren*, from disposing by Will and Testament any temporall estate. But no lawe prohibiteth any possessor of morall and spiritual riches, to impart them unto others, either in life by communicating, or in death by bequeathing. (A3r–A3v)

Goad describes the specific legal difficulties faced by women under coverture that followed parliamentary legislation in the mid-fourteenth century. This legislation, which overturned medieval ecclesiastical law, declared that "a wife could not make a will without a pre-marital agreement with her husband to do so" and "a husband could revoke his consent at any time up until his wife's will was proved in court."[49] As both wife and writer, Jocelin is constrained by this legal predicament; the manual she leaves to her son manifests the "morall and spiritual riches" that she is free to dispense, instead of the "temporall" goods that she is legally powerless to bequeath. Caught between the material limitations of coverture and the personal initiative and educative duty that shape her text, Jocelin thus draws on yet another generic model in constructing the *Legacie*: the genre of the will.

In her important argument about the popularity of early modern mothers' legacies, Wendy Wall contends that Jocelin and other authors of these texts utilize the language of wills in order to reclaim textually their right to bequeath. Wall maintains that "[i]n these mothers' 'wills,' we see the way in which the form of the last testament allowed women to participate in generational transmission as well as affording them an arena in which the legal/economic power denied by the culture could be simulated."[50] Women such as Jocelin and Grymeston who were married and therefore legally precluded from writing wills could use the legacy book as a culturally viable substitute, justified by the rhetoric of impending death.

Wall's thesis has been very influential, as it productively connects women's advice books to the economic conditions under which they were produced. But the genre of the will is only one of the many

textual forms that shapes these legacies, and the narrative of substitution that Wall articulates does not account for the many kinds
of female instruction and agency that these books make visible and
that are largely absent from the legal language of seventeenth-century
wills. Wills from this period were not, of course, purely economic
documents. However, they did rely extensively on religious preambles
and formulae penned (and often created) by scribes, resulting in limited structural flexibility.[51] Mothers' legacies, as we have seen, are
particularly notable for their innovative and fluid use of generic models, and I suggest that it is precisely this flexibility—this opportunity
to define, construct, and bequeath educational advice, practical guidance, and spiritual dictates—that helps to explain the appeal of the
legacy book as a genre to early modern women writers. In other words,
the expansiveness and supplemental qualities of the mothers' legacies
may ultimately have been more important to these authors than the
more limited ability of these texts to serve as legal surrogates.

Indeed, given that Leigh was a widow, we might reasonably ask:
why didn't she simply write a will, as she was legally entitled to do?
Or, if she *did* write a will, but it simply hasn't survived, then why did
she also choose to write and publish her *Blessing*?[52] Perhaps Leigh
made a purposeful decision not to leave a written will in order to
reinstate rhetorically her status as a dutiful wife. Instead of replicating
her husband's decision to leave a will for his children, Leigh obediently writes her "few lines" in order to fulfill her duty as executrix of
her husband's will while deliberately not taking advantage of her legal
rights as a widow (A7r). For another explanation, however, we might
take a hint from Leigh herself, who in Chapter 4 tells her children
to "remember to write a booke unto your children, of the right and
true way to happinesse" (B5v). Leigh insinuates that legacy books are
culturally useful texts that can play a key role in the moral and social
education of children. The legacy book, that is, offers a flexible formal
space in which its author can direct and shape her children's future
lives in a manner nearly impossible in a conventional will. Viewed
from this perspective, Leigh's specific motives for writing her legacy are immaterial since the choice itself—and the formal flexibility
afforded by the legacy genre—allows her to deploy a wide range of
textual strategies in order to narrate her educational labors.

Again, this is not a process that operates free of power differentials.
The educational exchange that these texts envision can only come
to fruition in the future and, crucially, since the mother is necessarily absent, only through the text itself. Though this deferral origi-
nates in the trope of impending death these women use to authorize

their writings, it is also a mechanism of control. Jocelin, Leigh, and Grymeston are each able to dictate the circumstances under which their children's education will occur, in part by imagining a reciprocal pedagogical relationship between mother and child. Though they cannot, of course, completely predict or control the ways in which their teachings will be interpreted or enacted, they can determine the organization and contents of their volume as well as the literary models that they will employ. And they can leave their children a much more expansive and eclectic legacy than they could with a will alone.

Early modern mothers' legacies were thus not simply substitutes for wills, nor can they be fully explained as depictions of temporary periods of female authority justified by the trope of impending death. Though they often operate according to the circumscribed narrative trajectory that we saw in *3 Henry VI* and *Two Angry Women*, they also complicate that narrative by representing household pedagogy in more flexible terms whereby women's sustained influence over the lives of their children is not ended or erased by death but begun by it. As a result, it becomes less certain that one generation "gives way" to the next and more apparent that education is a process constituted mutually by mothers and their children. As we have seen, this reciprocity does not necessarily entail an abdication of female authority; it can often solidify maternal power over children by maintaining familial hierarchy across the boundary of death. Furthermore, when reading these texts, it becomes impossible to tell when (or if) the educational values of their writers coincide with that of their absent husbands. Representing social education as an inheritable artifact, these texts thus divest that education of a stable ideological meaning. In doing so, they reveal quite strikingly the gap between coverture as a theoretical system and maternal pedagogy as a lived, textual practice.

This reciprocal relationship that we can trace between the authors of the mothers' manuals and the children to whom these texts are bequeathed suggests a subtle way in which these texts expose the limitations of strictly defined patrilineal inheritance patterns. Scholars have demonstrated that inheritance law in early modern England took as its model a process by which the land, goods, and name of the father were passed on to children, with a preference for sons. However, in her groundbreaking book *Women and Property in Early Modern England*, Amy Louise Erickson notes that women's wills reveal a "wider recognition of kin" than men's wills.[53] She argues that contemporary scholars have been slow to acknowledge this difference and its importance to the history of early modern inheritance practices, noting that for economic historians, "[t]he male line of descent *through* time is now perceived as more important than the horizontal claims of women and younger sons *at* the time."[54]

Erickson's argument about the "horizontal" logic of female testators offers a useful framework for reading the mothers' legacy books. Writers such as Grymeston and Jocelin display a concern *both* with the transmission of precepts through time *and* with the more "horizontal" or reciprocal mechanisms of education in the present time of their writing. These texts negotiate between the culturally sanctioned role of mothers as educators of children and the legal restrictions placed on women through practices such as coverture and primogeniture.[55] By drawing from genres as diverse as sermons, marriage manuals, and madrigals, the authors of these texts can redefine inheritance in more flexible terms, and they can represent more facets of their work as social educators than they could in a will alone. Formal experimentation, that is, expands the representational options for this form of labor, broadening and deepening the possible roles mothers can assume in the educative process. Though these texts do not pose radical challenges to patriarchal dictates for female behavior, and are in many ways predicated on the legitimacy of women's duties to raise and instruct their children, they do offer a productive contrast to the much more limited representations of women's educative functions in *3 Henry VI* and *Two Angry Women*. The mothers' legacies expose the fundamental inadequacy of narratives—however reassuring or culturally useful those narratives might have been—in which female instructors act only as substitutes for their husbands and are then quickly eliminated from the story. In authoring these texts, seventeenth-century women such as Leigh, Jocelin, and Grymeston are able to extend the usually truncated account of female pedagogy, rhetorically prolonging and legitimizing women's agency as maternal educators.

NURTURING A WELL-DERIVED NATURE IN *ALL'S WELL THAT ENDS WELL*

The strategies by which the mothers' legacy books vividly capture the paradoxical position of female educational agency within the discourse of coverture and carve out a limited space for female autonomy are worth keeping in mind as we return to the drama, where they can suggest a new way of reading a famous, as well as a famously problematic, play. The gaps in early modern educational ideology that the mothers' legacies bring to light are perhaps most clearly and complexly articulated on stage in Shakespeare's problem comedy,

All's Well That Ends Well. To a certain extent, this play follows the narrative trajectory that we have seen in *3 Henry VI* and *Two Angry Women:* it links women's educational work to narratives of inheritance and limits these labors to a precisely (and narrowly) defined timeline with a clear endpoint. But *All's Well* also develops further some of the complexities we saw in the mothers' legacies. Namely, we can see— particularly in the play's volatile second half—a narrative of education and inheritance that works against the strictly patrilineal process of handing down precepts from one generation to the next via a female agent. Through its convoluted plot structure and ideologically elusive ending, *All's Well* dramatically showcases the representational effects of coverture both in delimiting women's household pedagogies and (paradoxically) in articulating the available subject positions for female educators.

All's Well That Ends Well is at once a play suffused with nostalgia for the dead yet deeply invested in the transference of authority to the next generation of the living. From its opening lines, the play immerses the audience in a world riddled with nostalgia for dead fathers. But clothed in mourning black, the Countess of Rossillion, Bertram, and Lafew also insistently connect the dead Count of Rossillion with his still-living relations:

> *Countess:* In delivering my son from me, I bury a second husband.
> *Bertram:* And I in going, madam, weep o'er my father's death anew; but I must attend his majesty's command, to whom I am now in ward, evermore in subjection.
> *Lafew:* You shall find of the king a husband, madam; you, sir, a father. (1–7)[56]

These lines enact a series of grammatical substitutions: Bertram, the son, replaces the dead father, while the king simultaneously supplants Count Rossillion as both father and husband. Like Leigh in *The Mothers Blessing,* the Countess and Bertram each use participial phrases that deploy the present progressive tense ("[i]n delivering my son from me"; "in going, madam"), and this parallelism draws our attention to ongoing activities that involve both transference and momentum. Indeed, despite its nostalgic tone, the action of *All's Well* is heavily invested in the present progressive, in the ways in which the future comes into being through human action in the present. Bertram's inheritance, his succession as the rightful son of his father (and all his father's virtues) is the focus of this play from the beginning, and, as the conflicts of the plot make clear, this transition between past and future is directly dependant on the success of Bertram's social education.

The grammatical substitutions of the play's opening lines emphasize the transfer of inheritance from father to son, but the play's first scene establishes the Countess as a vital—indeed the only—link between the two men. The Countess as a character is entirely Shakespeare's invention; she does not exist in either Boccaccio's *Decameron* or in Shakespeare's primary source for *All's Well*, William Painter's *The Palace of Pleasure*.[57] Shakespeare's focus on the benevolent, widowed Countess brings into visibility the specific role that a woman plays in the education of her son and the work that she must do in order to ensure that his father's legacy and his "moral parts" are passed down to him. (1.2.21). But Shakespeare also makes it clear from the outset that her role is largely that of a substitute for an absent father; it is precisely paternal absence or, in Rose's words, a "defective patriarchy" that enables the Countess's intervention in Bertram's social education.[58] As is true in *3 Henry VI* and *Two Angry Women*, the shared parental duties of education and socialization are representationally subsumed under the discourse of coverture and delegated to a single parent.

One of the Countess's primary responsibilities in the play is to educate her son and see him well married. As we saw in the earlier plays, these tasks were key components of the socialization process, usually assumed to be shared parental duties. In *All's Well*, however, these important obligations fall entirely to the Countess. Her blessing to Bertram as he leaves for the court expresses her determination to bring him up, as Bentley would advise, "in nourture and learnyng":

> Be thou bless'd, Bertram, and succeed thy father
> In manners as in shape! Thy blood and virtue
> Contend for empire in thee, and thy goodness
> Share with thy birthright!...
> ...What heaven more will,
> That thee may furnish and my prayers pluck down,
> Fall on thy head! Farewell. My lord,
> 'Tis an unseason'd courtier; good my lord,
> Advise him.   (1.1.57–60; 64–68)

The Countess wishes to ensure an uninterrupted transference of both "manners" and "shape" from father to son; since Bertram's physical shape has already been determined, she focuses her attention and efforts on the successful transmission of "virtue" and "goodness" to Bertram. The Countess's blessing exemplifies the rhetorical figure of *diatyposis* (the giving of advice in the form of "profitable rules and precepts") and thereby helps to establish her moral authority as a speaker and parent.[59] But the Countess hints that some work will be required to make this transition successful. As she tells Lafew, Bertram is an "unseason'd courtier" who needs advising, and she insists that her prayers must supplement Bertram's own actions in order to bring about efficacious results. The Countess's onstage blessing, coupled, we are meant to presume, with her offstage prayers, are didactic tools that she uses to continue Bertram's socialization and ensure that he makes a transition to responsible manhood, in the legacy of his father.

The Countess is, of course, right to be skeptical, as Bertram proves to be a notoriously intractable son. Bertram's actions throughout the play demonstrate poor judgment: he rejects his mother's didactic process and the opportune marriage with Helena, and he seems stubbornly adverse to the very types of social relationships necessary for the maintenance and reproduction of a hierarchical society. He tells his mother: "I *must* attend his majesty's command, to whom I am now in ward, evermore *in subjection*" (1.1.3; emphasis added). Bertram can only comprehend his relationship with the king in terms of forced enthrallment. His resentful approach to state hierarchy coincides with his careless selection of companions, specifically his association with the dissolute and ambitionless Paroles. When the Countess learns that Bertram has left France in Paroles's company, she berates Paroles, calling him a "very tainted fellow, and full of wickedness; / My son corrupts a well-derived nature/ With his inducement" (3.2.87–89). The Countess pointedly names her son, not Paroles, as the corrupting influence; Bertram corrupts his own "well-derived nature" while Paroles is relegated to the subordinate clause and is syntactically dependent upon him. In his mother's eyes, Bertram is primarily to blame for the relationship because it signals his lack of self-control and social discernment. Indeed, in *The Education of children in learning* (1588), William Kempe dictates that children be brought up in "none other company than such as are both honest and civil, as well in behavior as in language," warning specifically against "clownish playmates and all rustical persons" (E3v).[60] Bertram's embarrassing relationship with Paroles thus signals quite early in the play his own self-corruption and misguided comportment. It is only much later that Bertram begins to question Paroles's virtue (asking a Lord, "Do you think I am so far deceived in him?" (3.6.6)), and he continues his own dissolute behavior well into the play's final act.[61]

Bertram's unwillingness to fulfill his role as Helena's husband triggers the central conflict of Shakespeare's play. Bertram initially rejects

Helena because of her lower social status; he tells the king that "[s]he had her breeding at my father's charge— / A poor physician's daughter my wife! Disdain / Rather corrupt me ever!" (2.3.114–116). Even though the king insists that nobility arises from virtuous actions ("From lowest place when virtuous things proceed, / The place is dignified by th'doer's deed" (2.3.125–126)), Bertram resents Helena and calls his marriage "a clog" (2.5.53). Bertram is officially married, but he still desperately needs to learn how to become a proper husband, a pedagogical process that he rejects. As the Countess notes when she learns about the marriage: "It hath happen'd all as I would have had it, save / that he comes not along with her" (2.2.1–2). The pause between "it" and "save," which drastically qualifies the Countess's confident "all," speaks volumes about Bertram's failure to live up to his mother's expectations. The Countess considers her son to be well bestowed in marriage and she is eager to make Helena her heir, but his enforced separation from his wife renders him not a dutiful son but a "rash and unbridled boy" (2.2.27). His attempt to win Diana's sexual favors in Florence further confirms his mother's indictment.

The Countess takes initial responsibility for properly socializing Bertram, whose actions mark him as a dissolute, "unbridled" son and husband who has neglected his own social education. But, as was true in *3 Henry VI, Two Angry Women*, and, to a lesser extent, in the mothers' advice books, her labor is significantly limited in both extent and duration. We can detect the Countess's gradually waning influence over her son as early as Act 1, during a seemingly innocuous conversation with the Clown:

> *Countess*: Tell me thy reason why thou wilt marry.
> *Clown*: My poor body, madam, requires it; I am driven on by the flesh, and he must needs go that the devil drives.
> *Countess*: Is this all your worship's reason?
> *Clown*: Faith, madam, I have other holy reasons, such as they are.
> *Countess*: May the world know them?
> *Clown*: I have been, madam, a wicked creature, as you and all flesh and blood are, and indeed I do marry that I may repent.   (1.3.19–35)

The Countess's persistent questioning is almost catechistical in nature, resembling some early casuistry treatises in its structure.[62] Here the Countess attempts to teach the Clown appropriate reasons for marrying by ferreting out and then critiquing his own rationales. Though the scene may reveal the Countess's admirable concern for the well-being of her household dependents, it also deflects attention away from her relationship to Bertram, who is vastly more in need of her scrutiny and apprehension. The Countess's dialogue with her servant is an ineffective substitute for the conversation she should be having with her son, and it signals her unsuccessful, if well-intended, role as a socializer and ethical instructor. Her failed pedagogy is notably marked by her prompt disappearance from the play's action following Bertram's ultimatum to Helena in Act 3; she returns to the stage only for the final scene. Once again, women's educational labors seem to be pointedly limited in duration and, in this case, efficacy.

We have seen this narrative trajectory at work in the other texts I've examined in this chapter: women's work as educators is discursively connected to inheritance and transference and limited to a neatly plotted and circumscribed timeframe. In the absence of fathers and husbands, women attempt to educate their children and then conveniently disappear from the scene. But while this narrative might be culturally useful, in that it both sanctions and delimits women's post-Reformation educational duties under coverture, it does not explain all that goes on in *All's Well*. As we saw most notably in the mothers' legacies, women's role in social education is not always as clearly defined or as slavishly patriarchal in ideology as it may initially appear to be in these texts. The second half of *All's Well*, loosely defined as the action that occurs following the Countess's disappearance in Act 3, complicates the model of education and inheritance established so clearly in Act 1. Just as Bertram and Helena's marriage is far from the end of this problem comedy, the Countess's failed socialization of her son is not the end of his education, or of women's role in it.

As the Countess disappears from the play's action in Act 3, the story shifts focus to Helena's pursuit of Bertram in Florence. In *Two Angry Women*, maternal failure resulted in paternal intervention, but in *All's Well*, Shakespeare summons another female character to finish the job of educating the recalcitrant lord. This transition is not mere coincidence. Because the Countess's education of Bertram has failed, the work of transforming this "unbridled boy" into an ethical and fully socialized husband and father must be transferred to Helena, a transference that is doubly meaningful because Helena has herself been educated by the Countess and is both surrogate daughter and actual daughter-in-law to her. The Countess claims Helena as her own child even before her marriage to Bertram, telling her: "I say I am your mother, / And put you in the catalogue of those / That were enwombed mine...I express to you a mother's care" (1.3.137–139, 142). After hearing Bertram's written ultimatum to Helena, the

Countess makes a clean break from her son, transferring her benevolent attention entirely to Helena: "He was my son, / But I do wash his name out of my blood / And thou art all my child" (3.2.66–68). As the Countess's delegate and virtuous successor in the play's final acts, Helena takes on the task of educating the recalcitrant Bertram and correcting his unruly attitudes toward marriage and social order.

This shift in the comic plot significantly compromises the patrilineal model of pedagogy and inheritance implied by the Countess's initial desire to see Bertram succeed his father, both in manners and shape. As soon as Helena takes over as the Countess's surrogate, social education in the play loses its connection to generation. Helena fulfills the role of more traditional romantic heroines, such as Rosalind in *As You Like It* (written in 1599), who train their wooers to follow social conventions and behave like proper lovers prior to marriage. The substitution of Helena for the Countess thus reveals that the coming into being of new knowledge and new social skills is not necessarily directly tied to the coming into being of a new generation. Furthermore, it seems unlikely that Helena will disappear following her instruction, as the Countess does; on the contrary, it is a fundamental (if often untested) premise of romantic comedy that the marital pair will remain together well after the final scene. But of course all of this is complicated in *All's Well* by the fact that Helena and Bertram are already married, one of the many idiosyncrasies that makes this play a problem comedy.[63] The closure promised by marriage is clearly not adequate to ensure that this comedy will end well, as Bertram has yet to accept his social responsibilities as a husband and future father. Bertram may technically be a husband, but he is not yet acting like one.

Bertram's ultimatum to Helena encapsulates his counterintuitive logic about generation. He demands of his wife what he believes to be impossible: "When thou canst get the ring upon my finger, which never shall come off, and show me a child begotten of thy body that I am father to, then call me husband; but in such a 'then' I write a 'never'" (3.2.56–59). The conditional syntax of the letter betrays both the backward logic of Bertram's threat and the loophole that will undermine it. Bertram demands to see the results of inheritance and generation (a ring and a child) before he will acknowledge and legitimize their origin by calling Helena his wife. As in *Two Angry Women*, where Mall's successful marriage can only belatedly validate the respectability of her mother, the inherited ring must be bequeathed again to Helena and the child must be born *before* Bertram will acknowledge the legal relationship that legitimizes both the bequeathal and the birth. Clearly this is not what either Bentley or Dod had in mind when they wrote about children's proper socialization through ideal marriage arrangements; the awkwardness of Bertram's ultimatum indicates just how far he has strayed from the exemplary marital path.

Helena's response to Bertram's demands, the mechanism by which she will ultimately instruct and reclaim her wayward husband, is the bed trick. Without rehearsing the many arguments that have been made previously about this "disquieting device," I want to focus on the peculiar logic of the bed trick and the ways in which it further complicates the narrative of Bertram's socialization.[64] On the one hand, the bed trick produces an heir for Bertram and ultimately convinces him to fulfill his duties as a husband and father. This process deflects attention away from Helena, now a mother in her own right, and restores the connection between Bertram's socialization and the process of generational transmission. The play thus seems to have returned full circle to the original vision of patrilineal education and inheritance presumed by the Countess in Act 1, and Helena's active role as an educator seems destined to be as short-lived as Margaret's in *3 Henry VI*. But the convoluted directional logic of the bed trick throws this simple teleology in doubt. Like Bertram's ultimatum to which it responds, the bed trick as a dramatic contrivance does not presuppose a neat or uninterrupted model of generation, but rather one that reverses the very process of inheritance that it intends to secure. The child must be produced before the marriage that legitimizes that child can be retroactively validated, and the ring must be exchanged before Bertram will acknowledge Helena as his wife, the rightful recipient of the "favor" that will "sparkle" in her spirits (5.3.74–75). The telos, that is, must come before the act of its origination, a reversal that suggests that it is the *marriage* and Bertram's proper role in it that needs to be secured, not the child. Though it is the child that convinces Bertram to reform his ways, the teleological impulse of the bed trick is to resuscitate a marriage badly in need of social legitimization. Helena's deployment of the bed trick thus produces a distinctive model of socialization, in which the two key participants in the process—Helena and her child—act in mutually constitutive ways to transform Bertram into a properly socialized man. Helena produces the child, and the child retroactively endorses the marriage. In this process, Helena retains authority as an educator, the instigator of a process that leads (circuitously) to social knowledge and legitimacy.

Helena's own recognition and description of her talents as a healer perhaps best exemplify the intricate way in which women's pedagogical agency emerges in the play. In the opening scene, the Countess tells Lafew that Helena has been "bequeathed to [her] overlooking" and that she has "those hopes of her good that her education promises her dispositions she inherits—which makes fair gifts fairer" (1.1.35–38). Unlike Bertram, Helena has bettered her own inheritance through careful instruction and the cultivation of "virtuous qualities" (1.1.39). This inheritance comes in part from her own deceased father, who has bequeathed her his skill in medicine ("my father left me some prescriptions / Of rare and prov'd effects...and that he will'd me" (1.3.216–217; 219)) and a more intangible legacy of knowledge and talent.[65] But Helena's own words to the Countess about this inheritance render the process of transmission more ambiguous:

> There's something in't
> More than my father's skill, which was the great'st
> Of his profession, that his good receipt
> Shall for my legacy be sanctified
> By th' luckiest stars in heaven   (1.3.237–241)

The "something in't" that exceeds her father's skill is precisely the "legacy" that will ensure heavenly sanctification of her treatment of the king. But the grammatical ambiguity of the phrase "my legacy" begs the question: is this her father's legacy to her or her legacy to someone else? Like the bed trick, the difficult syntax of this passage implies that inheritance is not simply transmitted through an uncomplicated patrilineal process but that it needs to be secured and improved through labor—in this case, Helena's medical treatment of the king. Helena's "value added" approach to her father's inheritance, reminiscent of the biblical parable of the talents, suggests that the inherited artifact, whether it is the body's physical shape, a particular skill, or even a child, does not on its own constitute a legacy.[66] Helena's legacy began as an inheritance from her father, but she has bettered it through her own "virtuous qualities."

Much of the dramatic energy and central conflict of *All's Well* derive from Shakespeare's negotiation of the paradoxical situation of female educators under coverture. The Countess's initial participation in Bertram's education reiterates the narrative we saw developed in *3 Henry VI* and *Two Angry Women* in which female pedagogy effects a generational transition and female authority is both precisely defined and shortly lived. But when Helena takes over the Countess's duties, the play shifts gears, revealing the inherent untenability of coverture as a legal construct. Through her involvement in Bertram's social education, the play offers a story in which women's educative functions are by necessity extended and pronounced. Education is not simply mimesis at these moments, but a reciprocal process between generations, most notably between Helena and her father and between Helena/Bertram and their unborn child. Indeed, Helena's education of Bertram exposes the fundamental problem of the mimetic model of education: while mimesis may be the educational ideal, perfect replication is never attainable in practice. Similarly—and here I return to Schwarz's point about the "lending" of power to women—*All's Well* openly displays one of the crucial flaws in post-Reformation culture's allegiance to patrilineality, namely, that paternal values must pass through women's hands in order for the system to function properly. This is the chink in the armor, so to speak, the circumstance that enables transformation, innovation, and newness to enter into inheritance practices and occasionally alter them. As is clear in texts such as *All's Well*, women are not only transmitters of paternal values but sources of domestic healing and knowledge. It is in this kind of incipient association between women, household pedagogy, and domestic authority that we can see the general contours of the eighteenth-century household beginning to emerge. Helena's claim to educational authority, that is, is a representational construct that prefigures the feminization of the household that would take hold more firmly in the next century, when women's status as the "good conscience of the family" would become a cultural commonplace.

But to add yet a final complication to the multifaceted discourses of household pedagogy at work in the play, we must consider the play's notoriously difficult ending, which largely undermines the security offered by Helena's social wisdom and authority. Though Bertram ultimately accepts his role as husband and father, the audience can't help but wonder just how successful or long-lasting this comfortable comic ending and the closure it attempts to ensure will be. Bertram's hasty and unconvincing exclamation that he will love Helena "dearly, ever, ever dearly" (5.3.310) suggests that the Countess and Helena have succeeded only nominally or temporarily in their work as educators and Bertram's socialization may be yet unfinished. Beginning as it does with a palpable nostalgia for dead fathers, *All's Well That Ends Well* shifts focus to the mothers and wives who must perform the living, active work of socialization in order to transform the vices of one generation into the remedy for future ones. But the uncertainty of the play's ending yields only an ambivalent representation of female pedagogy; it remains up to the audience to determine whether or not Bertram's reluctant road to manhood and maturity has truly ended "well."

All's Well thus brilliantly showcases the difficulties involved in representing women's post-Reformation educational duties in a culture governed by the dictates of coverture. Whereas Jonson in "To Penshurst" elided Barbara Gamage's agency by subsuming her under the rubric of "virtuous parents," Shakespeare explicitly draws his audience's attention to the paradoxes of women's educative roles by splitting his female educator into two characters. Female agency thus dominates the play, but only because fathers are notably absent. Women emerge as primary educators, but the effects of these efforts are rendered suspect by the play's vexed ending. And yet if women's authority as educators is circumscribed, it is nevertheless staged. As such, the theater joins the mothers' legacy books as a site and medium through which household pedagogy gets tangibly linked to female subjectivity. By exploring and staging the discrepancies within early modern educational ideologies, Shakespeare reveals that both pedagogical mimesis and patrilineal inheritance tenuously depend upon women's active involvement, however restricted. What *All's Well* reveals so strikingly, in other words, is the failure of coverture as an ideological system to do the very thing it theoretically claims to do: erase female agency.

All's Well, like the other texts I've discussed in this chapter, demonstrates that women's work as educators is often represented through narrative structures specifically demarcated by coverture. Women's household pedagogies proceed according to a clearly defined timeline that allows for female agency only at moments of substitution and transference. In these seventeenth-century representations, education is aligned with the discourse of inheritance and takes shape under specific narrative circumstances. Like service, it has a trajectory: women socialize their children and then quietly exit the scene, mimicking the process of bequeathal that their instruction is intended to reinforce. For early modern audiences, these narratives may have been socially satisfying in large part because they helped solve the problem of how to define the maternal authority of the feme covert. Prior to the fuller acceptance of women as educators of children, which would hinge on the ideologically powerful feminization of religion and the domestic and the clearer division between parental roles, both of which would take hold in the eighteenth century, women's pedagogical duties were inexactly defined and often lumped together in a general category of shared parental duties to children. At the same time, as the Reformation encouraged a heightened focus on domesticity and on the wife's role in religious education, some explanation and definition of her duties needed to emerge. What surfaces in the period are stories about women's socialization of children that project a myth of seamless transference between one generation and the next. These narratives advocate female agency, but they insist that women act solely as substitutes for husbands and fathers—rather than sharing these duties with them—and that any familial authority that they acquire is temporary.

But as becomes clear in *All's Well* and the mothers' legacies, this is a story that can only partially paper over the irreconcilable social presumptions that attend women's work as educators. If framing women's pedagogical authority as temporary and second-best is a compelling fiction, then the opportunities for female influence within the primary educational site of the family that are traceable in these texts reveal the limits of that fictionality. And it is perhaps not surprising that female agency often becomes visible in these narratives through the trope of reciprocity, in which mothers and children participate collectively—though not necessarily equally—in the process of education. That is, in these narrative renderings, women seem to gain educational authority only in nonexclusive terms. And yet, though limited and often ambivalent, these depictions of women's work as socializers, like the narratives I considered in the previous chapter that aligned women's household with introspective piety, begin to sketch out some of the subject positions available to women in the post-Reformation English household. In so doing, these texts inadvertently prefigure the changes to the family and to the ideology of motherhood that would become characteristic of eighteenth-century English society, when women's domestic authority would be explicitly embraced and idealized. This is not to say that women's inheritance rights would become less restrictive in the eighteenth century, as the opposite is true,[67] but to suggest that the glimpses of women's domestic initiative and personality that we see in texts such as Grymeston's *Miscelanea* and Shakespeare's *All's Well* would ultimately find a more stable, if also more segregated and limited, home within eighteenth-century domestic ideology.

We can begin to see this ideological shift in late seventeenth-century texts, such as the ballad *A Hundred Godly Lessons. That a Mother on her Death-Bed gave to her Children* (1674).[68] In this popular text, the dying female speaker addresses her children and offers them advice on choosing spouses, worshipping God, and assisting neighbors. At the end of the ballad, she tells her children:

> Print well in your Remembrance,
> the Lessons I have shown,
> Then shall you live in happy state
> when I am dead and gone.

Like Grymeston, the speaker of this ballad requests her children to transform her textual legacy into a mental one, suggesting a symbiosis between maternal advice and filial duty. But this ballad also shares with other late seventeenth-century and eighteenth-century texts a specific focus on a mother's unique responsibilities to educate her children. George Booth, Earl of Warrington, would write in 1739 that "[t]he Care and Education of children, both with respect to their Bodies and Minds, is by Nature given all along to the Mother, in a much greater Proportion than to the Father"(6).[69] This is clearly a different position from that taken by most sixteenth- and seventeenth-century writers, including Gouge and Perkins who, as we have seen, offered predominantly undifferentiated guidelines for parental authority. The "virtuous parents" of "To Penshurst" have all but disappeared, replaced by the figurative descendant of Jonson's fictionalized Barbara Gamage, the mother who will instruct her household in the "mysteries of manners, arms and arts." The act of imagining female pedagogy in terms of patrilineal succession thus produces a surprising literary legacy of its own, an oblique reminder of the ways in which women's intervention in inheritance practice can have unpredictable material effects.

The narratives that I have traced in this chapter vividly mark a period of historical change, a period in which the definition of motherhood and female authority within the post-Reformation, yet pre-Enlightenment, family was cautiously being negotiated. Many decades prior to *A Hundred Godly Lessons*, seventeenth-century texts such as *All's Well* and Grymeston's *Miscelanea* articulated narratives of female pedagogy that carve out a space of limited but significant authority for women within the early modern household. These texts certainly do not offer a final word on these issues, but they are nevertheless culturally useful stories that play an active role in the ongoing historical process of transforming the female worker—here the female educator—into a socially recognizable and classifiable figure.

EPILOGUE

The cultural changes of seventeenth-century England profoundly affected both the lived experience and the ideological construction of working women. By illuminating the stories about women's labor that animate early modern texts, I have argued for the central role of literary narrative in this historical process, a process by which women become discursively legible as working subjects. In their depictions, evasions, and occlusions of women's work, these narratives offer us a rich archive of cultural material. Romantic comedies and practical guidebooks alike imagine tales in which female servants find romantic happiness in marriage. City comedies such as Webster and Dekker's *Westward Ho* begin to circulate narratives about midwives and wet nurses who operate on the outskirts of London society. Domestic tragedies and women's private diaries envision Protestant housewives whose domestic competence is signaled by the piety that infuses their daily chores. And seventeenth-century advice books, such as Dorothy Leigh's *The Mothers Blessing*, vividly portray female teachers who educate their children, only to die shortly afterward. These were some of the enticing fictions, the "wishes, daydreams, reveries," that lured early modern readers and theatergoers.[1] Analyzing these narratives reveals not only how early modern writers and their audiences understood women's work but also how these cultural understandings changed over the course of the seventeenth century.

Indeed, texts written around the turn of the eighteenth century can serve as useful indices of these changes, as they begin to introduce some new stories about female workers that differ markedly from the ones explored in this book. William Congreve's brilliant Restoration comedy *The Way of the World* (1700), for instance, links

female service to marriage, but it does so by reversing the romantic teleology at work in earlier plays such as *Twelfth Night*. Lady Wishfort's
waiting maid Foible is married off to Mirabell's servant Waitwell near
the *beginning* of the play, as part of Mirabell's complex scheme to
win the hand of Millament, Lady Wishfort's niece. When the newly
married Waitwell and Foible first appear on stage in Act 2, Mirabell
takes note of their evident happiness and addresses them caustically:
"Sirrah, Waitwell, why sure you think you were married for your own
recreation, and not for my conveniency" (2.1 454–455).[2] Married
explicitly for (Mirabell's) convenience, Foible and Waitwell continue
to serve at the behest of their superiors throughout the play. There is
no sense either that marriage is a reward for good service or that service ends when marriage begins. Furthermore, Foible's marriage to
Waitwell is clearly not an upwardly mobile one, as it was for Viola and
Maria. When Lady Wishfort learns of the secret marriage later in the
play, she is furious because she has unwittingly become "a botcher of
secondhand marriages between Abigails and Andrews" (5.1. 48–49).
It seems that even the fantasy of upward mobility via marriage, which
lingered in texts such as Woolley's *The Compleat Servant-Maid*, was
gradually losing its luster by 1700, when the more mutable practices
that attended servant life in the seventeenth century were giving way
to the more rigid service hierarchy that would characterize eighteenth-
century English culture.[3] By staging the expedient marriage between
Foible and her fellow servant, *The Way of the World* subtly attests to
the gradual ossification of women's domestic service into a permanent occupation and class position by the early eighteenth century.

Like domestic service, the other forms of women's work I have
considered in this study changed significantly as the seventeenth century progressed, and popular literature played an integral role in that
process. Midwifery, wet-nursing, housework, and educational work
would all acquire new ideological valences in the eighteenth century, resolving some of the most urgent social concerns of the earlier
period as well as introducing new ones. We can trace some of these
historical and cultural shifts by returning to the figure of Lady Anne
Clifford, whose personal account of pious housewifery I examined in
chapter 3. Clifford is a useful barometer for such discursive changes
because she lived an unusually long eighty-six years, from 1589 to
1676. By the time of her death, the cultural paradigms associated
with working women were beginning to take new forms.

At Clifford's funeral, Edward Rainbowe, Lord Bishop of Carlisle,
preached a sermon (delivered in 1676, published in 1677) that speaks
both directly and indirectly to changing ideologies of housework,

childcare, and education. In discussing how the household should be properly ordered and governed, Rainbowe asserts that women should take primary responsibility for domestic duties, including the nurturing and education of children:

> Now this part of Family-Government chiefly belongs to Women; who, when mens occasions call them out, are commonly fix'd to the House, as Intelligences to their Sphear; who, although the man, as the *primum mobile*, directs the general motion of all; yet the particular and regular inclinations in the Children are commonly formed by the Woman; and if she be indeed intelligent and Wise, none can do it better. Children well instituted in *Gynaeceo*, as plants well ordered in the Nursery, will thrive, and prosper, and fill the World with good fruit.   (D2v)[4]

This passage neatly encapsulates several significant developments in seventeenth-century women's labor. Rainbowe clearly assumes that late seventeenth-century wives were not simply included in a general parental mandate to provide for one's family but were singled out as especially adept at nurturing the "particular and regular inclinations" of their children. In contrast to the sentiments expressed by William Gouge and William Perkins in the first two decades of the seventeenth century, Rainbowe clearly differentiates between the educational roles of mothers and fathers, unhesitatingly assigning the religious instruction and general education of children to mothers.[5] As Rainbowe goes on to claim, Anne Clifford—the "Wise Woman"—"built up" her children "in the nurture and fear of the Lord; season'd them with sound Principles of Religion, as was sufficiently evident to those who have known them" (D2v). Clifford's children in turn, he attests, taught their children "the same Principles which they had sucked with their Mothers milk" (D3r). By the end of the seventeenth century, then, we can begin to see the development of a separate sphere ("Sphear") ideology in relation to women's educative duties within the home. Along with the feminization of the domestic came the gendered division of domestic pedagogy.

In drawing on an emerging narrative of separate spheres, Rainbowe's sermon also suggests changing notions about women's housework.[6] As we saw in chapter 3, early seventeenth-century narratives about women's pious housewifery respond to particular post-Reformation concerns about domestic authority, but they also prefigure to a degree the eventual conflation of women, domesticity, and piety that would ideologically transform the eighteenth century. By 1676 at least, this process was well underway: Clifford in Rainbowe's account is "fix'd to the House" and governs its "particular and regular inclinations," including religious instruction. In reading Clifford's diary along-side other early seventeenth-century texts, I argued that the figure of the pious Protestant housewife emerges through evidentiary narrative structures. In other words, it is necessary to *prove* the housewife's domestic skills and piety to readers and audiences since, given the changes in wives' domestic responsibilities in post-Reformation England, these attributes cannot be automatically assumed. By the end of the century, however, the link between women, piety, and domestic order no longer needs to be proven rhetorically; it can just be stated as a given. This is not to say that either housework or female religiosity were unproblematic in eighteenth-century England, but simply to note that the alignment of women, housework, and piety had become an a priori assumption.

Finally, Rainbowe's sermon implies a shift in thinking about women, reproduction, and maternity. In arguing that "[c]hildren well instituted in *Gynaeceo*, as plants well ordered in the Nursery, will thrive," Rainbowe naturalizes the labor involved in reproduction and motherhood. His simile links the rearing and "ordering" of children to the natural thriving of plants in a nursery. And the word "nursery" itself, which could signify both a place for raising plants and a place for the feeding and education of children by a female nurse, helps to create an image that designates reproduction and child rearing as specifically female activities. Implicit in Rainbowe's comparison is the understanding that a good mother will also serve as a good nurse, producing "well ordered" children. The naturalization of maternal labor accomplished by this image reflects a gradually shifting cultural perception of maternity in early modern England. As we saw in chapter 2, as arguments in favor of maternal breast-feeding gained a stronghold in eighteenth-century English society, biological mothers would largely take over the jobs previously performed by wet nurses, and midwifery would disappear almost completely as a female profession. Women's reproductive work would thus gradually become associated exclusively with the figure of the mother and reified as part of a natural family order.

Looking at representations of women's work over the course of the seventeenth century in England, then, we see a gradual process of definitions being forged, parameters being established, social and economic dilemmas being worked out discursively, and new ideas about female subjectivity being brought into being. This does not mean that ideas about women and their labor would become fixed or rigid in the eighteenth century or that such changes occurred either neatly or linearly. However, certain categories of women's work, such as service, housewifery, and midwifery, would solidify into clearer occupational identities, becoming more precisely defined and more readily categorized as the seventeenth century drew to a close. In part, what makes the early modern period such a fascinating one in terms of women's work is the palpable sense of development and uncertainty that characterizes it. Women, of course, had always worked, but the scope and cultural *meanings* of that work were fundamentally altered in post-Reformation England. And by responding in creative and dynamic ways to the pressures of an increasingly complex consumer economy, writers of the period played a significant role in debating, imagining, and rewriting those meanings.

Taking narrative as a primary category of analysis, as this book has done, has led me to survey a broad canvas of literary evidence, from the famous and canonical tragedy *Romeo and Juliet* to the private meditations of Lady Margaret Hoby. As such, I hope that this project will instigate new and vibrant conversations between those scholars who work on early modern drama and those who work on women's writing. Reading early modern texts across gendered and generic lines has helped me to locate the stories about working women that proved most resilient throughout the period. These fictions allured seventeenth-century writers, readers, and theatrical audiences because they offered narrative resolutions to pressing social and economic problems. But this type of reading—one that is historicist, feminist, and formalist—can also encourage scholars more generally to bring together the full range of stories and images that profoundly shaped early modern culture and that continue to animate scholarship on the period. If we read this literature in terms of its (multiple and often contested) narratives, we are less likely to cut up the literary terrain of early modern England into its components and subfields, and more likely to cut across this rich territory, revealing its common concerns and shared ideologies.[7]

Women's Work in Early Modern English Literature and Culture has also argued that narratives of women's work were instrumental in constructing and delimiting female subjectivity in the seventeenth century. By exploring labor as a potential site of subject formation in the period, this book offers a subtle, though suggestive, counternarrative to theories of the early modern subject that emphasize interiority over physicality or the individual humoral body over its participation in England's economy.[8] Additionally, my study resists associating women's subject formation in the period exclusively with changing ideas about sexuality, which Michel Foucault and others have heralded as the key to modern or post-Enlightenment subjectivity. Instead, I would like to suggest briefly here—in part as an invitation for further research and comment—that over the course of the early modern period in England, "work" was becoming an important discourse of identity for women. That is, narratives about women's work, such as those I have considered in this book, established parameters for how the category of "women" was culturally articulated.

In seeking to elucidate the important economic components of gendered identity, recent historical scholarship on credit and gender in early modern England has likewise shifted focus from sexuality to work. In her study of female honor in the early modern period, for instance, Garthine Walker contends that women's reputation and social identity were defined as much by their housewifery as by their sexual behavior.[9] Similarly, Alexandra Shepard argues that working women (like working men) often associated their labor with "a positive sense of vocation" that could strengthen their social credit.[10] Early modern literature offers further evidence that work could stand in place of sexuality as a vital component of female subjectivity. In Rachel Speght's *A Dreame*, for example, a dream-vision poem that serves as a preface to her *Mortalities Memorandum* (1621), the speaker engages in dialogue with the allegorical figure of Industrie as she attempts to overcome the effects of Ignorance, who has turned her into a "brute" troubled by an "irksome grief" (A4v, B1v).[11] In response to Disswasion's discouraging remarks, which include a critique of the speaker's "dulnesse" and defective memory (B1v), Industrie insists that the speaker will be successful in her search for Knowledge if she pursues the task diligently. Industrie tells Disswasion:

> For with my sickle I will cut away
> All obstacles, that in her way can grow,
> And by the issue of her owne attempt,
> I'le make thee *labor omnia vincet* know.   (B2r)

In his rebuke, Industrie names "labor" instead of the more familiar and expected "amor" as the agent that will conquer all in the speaker's struggle against Ignorance. This fascinating substitution disrupts the usual conventions of romance narratives such as Speght's, but it also links female authority within the poem to a discourse of work.[12] It is the speaker's "owne attempt" to acquire knowledge in the poem—not Industrie's intervention—that will counteract Disswasion's catalog of obstacles. Industrie's metaphoric replacement of "amor" with "labor," I suggest, offers a potentially useful paradigm for studying early modern women's subject formation. As audience members attended a production of *Twelfth Night* or readers perused *The Countesse of Lincolnes Nurserie*, they were participating in a process whereby the subject-hood of early modern women was coming into being in accordance with the work they performed. The contours of female subjectivity were defined in part by how women's work was narrativized in popular literature and made available for a consuming public to scrutinize and discuss. By examining work as an emerging component of female subjectivity as it developed in the early modern period, we can expand our historical and theoretical vocabulary as we continue to analyze women's subject formation as a historically situated, discursive process.

The stories about working women that disturbed and delighted early modern audiences often bear little or no resemblance to twentieth- and twenty-first-century stories about gender and labor. Indeed, modern narratives about women, poverty, and blue-collar work (such as Barbara Ehrenreich's *Nickel and Dimed: On (Not) Getting By in America*) or even about women in domestic service (such as Mary Romero's *Maid in the U.S.A.*) reveal the enormous gap between modern and early modern ideologies about working women, though they certainly do not attest unequivocally to a progressive pattern of social reform.[13] However, the significance of these historical differences does not negate the power of narratological analysis, which can, I have proposed, support both historicist and formalist critical impulses. Reading and analyzing early modern narratives and formal arrangements not only can help us to produce better understandings of the specific historical roles played by these tales but also can enable us to recognize more clearly the social work performed by all stories, whatever their time, place, or structures. Our engagement with the alterity of the past and its fictions, in other words, need not involve a disavowal of form. Rather, I suggest that this type of historical analysis can help us sharpen our critical appraisal of narrative's transformative social power.

NOTES

INTRODUCTION

1. William Shakespeare, *Twelfth Night*, ed. J.M. Lothian and T.W. Craik (London: Methuen, 1975).

2. Even a cursory glance at the *Oxford English Dictionary* reveals that the word "work" could signify a surprisingly wide range of practices in the early modern period. "Work" could indicate a generic task or occupation, but it could also mean the act or product of needlework and embroidery, human birth, a moral or religious deed, sexual intercourse, or the act of committing a crime.

3. *A Womans Work is never done*, Roxburge Ballads I, fo. 534 (London, 1660?).

4. The fluid and wide-ranging nature of early modern women's labor prefigures to a certain degree the feminist critiques of Marxism and of labor relations within the modern family that emerged in the 1970s and 1980s. These analyses usefully broadened definitions of work in order to account for women's experiences. However, the hallmarks of these twentieth-century political critiques—such as the demand for equal pay for equal work and debates over the economic value of housework—are not particularly relevant to women in early modern England. See Wendy Wall's critique of the usefulness of "1970s family studies" for the analysis of early modern texts in *Staging Domesticity: Household Work and English Identity in Early Modern Drama* (Cambridge: Cambridge University Press, 2002), 9.

5. Katrina Honeyman and Jordan Goodman, "Women's Work, Gender Conflict, and Labour Markets in Europe, 1500–1900," *The Economic History Review* 44.4 (1991): 608–628, esp. 610. See also Sara Mendelson and Patricia Crawford, *Women in Early Modern England 1550–1720* (Oxford: Clarendon Press, 1998), 258; Peter Earle, "The Female Labour Market in London in the Late Seventeenth and Early Eighteenth Centuries," *The Economic History Review* 42.3 (1989): 328–353, esp. 342–344; and Marjorie Keniston McIntosh, *Working Women in English Society, 1300–1620* (Cambridge: Cambridge University Press, 2005), 7–8.

6. Earle, "The Female Labour Market in London," 337. See also Mendelson and Crawford, *Women in Early Modern England*, 256–260; and Natasha Korda, "Labours Lost: Women's Work and Early

Modern Theatrical Commerce," in *From Script to Stage in Early Modern England*, ed. Peter Holland and Stephen Orgel (Basinstoke: Palgrave, 2004), 195–230, esp. 198–205.

7. For England's demographic growth, see Keith Wrightson, *English Society 1580–1680* (New Brunswick: Rutgers University Press, 1982), 121–148; Wrightson, *Earthly Necessities: Economic Lives in Early Modern Britain* (New Haven: Yale University Press, 2000), 159–160; A.L. Beier, *Masterless Men: The Vagrancy Problem in England 1560–1640* (London: Methuen, 1985), 19–22; and *London 1500–1700: The Making of the Metropolis*, ed. A.L. Beier and Roger Finlay (London: Longman, 1986).

8. See Robert Brenner, *Merchants and Revolution: Commercial Change, Political Conflict and London's Overseas Traders, 1550–1653* (Cambridge: Cambridge University Press, 1993), 43. On the rise of England's consumer economy, see also Joan Thirsk, *Economic Policy and Projects: The Development of a Consumer Society in Early Modern England* (Oxford: Clarendon Press, 1978); Susan Cahn, *Industry of Devotion: The Transformation of Women's Work in England, 1500–1660* (New York: Columbia University Press, 1987), 40–46; Lena Cowen Orlin, *Private Matters and Public Culture in Post-Reformation England* (Ithaca: Cornell University Press, 1994), 1–13; and Wrightson, *Earthly Necessities*, 171–181.

9. See Wrightson, *Earthly Necessities*, 307–316; and Honeyman and Goodman, "Women's Work," 609–614.

10. For urban migration and the demographic growth of London, see Wrightson, *English Society*, 127–130; Ian W. Archer, *The Pursuit of Stability: Social Relations in Elizabethan London* (Cambridge: Cambridge University Press, 1991); Mark S.R. Jenner and Paul Griffiths, introduction to *Londinopolis: Essays in the Cultural and Social History of Early Modern London*, ed. Griffiths and Jenner (Manchester: Manchester University Press, 2000), 1–23; Steve Rappaport, *World Within Worlds: Structures of Life in Sixteenth-Century London* (Cambridge: Cambridge University Press, 1989), 61–67; Lena Cowen Orlin, introduction to *Material London, ca.1600*, ed. Orlin (Philadelphia: University of Pennsylvania Press, 2000), 1–13; Earle, "The Female Labour Market in London," 333; and Patricia Fumerton, *Unsettled: The Culture of Mobility and the Working Poor in Early Modern England* (Chicago: University of Chicago Press, 2006), 12–32.

11. For the "crisis" in gender relations during the early modern period, see David Underdown, "The Taming of the Scold: The Enforcement of Patriarchal Authority in Early Modern England," in *Order and Disorder in Early Modern England*, ed. Anthony Fletcher and John Stevenson (Cambridge: Cambridge University Press, 1985), 116–136, esp. 117. For useful critiques of this position, see Martin Ingram, " 'Scolding Women Cucked or Washed': A Crisis in Gender

Relations in Early Modern England?" in *Women, Crime and the Courts in Early Modern England*, ed. Jenny Kermode and Garthine Walker (Chapel Hill: University of North Carolina Press, 1994), 48–80; Laura Gowing, *Domestic Dangers: Women, Words, and Sex in Early Modern London* (Oxford: Clarendon Press, 1996); and Mary E. Fissell, *Vernacular Bodies: The Politics of Reproduction in Early Modern England* (Oxford: Oxford University Press, 2004), 1–13.

12. Gowing, *Domestic Dangers*, 28.

13. For an important challenge to the medieval "golden age" model of women's work, see Judith M. Bennett, *Ale, Beer, and Brewsters in England: Women's Work in a Changing World 1300–1600* (Oxford: Oxford University Press, 1996), 145–157; and Bennett, " 'History That Stands Still': Women's Work in the European Past," *Feminist Studies* 14.2 (1988): 269–283. See also McIntosh's useful historiographic overview in *Working Women*, 28–37.

14. For general trends in late medieval and early modern women's labor throughout Europe, see *Women and Work in Preindustrial Europe*, ed. Barbara A. Hanawalt (Bloomington: Indiana University Press, 1986); and Martha Howell, *The Marriage Exchange: Property, Social Place, and Gender in Cities of the Low Countries, 1300–1550* (Chicago: University of Chicago Press, 1998).

15. For characteristics of women's work in eighteenth-century England, see Bridget Hill, *Women, Work and Sexual Politics in Eighteenth-Century England* (Montreal: McGill-Queen's University Press, 1989), 259–267. See also Mendelson and Crawford, *Women in Early Modern England*, 343–344; and Anthony Fletcher, *Gender, Sex, and Subordination in England 1500–1800* (New Haven: Yale University Press, 1995), 283–413. For a good overview of the changes in female employment over the seventeenth, eighteenth, and nineteenth centuries, see *Women's Work: The English Experience 1650–1914*, ed. Pamela Sharpe (London: Arnold, 1998); and *European Women and Preindustrial Craft*, ed. Daryl M. Hafter (Bloomington: Indiana University Press, 1995).

16. Alice Clark, *Working Life of Women* (London: Routledge, 1919; 3rd ed., 1992). Though Clark's study is still extremely valuable to historians and literary scholars nearly a century after its first publication, many of her arguments have since been critiqued and refuted. Clark's main error was her chronology; she attributed events to the seventeenth century—such as mechanization and the removal of production from the home—that happened at least a century later. Clark has also been criticized for drawing too severe a line between precapitalist and capitalist economies in terms of their effects on women. For an excellent summary of these and other important addendums to Clark's study, see Amy Louise Erickson's introduction to the *Working Life of Women* (London: Routledge, 1992), vii–lv.

17. Notable studies include Bennett, *Ale, Beer, and Brewsters*; Barbara A. Hanawalt, "Peasant Women's Contribution to the Home Economy in

Late Medieval England," in *Women and Work in Preindustrial Europe*, ed. Hanawalt (Bloomington: Indiana University Press, 1986), 3–19; Natalie Zemon Davis, "Women in the Crafts in Sixteenth-Century Lyon," in *Women and Work in Preindustrial Europe*, 167–197; McIntosh, *Working Women*; Wall, *Staging Domesticity*; and Natasha Korda, *Shakespeare's Domestic Economies: Gender and Property in Early Modern England* (Philadelphia: University of Pennsylvania Press, 2002).

18. For a call to link formalist and feminist analyses of literature, see Janet Todd, *Feminist Literary History* (New York: Routledge, 1988), 99–102 and 136. See also Patricia Parker, *Literary Fat Ladies: Rhetoric, Gender, Property* (London: Methuen, 1987). It is worth noting that the concept of "feminist formalism" is not synonymous with "feminist aesthetics"—a term that refers to a critical approach to literature defined (and ably critiqued) by Rita Felski as "any theoretical position which argues a necessary or privileged relationship between female gender and a particular kind of literary structure, style, or form." See *Beyond Feminist Aesthetics: Feminist Literature and Social Change* (Cambridge, MA: Harvard University Press, 1989), 19.

19. Raymond Williams argues that literary forms are the material conditions that exist before any social interactions between authors and their audiences or readers can occur, in *Marxism and Literature* (Oxford: Oxford University Press, 1977), 187–188. Fredric Jameson defines genres as "literary *institutions*, or social contracts between a writer and a specific public, whose function is to specify the proper use of a particular cultural artifact," in *The Political Unconscious: Narrative as a Socially Symbolic Act* (Ithaca: Cornell University Press, 1981), 106.

20. Stephen Cohen, "Between Form and Culture: New Historicism and the Promise of a Historical Formalism," *Renaissance Literature and Its Formal Engagements*, ed. Mark David Rasmussen (New York: Palgrave, 2002), 17–42, esp. 33. Douglas Bruster defines the "new formalism" in similar terms, as "a critical genre dedicated to examining the social, cultural, and historical aspects of literary form, and the function of form for those who produce and consume literary texts," in "Shakespeare and the Composite Text," in *Renaissance Literature and Its Formal Engagements*, 43–66, esp. 44. For a good overview of the critical revival of formalist studies, see Mark David Rasmussen, "New Formalisms?" in *Renaissance Literature and Its Formal Engagements*, 1–14.

21. Jameson, *The Political Unconscious*, 130.

22. See Louis Althusser, "Ideology and Ideological State Apparatuses (Notes towards an Investigation)," in *Lenin and Philosophy and Other Essays*, trans. Ben Brewster (New York: Monthly Review, 1971), 127–186. For a useful narratological approach to the problematic

dualism of fiction and reality, see Wolfgang Iser, *The Fictive and the Imaginary: Charting Literary Anthropology* (Baltimore: Johns Hopkins University Press, 1993), 1–21.

23. See Jonathan Culler, *The Pursuit of Signs: Semiotics, Literature, Deconstruction* (London: Routledge, 1981), 169–187, esp. 175. For what is perhaps the most influential account of the distinction between story and discourse in American narratology, see Seymour Chatman, *Story and Discourse: Narrative Structure in Fiction and Film* (Ithaca: Cornell University Press, 1978).

24. David Herman, "Introduction: Narratologies," in *Narratologies: New Perspectives on Narrative Analysis*, ed. Herman (Columbus: Ohio State University Press, 1997), 1–30, esp. 8.

25. Hayden White, *The Content of the Form: Narrative Discourse and Historical Representation* (Baltimore: Johns Hopkins University Press, 1987), 24. Barthes's earlier essay, "Le discourse de l'histoire," (1967) which also denies the distinction between fictional and historical narrative, is regarded by many as the turning point in narratology between structuralism and poststructuralism. For an English translation, see Barthes, "The Discourse of History," trans. Stephen Bann, *Comparative Criticism* 3 (1981): 7–20.

26. See White, *The Content of the Form*, 24. For challenges to White's argument, see Louis O. Mink, "Everyman His or Her Own Annalist," in *On Narrative*, ed. W.J.T. Mitchell (Chicago: University of Chicago Press, 1980), 233–239; Marilyn Robinson Waldman, "'The Otherwise Unnoteworthy Year 711': A Reply to Hayden White," in *On Narrative*, 240–248; and Felicity A. Nussbaum, *The Autobiographical Subject: Gender and Ideology in Eighteenth-Century England* (Baltimore: Johns Hopkins University Press, 1989), 12–23.

27. See Northrop Frye, *Anatomy of Criticism* (Princeton: Princeton University Press, 1971). For the particular importance of historical specificity to feminist inquiries into the past, see Joan W. Scott, *Gender and the Politics of History* (New York: Columbia University Press, 1988), 28–52; and Margaret J. M. Ezell, *Writing Women's Literary History* (Baltimore: Johns Hopkins University Press, 1993).

28. For sedimentation as a part of the "ideology of form," see Jameson, *The Political Unconscious*, 98–100 and 144–145. For a feminist definition of sedimentation as a reiterative process whereby gender becomes naturalized—a process that nevertheless opens up discursive "gaps and fissures"—see Judith Butler, *Bodies That Matter: On the Discursive Limits of "Sex"* (New York: Routledge, 1993), 12–16; and "Performative Acts and Gender Constitution: An Essay in Phenomenology and Feminist Theory," in *Performing Feminisms: Feminist Critical Theory and Theatre*, ed. Sue-Ellen Case (Baltimore: Johns Hopkins University Press, 1990), 270–282.

29. The closing of the theaters by Parliament in 1642 has traditionally been understood to mark the end of early modern drama. See Walter

Cohen, *Drama of a Nation: Public Theater in Renaissance England and Spain* (Ithaca: Cornell University Press, 1985), 255–281; Martin Butler, *Theatre and Crisis, 1632–1642* (Cambridge: Cambridge University Press, 1984); and Andrew Gurr, *Playgoing in Shakespeare's London* (Cambridge: Cambridge University Press, 1996), 4 and 10. For a counterargument to this traditional account of the "end" of Renaissance drama, see David Scott Kastan, *Shakespeare After Theory* (New York: Routledge, 1999), 201–220.

30. Some classic examples of these studies include: Jean E. Howard, *The Stage and Social Struggle in Early Modern England* (London: Routledge, 1994); Karen Newman, *Fashioning Femininity and English Renaissance Drama* (Chicago: University of Chicago Press, 1991); Louis Montrose, *The Purpose of Playing: Shakespeare and the Cultural Politics of the Elizabethan Theatre* (Chicago: University of Chicago Press, 1996); Steven Mullaney, *The Place of the Stage: License, Play, and Power in Renaissance England* (Ann Arbor: University of Michigan Press, 1988); *Political Shakespeare: New Essays in Cultural Materialism*, ed. Jonathan Dollimore and Alan Sinfield (Ithaca: Cornell University Press, 1985); and *Staging the Renaissance: Reinterpretations of Elizabethan and Jacobean Drama*, ed. David Scott Kastan and Peter Stallybrass (New York: Routledge, 1991). For the size and diversity of early modern theater audiences, see Alfred Harbage, *Shakespeare and the Rival Traditions* (New York: Macmillan, 1952); Andrew Gurr, *The Shakespearean Stage 1574–1642* (Cambridge: Cambridge University Press, 1992); and Gurr, *Playgoing in Shakespeare's London*.

31. As the concept of autobiography was only beginning to be developed in seventeenth-century England, I use the term "semiautobiographical" somewhat loosely to describe personal narratives that take a variety of forms, ranging from diaries to poetic miscellanies. For the construction of women's autobiographical discourse in the early modern period, see the introduction to *Her Own Life: Autobiographical Writings by Seventeenth-Century Englishwomen*, ed. Elspeth Graham, Hilary Hinds, Elaine Hobby, and Helen Wilcox (London: Routledge, 1989), 1–27; Graham, "Women's writing and the self," in *Women and Literature in Britain 1500–1700*, ed. Helen Wilcox (Cambridge: Cambridge University Press, 1996), 209–233; Mary Beth Rose, "Gender, Genre, and History: Seventeenth-Century English Women and the Art of Autobiography," in *Women in the Middle Ages and the Renaissance: Literary and Historical Perspectives*, ed. Rose (Syracuse: Syracuse University Press, 1986), 245–278; and *Genre and Women's Life Writing in Early Modern England*, ed. Michelle M. Dowd and Julie A. Eckerle (Aldershot: Ashgate, 2007).

32. For a call to read early modern women writers in varied literary contexts, see Maureen Quilligan, "Completing the Conversation," *Shakespeare Studies* 25 (1997): 42–49.

33. For women as theatergoers, see Howard, *The Stage and Social Struggle*, 73–92. For women as readers and writers, see especially *Women and Literature in Britain 1500–1700*, ed. Helen Wilcox (Cambridge: Cambridge University Press, 1996); Ezell, *Writing Women's Literary History*; Margaret Spufford, *Small Books and Pleasant Histories: Popular Fiction and its Readership in Seventeenth-Century England* (Cambridge: Cambridge University Press, 1981); and Margaret W. Ferguson, "A Room Not Their Own: Renaissance Women as Readers and Writers," in *The Comparative Perspective on Literature: Approaches to Theory and Practice*, ed. Clayton Koelb and Susan Noakes (Ithaca: Cornell University Press, 1988), 93–116.

34. For the increased publication of women's writings at mid-century, see Patricia Crawford, "Women's Published Writings 1600–1700," in *Women in English Society 1500–1800*, ed. Mary Prior (London: Routledge, 1986), 211–282.

35. Critical studies have recently begun to acknowledge and investigate differences of age and marital status and their importance to the study of premodern women. See, for example, *Women and Aging in British Society Since 1500*, ed. Lynn Botelho and Pat Thane (Harlow, England: Longman, 2001); *Singlewomen in the European Past, 1250–1800*, ed. Judith M. Bennett and Amy M. Froide (Philadelphia: University of Pennsylvania Press, 1999); *Widowhood in Medieval and Early Modern Europe*, ed. Sandra Cavallo and Lyndan Warner (Harlow, England: Longman, 1999); Amy M. Froide, *Never Married: Singlewomen in Early Modern England* (Oxford: Oxford University Press, 2005); and Ilana Krausman Ben-Amos, *Adolescence and Youth in Early Modern England* (New Haven: Yale University Press, 1994), 133–155.

36. Barbara Harris, *English Aristocratic Women 1450–1550: Marriage and Family, Property and Careers* (Oxford: Oxford University Press, 2002), 6 and 8.

37. For some exceptions to this, such as apprenticeships in housewifery or rare paid positions as household governesses and tutors, see Mendelson and Crawford, *Women in Early Modern England*, 264–265, 286–287, and 321–327; McIntosh, *Working Women*, 133–139; and Kenneth Charlton, *Women, Religion and Education in Early Modern England* (London: Routledge, 1999), 114–117.

1 Labors of Love: Female Servants and the Marriage Plot

1. For the gradual replacement of the feudal ideology of service with a wage labor system in the period, see Michael Neill, *Putting History to the Question: Power, Politics, and Society in English Renaissance Drama* (New York: Columbia University Press, 2000), 28–39; Wall, *Staging Domesticity*, 201–203; Mark Thornton Burnett, *Masters and Servants in English Renaissance Drama and Culture: Authority and*

Obedience (New York: St. Martin's, 1997), 4–5 and 8–9; and Mary Ellen Lamb, "Tracing a Heterosexual Erotics of Service in *Twelfth Night* and the Autobiographical Writings of Thomas Whythorne and Anne Clifford," *Criticism* 40.1 (1998): 1–25, esp. 1–7.

2. See Lamb, "Tracing a Heterosexual Erotics," 5–6.

3. See Neill, *Putting History to the Question*, 22.

4. Beier, *Masterless Men*, 23.

5. Neill, *Putting History to the Question*, 33.

6. See Walter Darell, *A Short discourse of the life of Servingmen* (London, 1578); and I.M., *A Health to the Gentlemanly profession of Servingmen* (London, 1598). For public concerns about service and social control in early modern England, see Madonna J. Hettinger, "Defining the Servant: Legal and Extra-Legal Terms of Employment in Fifteenth-Century England," in *The Work of Work: Servitude, Slavery, and Labor in Medieval England*, ed. Allen J. Frantzen and Douglas Moffat (Glasgow: Cruithne, 1994), 206–228, esp. 210–212; and Beier, *Masterless Men*.

7. William Shakespeare, *As You Like It*, in *The Riverside Shakespeare*, ed. G. Blakemore Evans, 2nd ed. (Boston: Houghton Mifflin, 1997), 403–436. All citations refer to this edition of the play. On Adam's faithful service, see Burnett, *Masters and Servants*, 82–83; and Linda Anderson, *A Place in the Story: Servants and Service in Shakespeare's Plays* (Newark: University of Delaware Press, 2005), 122–123. For Shakespeare's representation of ideologies of faithful service more generally, see David Evett, *Discourses of Service in Shakespeare's England* (New York: Palgrave, 2005), 109–132.

8. See Ann Kussmaul, *Servants in Husbandry in Early Modern England* (Cambridge: Cambridge University Press, 1981), 8–10; Wrightson, *English Society*, 42 and 74; Fumerton, *Unsettled*, 12–32; McIntosh, *Working Women*, 46–47; and Beier, *Masterless Men*, 22–25.

9. See Mendelson and Crawford, *Women in Early Modern England*, 92–94. For medieval England, see Maryanne Kowaleski, "Women's Work in a Market Town: Exeter in the Late Fourteenth Century," in *Women and Work in Preindustrial Europe*, ed. Barbara A. Hanawalt (Bloomington: Indiana University Press, 1986), 145–164, esp. 153. For the increase in female household servants during the early modern period, see Anne Laurence, *Women in England 1500–1760: A Social History* (London: Phoenix Giant, 1996), 134–135; and Ben-Amos, *Adolescence and Youth*, 151. For both men and women in the period, youth was virtually synonymous with service; about 60 percent of those aged fifteen to twenty-four were servants living in the households of families other than their birth families. See Kussmaul, *Servants in Husbandry*, 3; and Wrightson, *Earthly Necessities*, 32–33.

10. For service as a transitional position, see Kussmaul, *Servants in Husbandry*, 4; Wrightson, *Earthly Necessities*, 32; Mendelson and Crawford, *Women in Early Modern England*, 92–96; and Judith

Weil, *Service and Dependency in Shakespeare's Plays* (Cambridge: Cambridge University Press, 2005), 18–23. For the gender distinctions that characterized this transition, see Paul Griffiths, *Youth and Authority: Formative Experiences in England 1560–1640* (Oxford: Clarendon Press, 1996), 28–29; and Ben-Amos, *Adolescence and Youth*, 133. On service as preparation for marriage, see Judith M. Bennett and Amy M. Froide, "A Singular Past," in *Singlewomen in the European Past, 1250–1800,* ed. Bennett and Froide (Philadelphia: University of Pennsylvania Press, 1999), 1–37, esp. 9–10; and Ben-Amos, *Adolescence and Youth*, 227–232.

11. In this chapter, I am interested in the category of the domestic servant, the most common form of female service in the period, particularly in urban settings (Wrightson, *Earthly Necessities*, 32; Mendelson and Crawford, *Women in Early Modern England*, 99–100; Ben-Amos, *Adolescence and Youth*, 150–151). These women were expected to perform a wide range of household tasks that varied depending on the economic status of the household and the hierarchical status of an individual servant within that household. For servants in husbandry, see Mendelson and Crawford, *Women in Early Modern England*, 99–101; and Kussmaul, *Servants in Husbandry*, 4–5.

12. The body of literature on the subject of cross-dressing is extremely large. Particularly noteworthy examples that discuss *Twelfth Night* include: Stephen Greenblatt, *Shakespearean Negotiations: The Circulation of Social Energy in Renaissance England* (Berkeley: University of California Press, 1988), 66–93; Lisa Jardine, *Still Harping on Daughters: Women and Drama in the Age of Shakespeare* (New York: Columbia University Press, 1983), 9–36; Howard, *The Stage and Social Struggle*, 93–128; Stephen Orgel, "Nobody's Perfect: Or Why Did the English Stage Take Boys for Women?" *The South Atlantic Quarterly* 88 (1989): 7–29; Katherine McLuskie, "The Act, the Role and the Actor: Boy Actresses on the Elizabethan Stage," *New Theatre Quarterly* 3 (1987): 120–30; Valerie Traub, *Desire and Anxiety: Circulations of Sexuality in Shakespearean Drama* (London: Routledge, 1992), 117–144; and Dympna Callaghan, *Shakespeare Without Women* (London: Routledge, 2000), 26–48.

13. Howard, *The Stage and Social Struggle*, 113.

14. See Mendelson and Crawford, *Women in Early Modern England*, 94; Sue Wright, "'Churmaids, Huswyfes, and Hucksters': The Employment of Women in Tudor and Stuart Salisbury," in *Women and Work in Pre-Industrial England*, ed. Lindsey Charles and Lorna Duffin (London: Croom Helm, 1985), 100–121, esp.102–103; Kussmaul, *Servants in Husbandry*, 9; and Lu Emily Pearson, *Elizabethans at Home* (Stanford: Stanford University Press, 1957), 442.

15. William Shakespeare, *Twelfth Night*, ed. J.M. Lothian and T.W. Craik (London: Methuen, 1975). All citations refer to this edition of the play. For Viola's ambiguous class status and the play's elision

of the feudal elements of service, see Cristina Malcolmson, "'What You Will': Social Mobility and Gender in *Twelfth Night*," in *The Matter of Difference: Materialist Feminist Criticism of Shakespeare*, ed. Valerie Wayne (Ithaca: Cornell University Press, 1991), 29–57. On the fantastic aspects of the play in regard to Viola's marriage and financial situation, see Ann Jennalie Cook, *Making a Match: Courtship in Shakespeare and His Society* (Princeton: Princeton University Press, 1991), 133–134. On Viola's speech to the captain as indicative of the play's disavowal of its capitalist contexts, see Valerie Forman, "Material Dispossessions and Counterfeit Investments: The Economies of *Twelfth Night*," in *Money and the Age of Shakespeare: Essays in New Economic Criticism*, ed. Linda Woodbridge (New York: Palgrave, 2003), 113–127, esp. 115–118.

16. Compare Viola's decision, for example, to that of Rosalind in *As You Like It*, who explicitly dons male attire because of the physical danger that attends her and Celia's travel to Arden. See 1.3.106–122.

17. For a discussion of royal service and its particular rewards in the context of Queen Elizabeth and her waiting women, see Elizabeth A. Brown, "'Companion Me With My Mistress': Cleopatra, Elizabeth I, and Their Waiting Women," in *Maids and Mistresses, Cousins and Queens: Women's Alliances in Early Modern England*, ed. Susan Frye and Karen Robertson (New York: Oxford University Press, 1999), 131–145. For Queen Anne's court, see Leeds Barroll, "The Court of the First Stuart Queen," in *The Mental World of the Jacobean Court*, ed. Linda Levy Peck (Cambridge: Cambridge University Press, 1991), 191–208, esp. 203–205.

18. See Mendelson and Crawford, *Women in Early Modern England*, 102–106; Ben-Amos, *Adolescence and Youth*, 152–153; Marjorie Keniston McIntosh, "Servants and the Household Unit in an Elizabethan English Community," *Journal of Family History* 9.1 (1984): 3–23, esp. 15–16 and 18–19; and Vivian Brodsky, "Single Women in the London Marriage Market: Age, Status and Mobility, 1598–1619," *The Newberry Papers in Family and Community History* 80.2 (1980): 1–29, esp. 4.

19. See Malcolmson, "'What You Will,'" 51. For the conflation of love, eroticism, and service in the play, see also David Schalkwyk, "Love and Service in *Twelfth Night* and the Sonnets," *Shakespeare Quarterly* 56.1 (2005): 76–100; and Michael Neill, "'A woman's service': Gender, Subordination, and the Erotics of Rank in the Drama of Shakespeare and his Contemporaries," *Shakespearean International Yearbook* 5 (2005): 127–144, esp. 134–137. For Feste as an example of a servant whose poverty demands that he increase his wages via tips, see Lamb, "Tracing a Heterosexual Erotics," 6 and 21. See also Anderson, *A Place in the Story*, 46; and Ralph Berry, *Shakespeare and Social Class* (Atlantic Highlands, NJ: Humanities International, 1988), 74.

20. For Malvolio's fantasies of social advancement, see especially Lamb, "Tracing a Heterosexual Erotics"; and Barbara Correll, "Malvolio at Malfi: Managing Desire in Shakespeare and Webster," *Shakespeare Quarterly* 58.1 (2007): 65–92.

21. Mendelson and Crawford, *Women in Early Modern England*, 108. On the importance for female servants of saving up wages to amass a marriage portion, see Ben-Amos, *Adolescence and Youth*, 154; Burnett, *Masters and Servants*, 118–119; McIntosh, "Servants and the Household Unit," 4 and 18; and Ilona Bell, "In Defense of Their Lawful Liberty: *A Letter sent by the Maydens of London*," in *Women, Writing, and the Reproduction of Culture in Tudor and Stuart Britain*, ed. Mary E. Burke, Jane Donawerth, Linda L. Dove, and Karen Nelson (Syracuse: Syracuse University Press, 2000), 177–192, esp. 186. For the low wages of female servants, see Maryanne Kowaleski, "Singlewomen in Medieval and Early Modern Europe: The Demographic Perspective," in *Singlewomen in the European Past, 1250–1800*, ed. Judith M. Bennett and Amy M. Froide (Philadelphia: University of Pennsylvania Press, 1999), 38–82, esp. 57; and Amy Louise Erickson, *Women and Property in Early Modern England* (London: Routledge, 1993), 85.

22. *A Letter sent by the Maydens of London, to the vertuous Matrones & Mistresses of the same* (London, 1567). For more extensive commentary on this pamphlet, see Ann Rosalind Jones, "Maidservants of London: Sisterhoods of Kinship and Labor," in *Maids and Mistresses, Cousins and Queens: Women's Alliances in Early Modern England*, ed. Susan Frye and Karen Robertson (New York: Oxford University Press, 1999), 21–32; and Bell, "In Defense of Their Lawful Liberty." For the suppression of narratives of poor women in the play, see also Fiona McNeill, *Poor Women in Shakespeare* (Cambridge: Cambridge University Press, 2007), 48–57.

23. White, *The Content of the Form*, 10.

24. See Michael Goodich, "*Ancilla Dei:* The Servant as Saint in the Late Middle Ages," in *Women of the Medieval World: Essays in Honor of John H. Mundy*, ed. Julius Kirshner and Suzanne F. Wemple (Oxford: Basil Blackwell, 1985), 119–136, esp. 121–125.

25. Susan Dwyer Amussen, "Punishment, Discipline, and Power: The Social Meanings of Violence in Early Modern England," *Journal of British Studies* 34.1 (1995): 1–34, esp. 15–16. For the sexual vulnerability of female servants, see also Garthine Walker, "Rereading Rape and Sexual Violence in Early Modern England," *Gender and History* 10.1 (1998): 1–25; McIntosh, "Servants and the Household Unit," 20–21; Griffiths, *Youth and Authority*, 273–274; Laura Gowing, *Common Bodies: Women, Touch and Power in Seventeenth-Century England* (New Haven: Yale University Press, 2003), 59–65; and Tim Meldrum, "London Domestic Servants from Depositional Evidence, 1660–1750: Servant-Employer Sexuality in the Patriarchal Household," in *Chronicling Poverty: The Voices and Strategies of the*

English Poor, 1640–1840, ed. Tim Hitchcock, Peter King, and Pamela Sharpe (New York: St. Martin's, 1997), 47–69, esp. 52–57.

26. Thomas Dekker, John Ford, and William Rowley, *The Witch of Edmonton,* ed. Arthur F. Kinney (London: A & C Black, 1998).

27. Thomas Middleton and William Rowley, *The Changeling,* ed. Joost Daalder (London: A & C Black, 1990).

28. Isabella Whitney, *A Sweet Nosgay* (London, 1573). All citations refer to this edition of the text.

29. See for example the sixtieth aphorism, which claims:
    i. The poore, they have no frends at al
    ii. for to participate,
    iii. The sorow and the griefe they finde
    iv. in their most wretched state.   (B8r)
    For Whitney's self-representations as an impoverished former servant, see Jones, "Maidservants of London," 23–25.

30. In addition, the verse "Wyll and Testament" that concludes the *Nosgay,* written as a farewell to London, begins with Whitney sardonically describing herself as "Whole in body, and in minde, / but very weake in Purse" (E3r). For fuller analyses of this concluding poem, see Betty Travitsky, "The 'Wyll and Testament' of Isabella Whitney," *English Literary Renaissance* 10.1 (1980): 76–94; and Wendy Wall, "Isabella Whitney and the Female Legacy," *ELH* 58.1 (1991): 35–62.

31. See Wall, "Isabella Whitney," 46–55, esp. 54. On the nostalgia and isolation expressed by Whitney's speaker, see also Laurie Ellinghausen, "Literary Property and the Single Woman in Isabella Whitney's *A Sweet Nosgay,*" *Studies in English Literature 1500–1900* 45.1 (2005): 1–22.

32. See especially Jones, "Maidservants of London," 23–27.

33. For a fuller discussion of the etymology of "anthology" and its early modern implications, see Douglas Pfeiffer, "'A Life Beyond Life': The Rise of English Literary Biography" (Ph.D. diss., Columbia University, 2005), 77–137.

34. Pfeiffer, "'A Life Beyond Life,'" 115–116.

35. Wall makes a related point about Whitney's "Wyll and Testament," arguing that the poem "creates a myth of ownership" and grants Whitney "possession rhetorically (in the space of the poem) of material things that were denied in reality." See Wall, "Isabella Whitney," 50 and 54.

36. Malcolmson argues that both Viola and Maria's marriages are upwardly mobile, though there is no direct evidence from the play to establish whether or not Sir Toby's social rank is indeed higher than Maria's. See "'What You Will,'" 34.

37. Martha Moulsworth, "The Memorandum of Martha Moulsworth Widdowe," in *"My Name Was Martha": A Renaissance Woman's Autobiographical Poem,* ed. Robert C. Evans and Barbara Wiedemann (West Cornwall, CT: Locust Hill, 1993), 4–8.

38. For an excellent discussion of Moulsworth's puns, see Anne Lake Prescott, "Marginally Funny: Martha Moulsworth's Puns," in *"The Muses Females Are": Martha Moulsworth and Other Women Writers of the English Renaissance,* ed. Robert C. Evans and Anne C. Little (West Cornwall, CT: Locust Hill, 1995), 85–90.

39. Malcolmson, "'What You Will,'" 41. Burnett cites the Penthesilea reference as evidence that Maria turns gender boundaries "upside-down" (*Masters and Servants*, 142).

40. Mendelson and Crawford, *Women in Early Modern England,* 96. For the potential challenge to social order posed by singlewomen, see also Griffiths, *Youth and Authority*, 358–359; and Froide, *Never Married*.

41. Edith Snook, "'Fellowshippe in Their Apparrell, [...] obedience in their fashions': Clothing the Subject in Lady Mary Wroth's *Countess of Montgomery's Urania*," unpublished essay, 2004. On clothing as a marker of social status, see Ann Rosalind Jones and Peter Stallybrass, *Renaissance Clothing and the Materials of Memory* (Cambridge: Cambridge University Press, 2000), 17–21. For the sumptuary regulations governing mourning garments, see Ralph Houlbrooke, *Death, Religion and the Family in England 1480–1750* (Oxford: Clarendon Press, 1998), 248–254; and Lou Taylor, *Mourning Dress: A Costume and Social History* (London: George Allen and Unwin, 1983), 66.

42. William Shakespeare, *The Merchant of Venice,* in *The Riverside Shakespeare,* ed. G. Blakemore Evans, 2nd ed. (Boston: Houghton Mifflin, 1997), 288–319, esp. 4.1.174. *Merchant* was written in 1596–1597.

43. Juan Luis Vives, *A Very frutefull and pleasant boke called the Instruction of a Christen Woman,* trans. Richard Hyrde (London, 1529). All citations refer to this edition of the text. For the publication history of Vives's text, see the introduction to the edition prepared by Virginia Walcott Beauchamp, Elizabeth H. Hageman, and Margaret Mikesell (Urbana: Illinois University Press, 2002), xv–xciii, esp. lxxvii–xciii.

44. Eve Rachele Sanders, *Gender and Literacy on Stage in Early Modern England* (Cambridge: Cambridge University Press, 1998), 172.

45. For a good discussion of Woolley as a writer of domestic household guides, see Wall, *Staging Domesticity,* 54–58. See also Elaine Hobby, *Virtue of Necessity: English Women's Writing 1649–88* (London: Virago, 1988), 166–175. On the relationship between service, epistolary networks, and the early modern household, see Jennifer Summit, "Writing Home: Hannah Wolley, the Oxinden Letters, and Household Epistolary Practice," in *Women, Property, and the Letters of the Law in Early Modern England,* ed. Nancy E. Wright, Margaret W. Ferguson, and A.R. Buck (Toronto: University of Toronto Press, 2004), 201–218.

46. Hannah Woolley's description of her own experience as a servant appears in *The Gentlewomans Companion; Or, a Guide to the*

Female Sex (London, 1673), A4r. All citations refer to this edition of the text.

47. Hannah Woolley, *The Compleat Servant-Maid; Or, The Young Maidens Tutor* (London, 1677). All citations refer to this edition of the text. For mixed hand and its relationship to gender, see Sanders, *Gender and Literacy*, 173–174.

48. Sanders, *Gender and Literacy*, 181.

49. Neill, *Putting History to the Question*, 173. See also Jonathan Goldberg's discussion of the ideological contradictions of women's writing-literacy in *Writing Matter: From the Hands of the English Renaissance* (Stanford: Stanford University Press, 1990), 137–155. For servants' literacy as a route to "social advancement," see Lori Humphrey Newcomb, "The Romance of Service: The Simple History of *Pandosto*'s Servant Readers," in *Framing Elizabethan Fictions: Contemporary Approaches to Early Modern Narrative Prose*, ed. Constance C. Relihan (Kent, OH: Kent State University Press, 1996), 117–139, esp. 125–127.

50. See Neill, *Putting History to the Question*, 173. Of course, the particular letters that Maria has copied effect a sexual pun that Callaghan discusses nicely and at length (*Shakespeare Without Women*, 36–47). One could also argue, therefore, that Maria's letter-writing threatens not only social place but also sexual decorum and gender roles.

51. There is some dispute about Woolley's authorship of *The Gentlewomans Companion* due to a disclaimer she makes in *A Supplement to the Queen-Like Closet*, but the text was clearly attributed to her in the period.

52. See Jameson, *The Political Unconscious*, 106.

53. For a detailed analysis of eighteenth-century versions of the Cinderella myth, see Huang Mei, *Transforming the Cinderella Dream: From Frances Burney to Charlotte Brontë* (New Brunswick: Rutgers University Press, 1990).

54. For the "feminization of domestic service," see Hill, *Women, Work and Sexual Politics*, 260. For the gradual professionalization and increasingly permanent status of women's service, see especially Kussmaul, *Servants in Husbandry*, 83; Bridget Hill, *Servants: English Domestics in the Eighteenth Century* (Oxford: Oxford University Press, 1996); and Tim Meldrum, *Domestic Service and Gender 1660–1750* (Harlow, England: Pearson, 2000).

55. Newcomb, "The Romance of Service," 122.

56. Korda, *Shakespeare's Domestic Economies*, 33–38. For the growth of mercantilism and consumer culture throughout the early modern period, see Brenner, *Merchants and Revolution*, 39–50; and Thirsk, *Economic Policy and Projects*, 1–23 and 177. For the housewife's role in the eighteenth century, see Meldrum, *Domestic Service and Gender*, 139, 179, and 181; and Hill, *Women, Work and Sexual Politics*, 125–147.

57. See Wall, *Staging Domesticity*, 54. For the continuity between the work of female servants and that of married women, see Mendelson and Crawford, *Women in Early Modern England*, 108; and Wrightson, *Earthly Necessities*, 309–310.

58. For city comedy's focus on urban social classes, see Jean E. Howard, *Theater of a City: The Places of London Comedy, 1598–1642* (Philadelphia: University of Pennsylvania Press, 2007), 19–22. For city comedy's combined focus on economics and sexuality, see Theodore Leinwand, *The City Staged: Jacobean Comedy, 1603–1613* (Madison: University of Wisconsin Press, 1986), 51.

59. See Mendelson and Crawford, *Women in Early Modern England*, 100 and 264–265; Ben-Amos, *Adolescence and Youth*, 135–150; Natalie Zemon Davis, "Women in the Crafts," 177; and McIntosh, *Working Women*, 135–139. For the apprenticeship of girls to retail trades, see Clark, *Working Life of Women*, 200–201; Bennett and Froide, "A Singular Past," 9; Rappaport, *Worlds Within Worlds*, 36–42; and Mendelson and Crawford, *Women in Early Modern England*, 99.

60. Thomas Heywood (?), *The Fair Maid of the Exchange*, ed. Arthur Brown (Oxford: Malone Society Reprints, 1962–1963). All citations refer to this edition of the play.

61. See for example scene 11, where Mistress Flower, eager to plead on behalf of Anthony Golding to her daughter, informs the audience in an aside that she has sent for her daughter and ordered her servants to bring Phillis to her "presently upon her repaire hither from her Mistrisses" (1768–1769).

62. For criticism that discusses women's figurative role as sexual commodities in city comedy, see Newman, *Fashioning Femininity*, 131–143; and Richard Horwich, "Wives, Courtesans, and the Economics of Love in Jacobean City Comedy," in *Drama in the Renaissance: Comparative and Critical Essays*, ed. Clifford Davidson, C.J. Gianakaris, and John H. Stroupe (New York: AMS, 1986), 255–273. For specific discussions of *Fair Maid*, see Juana Green, "The Sempster's Wares: Merchandising and Marrying in *The Fair Maid of the Exchange* (1607)," *Renaissance Quarterly* 53.4 (2000): 1084–1118; and Howard, *Theater of City*, 60–67.

63. For a more detailed description of the work done by sempsters, see Green, "The Sempster's Wares," 1092, n. 23. In *Staging Domesticity*, Wall briefly discusses a similar incident in Thomas Dekker's *The Shoemaker's Holiday*, where Hammon and Simon Eyre make contradictory references to Jane's working hands (155).

64. A "drawer," as Juana Green points out, is "the draughtsman who quite literally 'draws' the image or motif to be embroidered onto either a reusable pattern or the fabric itself," in Cripple's case, women's handkerchiefs ("The Sempster's Wares," 1093).

65. Scene 13, line 2375. For a detailed discussion of the marriage negotiations in the play, see Green, "The Sempster's Wares," 1110–1112.

66. Woolley's body of work is consistently interested in upper-class domesticity, and, therefore, her representation of female service work attends only to this privileged group of servants. See Erickson, *Women and Property*, 56; and Wall, *Staging Domesticity*, 54. For Woolley's description of her own background and training as a servant, see *The Gentlewomans Companion*, B5v–B7v.

67. Newcomb, "The Romance of Service," 122.

68. See Wrightson, *Earthly Necessities*, 309–310.

69. London, 1671–1704? Bodleian, Douce Ballads 1(63a).

70. See White, *The Content of the Form*, esp. 24.

2 THE SPATIAL SYNTAX OF MIDWIFERY AND WET-NURSING

1. Michel de Certeau, *The Practice of Everyday Life*, trans. Steven Rendall (Berkeley: University of California Press, 1984), 115.

2. de Certeau, *The Practice of Everyday Life*, 118.

3. For the much-documented historical shift between female midwives and male physicians, see Hilda Smith, "Gynecology and Ideology in Seventeenth-Century England," in *Liberating Women's History: Theoretical and Critical Essays*, ed. Berenice A. Carroll (Urbana: University of Illinois Press, 1976), 97–114, esp. 107–113; Audrey Eccles, *Obstetrics and Gynaecology in Tudor and Stuart England* (London: Croom Helm, 1982), 119–124; Renate Blumenfeld-Kosinski, *Not of Woman Born: Representations of Caesarean Birth in Medieval and Renaissance Culture* (Ithaca: Cornell University Press, 1990), 91–119; Caroline Bicks, *Midwiving Subjects in Shakespeare's England* (Aldershot: Ashgate, 2003), esp. 9–14; David Harley, "Provincial Midwives in England: Lancashire and Cheshire, 1660–1760," in *The Art of Midwifery: Early Modern Midwives in Europe*, ed. Hilary Marland (London: Routledge, 1993), 27–48, esp. 39–42; and Lisa Forman Cody, "The Politics of Reproduction: From Midwives' Alternative Public Sphere to the Public Spectacle of Man Midwifery," *Eighteenth-Century Studies* 32.4 (1999): 477–495, esp. 477–478.

4. Gowing, *Common Bodies*, 48.

5. See Valerie Fildes, *Breasts, Bottles and Babies: A History of Infant Feeding* (Edinburgh: Edinburgh University Press, 1986), 162; Fildes, *Wet Nursing: A History from Antiquity to the Present* (New York: Basil Blackwell, 1988), 79 and 111–126; and Wall, *Staging Domesticity*, 134–136.

6. See Lena Cowen Orlin, "Boundary Disputes in Early Modern London," in *Material London ca. 1600*, ed. Orlin (Philadelphia: University of Pennsylvania Press, 2000), 345–376.

7. Mary Beth Rose, "Where Are the Mothers in Shakespeare? Options for Gender Representation in the English Renaissance," *Shakespeare Quarterly* 42.3 (1991): 290–314, esp. 296. See also Janet Adelman,

Suffocating Mothers: Fantasies of Maternal Origin in Shakespeare's Plays, Hamlet to The Tempest (New York: Routledge, 1992); Frances E. Dolan, "Marian Devotion and Maternal Authority in Seventeenth-Century England," in *Maternal Measures: Figuring Caregiving in the Early Modern Period*, ed. Naomi J. Miller and Naomi Yavneh (Aldershot: Ashgate, 2000), 282–292, esp. 283–284; Patricia Crawford, "The Construction and Experience of Maternity in Seventeenth-Century England," in *Women as Mothers in Pre-Industrial England: Essays in Memory of Dorothy McLaren*, ed. Valerie Fildes (London: Routledge, 1990), 3–38; Fissell, *Vernacular Bodies*; and Linda A. Pollock, "Embarking on a Rough Passage: The Experience of Pregnancy in Early-Modern Society," in *Women as Mothers in Pre-Industrial England: Essays in Memory of Dorothy McLaren*, ed. Valerie Fildes (London: Routledge, 1990), 39–67.

8. Dolan, "Marian Devotion," 283.

9. Ruth Perry, "Colonizing the Breast: Sexuality and Maternity in Eighteenth-Century England," *Eighteenth-Century Life* 16 (1992): 185–213, esp. 185. See also Gowing, *Common Bodies*, 193–194.

10. For overviews of midwives responsibilities, see David Cressy, *Birth, Marriage and Death: Ritual, Religion, and the Life-Cycle in Tudor and Stuart England* (Oxford: Oxford University Press, 1997), 59–63; Eccles, *Obstetrics and Gynaecology*, 87–93; Adrian Wilson, "The Ceremony of Childbirth and Its Interpretation," in *Women as Mothers in Pre-Industrial England: Essays in Memory of Dorothy McLaren*, ed. Valerie Fildes (London: Routledge, 1990), 68–107, esp. 72–83; and McIntosh, *Working Women*, 80–83.

11. For this phrase, see Thomas Raynalde, *The Byrth of mankynd, otherwyse named the womans Boke* (London, 1552), B5r. See also Gail Paster, *The Body Embarrassed: Drama and the Disciplines of Shame in Early Modern England* (Ithaca: Cornell University Press, 1993), 163–214; Bicks, *Midwiving Subjects*; and Cressy, *Birth, Marriage and Death*.

12. Doreen Evenden, "Mothers and Their Midwives in Seventeenth-Century London," in *The Art of Midwifery: Early Modern Midwives in Europe*, ed. Hilary Marland (London: Routledge, 1993), 9–26, esp. 13.

13. Cressy, *Birth, Marriage and Death*, 61.

14. William Shakespeare, *Titus Andronicus*, in *The Riverside Shakespeare*, ed. G. Blakemore Evans, 2nd ed. (Boston: Houghton Mifflin, 1997), 1069–1100. All citations refer to this edition of the play.

15. John Webster, *The Duchess of Malfi*, ed. Elizabeth M. Brennan (New York: Norton, 1993). All citations refer to this edition of the play.

16. Ben Jonson, *The Magnetic Lady*, ed. Peter Happé (Manchester: Manchester University Press, 2000). All citations refer to this edition of the play.

17. For fuller discussions of the play's representation of midwifery and the birthroom, see Julie Sanders, "Midwifery and the New Science

in the Seventeenth Century: Language, Print and the Theatre," in *At the Borders of the Human: Beasts, Bodies and Natural Philosophy in the Early Modern Period*, ed. Erica Fudge, Ruther Gilbert, and Susan Wiseman (London: Macmillan, 1999), 74–90; and Helen Ostovich, "The Appropriation of Pleasure in *The Magnetic Lady*," in *Maids and Mistresses, Cousins and Queens: Women's Alliances in Early Modern England*, ed. Susan Frye and Karen Robertson (Oxford: Oxford University Press, 1999), 98–113.

18. Thomas Dekker and John Webster, *Westward Ho*, in *The Dramatic Works of Thomas Dekker*, ed. Fredson Bowers, vol. 2 (Cambridge: Cambridge University Press, 1955), 318–403. All citations refer to this edition of the play.

19. On this scene, see Jean E. Howard, "Women, Foreigners, and Urban Space in *Westward Ho*," in *Material London, c.1600*, ed. Lena Cowen Orlin (Philadelphia: University of Pennsylvania Press, 2000), 150–167, esp. 154–155. For the fear that a desire for foreign luxuries would lead women away from the household and into illicit sexual relationships, see Newman, *Fashioning Femininity*, 131–143.

20. Laura Gowing, "'The freedom of the streets': Women and Social Space, 1560–1640," in *Londinopolis: Essays in the Cultural and Social History of Early Modern London*, ed. Paul Griffiths and Mark S.R. Jenner (Manchester: Manchester University Press, 2000), 130–151, esp. 145. See also Ruth Karras, *Common Women: Prostitution and Sexuality in Medieval England* (Oxford: Oxford University Press, 1996), 15, 37–43, and 75–76; Archer, *The Pursuit of Stability*, 211; E.J. Burford and Joy Wotton, *Private Vices—Public Virtues: Bawdry in London from Elizabethan Times to the Regency* (London: Robert Hal, 1995), 15; and Faramerz Dabhoiwala, "The Pattern of Sexual Immorality in Seventeenth- and Eighteenth-Century London," in *Londinopolis: Essays in the Cultural and Social History of Early Modern London*, ed. Paul Griffiths and Mark S.R. Jenner (Manchester: Manchester University Press, 2000), 86–106, esp. 92–94.

21. Gowing, "'The freedom of the streets,'" 141–144 and 145.

22. See Howard, "Women, Foreigners, and Urban Space," 158; and Simon Morgan-Russell, "'No Good Thing Ever Comes Out of It': Male Expectation and Female Alliance in Dekker and Webster's *Westward Ho*," in *Maids and Mistresses, Cousins and Queens: Women's Alliances in Early Modern England*, ed. Susan Frye and Karen Robertson (Oxford: Oxford University Press, 1999), 70–84, esp. 72–77. On Birdlime's connection to the play's topography, see Henry S. Turner, *The English Renaissance Stage: Geometry, Poetics, and the Practical Spatial Arts 1580–1630* (Oxford: Oxford University Press, 2006), 204–206.

23. de Certeau, *The Practice of Everyday Life*, 123.

24. Indeed, it is made clear earlier in the play (at 1.1.8 and 4.1) that Birdlime operates a brothel in Gunpowder Ally in London, within the city walls.

25. Gowing, *Common Bodies*, 51.

26. See Gowing, *Common Bodies*, 55–58.

27. For the wages of seventeenth-century English wet nurses, see Fildes, *Breasts, Bottles and Babies*, 159–163. On the practice of hiring wet nurses more generally in the period, see Paster, *The Body Embarrassed*, 199–201; Dorothy McLaren, "Marital Fertility and Lactation 1570–1720," in *Women in English Society 1500–1800*, ed. Mary Prior (London: Methuen, 1985), 22–53, esp. 26 and 43–46; Fildes, *Wet Nursing*, 79–100; Wall, *Staging Domesticity*, 70–74 and 134–142; and Eccles, *Obstetrics and Gynaecology*, 97.

28. For a reproduction of this particular tombstone, see Fildes, *Wet Nursing*, 86.

29. Wall, *Staging Domesticity*, 137.

30. See Fildes, *Wet Nursing*, 79–81.

31. Orlin, "Boundary Disputes in Early Modern London," 369–370. See also Fildes, *Wet Nursing*, 83.

32. William Shakespeare, *Romeo and Juliet*, ed. Brian Gibbons (London: Arden, 1980). All citations refer to this edition of the text.

33. Relevant studies include: Stanley Wells, "Juliet's Nurse: The Uses of Inconsequentiality," in *Shakespeare's Styles: Essays in Honour of Kenneth Muir*, ed. Philip Edwards, Inga-Stina Ewbank, and G.K. Hunter (Cambridge: Cambridge University Press, 1980), 51–66; Barbara Everett, *Young Hamlet: Essays on Shakespeare's Tragedies* (Oxford: Oxford University Press, 1989), 109–123; Mitsuo Shikoda, "Juliet, the Nursling of the Nurse," *Shakespeare Studies* (Tokyo) 25 (1987): 25–39; and Martin Stevens, "Juliet's Nurse: Love's Herald," *Papers on Language and Literature* 2.3 (1966): 195–206.

34. Paster, *The Body Embarrassed*, 220–231, esp. 229.

35. Paster, *The Body Embarrassed*, 221.

36. Fildes, *Wet Nursing*, 100 and *Breasts, Bottles and Babies*, 158–162.

37. See Paster, *The Body Embarrassed*, 221.

38. For the figure of the wet nurse in Spenser and its precedents, see Sandra S. Clark, "Glauce," *The Spenser Encyclopedia*, ed. A.C. Hamilton (London: Routledge, 1990), 333. On Shakespeare's sources for the Nurse, see Everett, *Young Hamlet*, 154–155; Wells, "Juliet's Nurse," 52 and 59–60; and Stevens, "Juliet's Nurse," 195–196.

39. See Lena Cowen Orlin, *Elizabethan Households* (Washington, D.C.: Folger Shakespeare Library, 1995), 3–5 and 21–23.

40. For contemporary texts that discuss breast milk, see Jane Sharp, *The Midwives Book or the Whole Art of Midwifery Discovered*, ed. Elaine Hobby (New York: Oxford University Press, 1999), 264–271, esp. 268; Raynalde, *The Byrth of mankynd*, L6v–M1r; and Nicholas Culpepper, *A Directory for Midwives* (London, 1651), L4v–L7v. For critical accounts of early modern humoral theory as it relates to breast milk, see Kathryn Schwarz, "Missing the Breast: Desire, Disease, and the Singular Effect of Amazons," in *The Body in Parts: Fantasies*

of Corporeality in Early Modern Europe, ed. David Hillman and Carla Mazzio (New York: Routledge, 1997), 147–169, esp. 152–153; Thomas Laqueur, *Making Sex: Body and Gender from the Greeks to Freud* (Cambridge, MA: Harvard University Press, 1990), 35–43; Marylynn Salmon, "The Cultural Significance of Breastfeeding and Infant Care in Early Modern England and America," *Journal of Social History* 28.2 (1994): 247–269, esp. 251–252 and 255; and Patricia Crawford, "Attitudes to Menstruation in Seventeenth-Century England," *Past and Present* 91 (1981): 47–73, esp. 52–53.

41. Edmund Spenser, *A View of the Present State of Ireland*, in *The Works of Edmund Spenser*, ed. R. Morris (London: Macmillan, 1902), 609–683.

42. See especially Wall, *Staging Domesticity*, 70–76 and 134–142; Sharp, *The Midwives Book*, 264–271; and Rachel Trubowitz, "'But Blood Whitened': Nursing Mothers and Others in Early Modern Britain," in *Maternal Measures: Figuring Caregiving in the Early Modern Period*, ed. Naomi J. Miller and Naomi Yavneh (Aldershot: Ashgate, 2000), 82–101, esp. 85.

43. For a careful analysis of the stylistic elements of the Nurse's language, see Wells, "Juliet's Nurse," 52–53.

44. See Trubowitz, "'But Blood Whitened,'" 84. For the bawdiness of the Nurse's story and its (inherited) effects on Juliet, see also Dympna Callaghan, "The Ideology of Romantic Love: The Case of *Romeo and Juliet*," in *The Weyward Sisters: Shakespeare and Feminist Politics*, ed. Callaghan, Lorraine Helms, and Jyotsna Singh (Oxford: Oxford University Press, 1994), 59–101, esp. 84–86; and Shikoda, "Juliet, the Nursling of the Nurse."

45. See in particular Johannes Fabian, *Time and the Other: How Anthropology Makes Its Object* (New York: Columbia University Press, 1983).

46. See David Cressy, *Bonfires and Bells: National Memory and the Protestant Calendar in Elizabethan and Stuart England* (London: Weidenfeld and Nicolson, 1989), 28–29; and Everett, *Young Hamlet*, 113–114. For the importance of the festal calendar in pre-Reformation England, see Eamon Duffy, *The Stripping of the Altars: Traditional Religion in England 1400–1580* (New Haven: Yale University Press, 1992), 11–52.

47. For the break between Juliet and the Nurse, see Shikoda, "Juliet, the Nursling of the Nurse," 36–37; and Stevens, "Juliet's Nurse," 200–201.

48. Numerous texts advocated maternal breast-feeding in the period. Some notable ones include: Erasmus's colloquy, *The New Mother*, in *Collected Works of Erasmus: Colloquies*, trans. Craig R. Thompson, vol. 39 (Toronto: University of Toronto Press, 1997); Henry Smith, *A Preparative to Mariage* (London, 1591); William Gouge, *Of Domesticall Duties* (London, 1622); Henry Newcome, *The Compleat*

Mother. Or An Earnest Perswasive to all Mothers (especially those of Rank and Quality) to Nurse their own Children (London, 1695); Culpepper, *A Directory for Midwives;* and Sharp, *The Midwives Book.*

49. Clinton, the daughter of Sir Henry Knevet of Charlton, Wiltshire, and the wife of Thomas Clinton, later the third earl of Lincoln, was the only known aristocratic woman to criticize the practice of wet-nursing in print. Critical studies of *The Nurserie* include Marilyn Luecke, "The Reproduction of Culture and the Culture of Reproduction in Elizabeth Clinton's *The Countesse of Lincolnes Nurserie,*" in *Women, Writing, and the Reproduction of Culture in Tudor and Stuart Britain,* ed. Mary E. Burke, Jane Donawerth, Linda L. Dove, and Karen Nelson (Syracuse: Syracuse University Press, 2000), 238–252; Elaine V. Beilin, *Redeeming Eve: Women Writers of the English Renaissance* (Princeton: Princeton University Press, 1987), 280–282; Betty S. Travitsky, "The New Mother of the English Renaissance," in *The Lost Tradition: Mothers and Daughters in Literature,* ed. Cathy N. Davidson and E.M. Broner (New York: F. Ungar, 1980), 33–43, esp. 36–37; and Valerie Wayne, "Advice for Women from Mothers and Patriarchs," in *Women and Literature in Britain 1500–1700,* ed. Helen Wilcox (Cambridge: Cambridge University Press, 1996), 56–79, esp. 60–62.

50. Elizabeth Clinton, *The Countesse of Lincolnes Nurserie,* reprinted in *The English Experience,* vol. 720 (Amsterdam: Walter J. Johnson, Inc., 1975). All citations refer to this edition of Clinton's text.

51. Clinton's daughter, Arbella, married Isaac Johnson, one of the "Winthrop fleet" that transported puritans in the Massachusetts Bay Company to Salem in the 1630s. See Fildes, *Breasts, Bottles and Babies,* 99; and Luecke, "The Reproduction of Culture," 242–243 and n. 14.

52. For the physical problems that prevented many early modern mothers from breast-feeding, see Paster, *The Body Embarrassed,* 202–205; Fildes, *Wet Nursing,* 83; Fildes, *Breasts, Bottles and Babies,* 134–150; and Sharp, *The Midwives Book,* 258–260 and 265.

53. de Certeau, *The Practice of Everyday Life,* 129.

54. Sharp similarly criticizes "City Dames" in *The Midwives Book,* arguing that they do not have many children because they do not perform enough physical labor, and "idleness is a great enemy to conception" (137).

55. See Fildes, *Breasts, Bottles and Babies,* 178.

3   DIVINE DRUDGERY: THE SPIRITUAL LOGIC OF HOUSEWORK

1. The multiple hands of the text and the historical span of the individual entries (over one hundred years) preclude a precise attribution of authorship to this text. However, the name of "Dorothy Philips," who married John Hanmer in 1652, appears in multiple places on the

flyleaf, suggesting that she had at least a tangential role to play in the book's compilation. For the difficulty of ascribing authorship to manuscript miscellanies and commonplace books, see Elizabeth Clarke, "Women's Manuscript Miscellanies in Early Modern England," in *Teaching Tudor and Stuart Women Writers*, ed. Susanne Woods and Margaret P. Hannay (New York: MLA, 2000), 52–60, esp. 54–57; Earle Havens, *Commonplace Books: A History of Manuscripts and Printed Books from Antiquity to the Twentieth Century* (New Haven: Yale University Press, 2001), 68; and Victoria Burke, "Women and Early Seventeenth-Century Manuscript Culture: Four Miscellanies," *The Seventeenth Century* 12.2 (1997): 135–150, esp. 135–136. For biographical information about the Hanmer family, see *Wales and the Marches: Catalog of Stanley Crowe, Bookseller and Printseller*, No. 64. (London: Stanley Crowe, 1960), 41.

2. For the variety and irregularity that exists even within the genre of the commonplace book, see Havens, *Commonplace Books*, 65; and Janet Theophano, *Eat My Words: Reading Women's Lives through the Cookbooks They Wrote* (New York: Palgrave, 2002). For the connection between commonplace book compilation and patterns of thought, see Ann Moss, *Printed Commonplace-Books and the Structuring of Renaissance Thought* (Oxford: Clarendon Press, 1996).

3. See Wall, *Staging Domesticity*; Orlin, *Private Matters and Public Culture*; and Korda, *Shakespeare's Domestic Economies*.

4. Korda, *Shakespeare's Domestic Economies*, 38.

5. Writing specifically about women's diaries, for example, Sara Heller Mendelson argues that "[a]lthough incidents recorded in spiritual journals are apt to be distorted by the religious lens through which they are viewed, we can nevertheless glimpse women's daily round." See "Stuart Women's Diaries and Occasional Memoirs," in *Women in English Society 1500–1800*, ed. Mary Prior (London: Routledge, 1985), 181–201, esp. 189. This type of formulation assumes that religious practices and household chores were separate, even contradictory, elements of an early modern woman's life, rather than interrelated activities.

6. For women's management of domestic properties, see Erickson, *Women and Property*; and Korda, *Shakespeare's Domestic Economies*, 15–51. For the decline in the number of official positions open to devout women (whether Catholic or Protestant) see Patricia Crawford, *Women and Religion in England 1500–1720* (London: Routledge, 1993), 75; Margaret King, *Women of the Renaissance* (Chicago: University of Chicago Press, 1991), 136; and Laurence, *Women in England*, 196. As Kathleen Davies and Margo Todd have argued, it is important not to exaggerate the changes in family life and women's roles brought about by the Reformation. See Davies, "Continuity and Change in Literary Advice on Marriage," in *Marriage and Society: Studies in the History of Marriage*, ed. R.B. Outwaite (New York: St. Martin's,

1981), 58–80; and Todd, *Christian Humanism and the Puritan Social Order* (Cambridge: Cambridge University Press, 1987). However, as Patrick Collinson and others have shown, real changes—including the increased focus on the family unit and the wife's household responsibilities—did occur, though they did so gradually. See Collinson, *The Birthpangs of Protestant England: Religious and Cultural Change in the Sixteenth and Seventeenth Centuries* (Basingstoke: Macmillan, 1988), 92–93; and Crawford, *Women and Religion*, 40.

7. Christine Peters, *Patterns of Piety: Women, Gender and Religion in Late Medieval and Reformation England* (Cambridge: Cambridge University Press, 2003), 201.

8. For the emphasis placed on interiority and self-scrutiny by Protestant reformers, see Huston Diehl, *Staging Reform, Reforming the Stage: Protestantism and Popular Theater in Early Modern England* (Ithaca: Cornell University Press, 1997); Peters, *Patterns of Piety*, 195–206; William J. Bouwsma, *John Calvin: A Sixteenth-Century Portrait* (Oxford: Oxford University Press, 1988), 179–180; Alexandra Walsham, *Providence in Early Modern England* (Oxford: Oxford University Press, 1999), 19–20; and Peter Lake, *Moderate Puritans and the Elizabethan Church* (Cambridge: Cambridge University Press, 1982), 116–168. For the importance of personal piety to the lives of Christian women in the early modern period, see *A History of Private Life: Passions of the Renaissance*, vol. 3, ed. Roger Chartier (Cambridge, MA: Harvard University Press, 1989), 71; Akiko Kusunoki, " 'Their Testament at Their Apron-Strings': The Representation of Puritan Women in Early-Seventeenth-Century England," in *Gloriana's Face: Women, Public and Private, in the English Renaissance*, ed. S.P. Cerasano and Marion Wynne-Davies (New York: Harvester Wheatsheaf, 1992), 185–204, esp. 186–189; and Diane Willen, "Women and Religion in Early Modern England," in *Women in Reformation and Counter-Reformation Europe: Public and Private Worlds*, ed. Sherrin Marshall (Bloomington: Indiana University Press, 1989), 140–165. Though men were certainly enjoined to practice devotion at home, the pious regime was more strongly associated with women in cultural discourse. In *Recreations with the Muses* (London, 1637), the Earl of Stirling famously argued that "[t]he weaker sex" was "to piety more prone" (107).

9. Though my own study is limited to Protestant texts, the link between housework and piety was certainly not unique to Protestant women. See especially Frances E. Dolan, "Reading, Work, and Catholic Women's Biographies," *English Literary Renaissance* 33.3 (2003): 328–357; and Claire Walker, "Combining Martha and Mary: Gender and Work in Seventeenth-Century English Cloisters," *Sixteenth Century Journal* 30.2 (1999): 397–417.

10. See for example Gouge, *Of Domesticall Duties*, C1v; and William Perkins, *Christian Oeconomie: Or, A Short Survey of the Right*

Manner of erecting and ordering a Familie, according to the Scriptures (London, 1609), B1v–B5r. For puritan concepts of the spiritualized household, see Christopher Durston and Jacqueline Eales, "Introduction: The Puritan Ethos, 1560–1700," in *The Culture of English Puritanism, 1560–1700*, ed. Durston and Eales (New York: St. Martin's, 1996), 1–31, esp. 27.

11. Like women's domestic service, housework cut across social classes; women at nearly all levels of society were expected to contribute to food preparation and household cleaning. See Mendelson and Crawford, *Women in Early Modern England*, 269, 307 and 313; Wrightson, *English Society*, 93; Wrightson, *Earthly Necessities*, 44–46; Erickson, *Women and Property*, 54–55; Cahn, *Industry of Devotion*, 91; and Laurence, *Women in England*, 109–115.

12. Robert Cleaver, *A Godlie Forme of Householde Government: For the Ordering of Private Families, according to the direction of Gods word* (London, 1598), L5v–L6r. See also Gervase Markham, *The English Housewife*, ed. Michael R. Best (Kingston: McGill-Queen's University Press, 1986), 5; and Thomas Tusser, *Five hundreth points of good husbandry united to as many of good husswiferie* (London, 1573), S3v. For the sexual division of labor in the early modern home, see Merry E. Wiesner, *Women and Gender in Early Modern Europe* (Cambridge: Cambridge University Press, 1993), 189; Laurence, *Women in England*, 196; Lyndal Roper, *The Holy Household: Women and Morals in Reformation Augsburg* (Oxford: Clarendon Press, 1989), 42 and 252; and Susan Dwyer Amussen, *An Ordered Society: Gender and Class in Early Modern England* (New York: Columbia University Press, 1988), 68–70.

13. See Mendelson, "Stuart Women's Diaries," 189.

14. Elizabeth Clarke, "Diaries," in *A Companion to English Renaissance Literature and Culture*, ed. Michael Hattaway (Malden, MA: Blackwell, 2000), 609–613, esp. 609–610.

15. Richard Rogers, *Seven Treatises* (London, 1603); John Featley, *A Fountaine of Teares* (London, 1646); and John Beadle, *The Journal or Diary of a Thankful Christian* (London, 1656). All citations will refer to these editions of the texts. See also Mendelson, "Stuart Women's Diaries," 185–186; Crawford, *Women and Religion*, 76; Sara Heller Mendelson, *The Mental World of Stuart Women* (Amherst: University of Massachusetts Press, 1987), 94–95; Owen C. Watkins, *The Puritan Experience: Studies in Spiritual Autobiography* (New York: Schocken Books, 1972), 11; Valerie Raoul, "Women and Diaries: Gender and Genre," *Mosaic* 22.3 (1989): 57–65, esp. 61; Durston and Eales, "Introduction," 10; John Stachniewski, *The Persecutory Imagination: English Puritanism and the Literature of Religious Despair* (Oxford: Clarendon Press, 1991), 85–126; and Effie Botonaki, "Seventeenth-Century Englishwomen's Spiritual

Diaries: Self-Examination, Covenanting, and Account Keeping," *Sixteenth Century Journal* 30.1 (1999): 3–21.

16. John Fuller's "To the reader," which introduces Beadle's tract, explicitly refers to the Christian journal as a text with the same function as a tradesman's "shop book" or a merchant's "accompt book" (B1v).

17. For biographical information on Lady Hoby, see Joanna Moody, introduction to *The Private Life of an Elizabethan Lady: The Diary of Lady Margaret Hoby 1599–1605*, ed. Moody (Phoenix Mill: Sutton, 1998), xv–lii. For Hoby's association with puritan theology, see also Mary Ellen Lamb, "Margaret Hoby's Diary: Women's Reading Practices and the Gendering of the Reformation Subject," in *Pilgrimage for Love: Essays in Early Modern Literature in Honor of Josephine A. Roberts*, ed. Sigrid King (Tempe: ACMR, 1999), 63–94. Other important critical studies of the Hoby diary include: Elspeth Graham, "Women's Writing and the Self," in *Women and Literature in Britain 1500–1700*, ed. Helen Wilcox (Cambridge: Cambridge University Press, 1996), 209–233, esp. 226; Margaret P. Hannay, " 'O Daughter Heare': Reconstructing the Lives of Aristocratic Englishwomen," in *Attending to Women in Early Modern England*, ed. Betty S. Travitsky and Adele F. Seeff (Newark: University of Delaware Press, 1994), 35–63; Sharon Cadman Seelig, *Autobiography and Gender in Early Modern Literature: Reading Women's Lives, 1600–1680* (Cambridge: Cambridge University Press, 2006), 15–33; and Helen Wilcox, "Private Writing and Public Function: Autobiographical Texts by Renaissance Englishwomen," in *Gloriana's Face: Women, Public and Private, in the English Renaissance*, ed. S.P. Cerasano and Marion Wynne-Davies (New York: Harvester Wheatsheaf, 1992), 47–62.

18. For useful discussions of puritan beliefs and the historical context of puritanism in early modern England, see Durston and Eales, "Introduction," 1–31; Peter Lake, "Defining Puritanism—Again?" in *Puritanism: Transatlantic Perspectives on a Seventeenth-Century Anglo-American Faith*, ed. Francis J. Bremer (Boston: Massachusetts Historical Society, 1993), 3–29; and Christopher Hill, *Society and Puritanism in Pre-Revolutionary England* (New York: St. Martin's, 1997), 1–15.

19. British Library MS Egerton 2614, Diary of Lady Margaret Hoby. Unless otherwise noted, all citations from the diary refer to this manuscript edition.

20. Dorothy M. Meads, ed., *The Diary of Lady Margaret Hoby 1599–1605* (London: Routledge, 1930); and Joanna Moody, ed., *The Private Life of an Elizabethan Lady: The Diary of Lady Margaret Hoby 1599–1605* (Phoenix Mill: Sutton, 1998). Moody adopts the punctuation of Meads's 1930 edition.

21. November 28, 1599; Moody, ed., *The Private Life*, 40.

22. *The Oxford English Dictionary Online*, entry 1.a. for wrought, ppl. a.

23. Thomas Wilson, *The Arte of Rhetorique* (London, 1553). For further discussion of epideictic rhetoric, see Marjorie Donker and George M. Mulldrow, *Dictionary of Literary-Rhetorical Conventions of the English Renaissance* (Westport, CT: Greenwood, 1982), 91–94; and Richard A. Lanham, *A Handlist of Rhetorical Terms*, 2nd ed. (Berkeley: University of California Press, 1991), 131–135.

24. Katherine Philips, "In memory of that excellent person Mrs. Mary Lloyd of Bodidrist," in *The Collected Works of Katherine Philips, The Matchless Orinda*, ed. Patrick Thomas, vol. 1 (Essex: Stump Cross Books, 1990), 111–114.

25. Clifford's diaries are spread out across several different documents. A 1603 memoir was appended to the manuscripts of the 1616–1619 diary, which I will refer to as the Knole Diary, following the D.J.H. Clifford edition of the diaries. The later diary, 1650–1675, will be referred to as the Kendall Diary. During the last year of her life (1676), Clifford dictated her diary entries to as many as four different scribes. This record exists as a separate document, though I will refer to it here as part of the Kendall Diary for the sake of simplicity. For more information on the different diaries and manuscripts, see D.J.H. Clifford, introduction to *The Diaries of Lady Anne Clifford*, ed. Clifford (Phoenix Mill: Sutton, 1990), x–xvi; and Katherine Osler Acheson, "The Modernity of the Early Modern: The Example of Anne Clifford," in *Discontinuities: New Essays on Renaissance Literature and Criticism*, ed. Viviana Comensoli and Paul Stevens (Toronto: University of Toronto Press, 1998), 27–51, esp. 36 n.6 and 44.

26. Wilcox, "Private Writing," 48. Barbara Lewalski also separates the Clifford diary from the Hoby diary on the basis of religious content and analytical commentary. See *Writing Women in Jacobean England* (Cambridge, MA: Harvard University Press, 1993), 140–141 and n.71. Other important critical studies of Clifford include: Mary O'Connor, "Representations of Intimacy in the Life-Writing of Anne Clifford and Anne Dormer," in *Representations of the Self from the Renaissance to Romanticism*, ed. Patrick Coleman, Jayne Lewis, and Jill Kowalik (Cambridge: Cambridge University Press, 2000), 79–96; and Seelig, *Autobiography and Gender*, 34–72.

27. Anne Clifford, *The Diaries of Lady Anne Clifford*, ed. D.J.H. Clifford (Phoenix Mill: Sutton, 1990). All citations refer to this edition of the diaries.

28. For more detailed discussion of the legal disputes, see Lewalski, *Writing Women*, 125–151; Mary Ellen Lamb, "The Agency of the Split Subject: Lady Anne Clifford and the Uses of Reading," *English Literary Renaissance* 22.3 (1992): 347–368; Acheson, "The Modernity of the Early Modern," 36–39; and D.J.H. Clifford, prologue to *The Diaries of Lady Anne Clifford*, ed. Clifford (Phoenix Mill: Sutton, 1990), 1–18.

29. See Megan Matchinske, "Serial Identity: History, Gender, and Form in the Diary Writing of Lady Anne Clifford," in *Genre and Women's Life Writing in Early Modern England*, ed. Michelle M. Dowd and Julie A. Eckerle (Aldershot: Ashgate, 2007), 65–80, esp. 67.

30. Lewalski, *Writing Women*, 126. See also Lamb, "The Agency of the Split Subject," 357–358.

31. For Clifford's implicit citation of Foxe, see Lewalski, *Writing Women*, 127.

32. See Lewalski, *Writing Women*, 129–130.

33. For detailed discussions of Clifford's building projects and their traces in her diaries, see O'Connor, "Representations of Intimacy," 86–88; Wilcox, "Private Writing," 51–52; and Susan Comilang, "English Noblewomen and the Organization of Space: Gardens, Mourning Posts, and Religious Recesses" (Ph.D. diss., The George Washington University, 2001), 106–146.

34. For Clifford's reading practices, see Lamb, "The Agency of the Split Subject," 353–357.

35. D.J.H. Clifford, "The Years Between, 1620–1649," in *The Diaries of Lady Anne Clifford*, ed. Clifford (Phoenix Mill: Sutton, 1990), 83–102, esp. 91.

36. Helen Wilcox, "Entering *The Temple*: Women, Reading, and Devotion in Seventeenth-Century England," in *Religion, Literature and Politics in Post-Reformation England, 1540–1688*, ed. Donna B. Hamilton and Richard Strier (Cambridge: Cambridge University Press, 1996), 187–207, esp. 192.

37. George Herbert, "The Family," in *The Temple, The Complete English Poems*, ed. John Tobin (London: Penguin, 1991), 128.

38. George Herbert, "The Church Porch," in *The Temple, The Complete English Poems*, ed. John Tobin (London: Penguin, 1991), 6–22.

39. Scholars have debated the exact nature of Herbert's religious allegiances (the so-called "religious wars" in Herbert criticism). Relevant studies include Helen Vendler, *The Poetry of George Herbert* (Cambridge, MA: Harvard University Press, 1975); Stanley Fish, *The Living Temple: George Herbert and Catechizing* (Berkeley: University of California Press, 1978); Rosemond Tuve, *A Reading of George Herbert* (Chicago: University of Chicago Press, 1978); Barbara Lewalski, "Emblems of the Religious Lyric: George Herbert and Protestant Emblematics," *Hebrew University Studies in Literature* 6 (1978): 32–56; Leah S. Marcus, "George Herbert and the Anglican Plain Style," in *'Too Rich to Clothe the Sunne': Essays on George Herbert*, ed. Claude J. Summers and Ted-Larry Pebworth (Pittsburgh: University of Pittsburgh Press, 1980), 179–193; Chana Bloch, *Spelling the Word: George Herbert and the Bible* (Berkeley: University of California Press, 1985); Christopher Hodgkins, *Authority, Church, and Society in George Herbert: Return to the Middle Way* (Columbia: University of Missouri Press, 1993);

and Christina Malcolmson, *Heart-Work: George Herbert and the Protestant Ethic* (Stanford: Stanford University Press, 1999).

40. George Herbert, "Discipline," in *The Temple, The Complete English Poems*, ed. John Tobin (London: Penguin, 1991), 168–169.

41. George Herbert, "Business," in *The Temple, The Complete English Poems*, ed. John Tobin (London: Penguin, 1991), 105–106.

42. George Herbert. "The Elixir," in *The Temple, The Complete English Poems*, ed. John Tobin (London: Penguin, 1991), 174. Malcolmson reads this poem as demonstrative of "the coordination of holy motive and sanctified action" (*Heart-Work*, 170).

43. Indeed, Crawford notes that wealthier women might often perform the menial household chores usually left to servants as part of a regime of self-denial. See *Women and Religion*, 92.

44. For Clifford's use of this phrase, see the entry in the Kendall Diary for April/May of 1651 (112).

45. For studies of domestic drama and its popularity during this period, see Andrew Clark, *Domestic Drama: A Survey of the Origins, Antecedents, and Nature of the Domestic Play in England, 1500–1640* (Salzburg: Institut für Englische Sprache und Literatur, 1975); Viviana Comensoli, *"Household" Business: Domestic Plays of Early Modern England* (Toronto: University of Toronto Press, 1996); Diana E. Henderson, "The Theater and Domestic Culture," in *A New History of Early English Drama*, ed. John D. Cox and David Scott Kastan (New York: Columbia University Press, 1997), 173–194; and Orlin, *Private Matters and Public Culture*.

46. For the particular problems faced by early modern dramatists as they wrestled with issues of iconography and the nature of religious spectacle within a decidedly visual and representational generic medium, see Diehl, *Staging Reform*; Paul Whitfield White, *Theatre and Reformation: Protestantism, Patronage, and Playing in Tudor England* (Cambridge: Cambridge University Press, 1993); and Margot Heinemann, *Puritanism and Theater: Thomas Middleton and Opposition Drama under the Early Stuarts* (Cambridge: Cambridge University Press, 1982).

47. He is ultimately pardoned and given a knighthood for bringing the two pirates to justice. See Barbara Fuchs, "Faithless Empires: Pirates, Renegadoes, and the English Nation," *ELH* 67.1 (2000): 45–69, esp. 52–57 for a compelling discussion of Forest's piracy in the play and the difficulty of distinguishing between licit and illicit commerce in the text.

48. Though Anne is first introduced "as newly come from the Wedding," (1.2), the actions of the rest of the play suggest that a great deal of time elapses before Act 5. Indeed, Old Harding dies in Act 4, leaving Anne a widow and available to marry Forest at the end of the play. In other words, even though Anne is introduced as a new wife, she does not remain in that position throughout the course of the play.

We will see a similar time scheme present in *A Woman Killed with Kindness*. See Thomas Heywood and William Rowley, *Fortune By Land and Sea*, in *The Dramatic Works of Thomas Heywood*, ed. R.H. Shepherd, vol. 6 (London: John Pearson, 1874), 359–435. All citations refer to this edition of the play. This edition has no lineation.

49. Kathleen E. McLuskie locates Heywood's plays within the context of popular Protestantism in *Dekker and Heywood: Professional Dramatists* (London: St. Martin's, 1994), 41–48. Marilyn L. Johnson compares the representation of women in Heywood's plays, including *Fortune*, to contemporary Protestant marriage manuals in *Images of Women in the Works of Thomas Heywood* (Salzburg: Institut für Englische Sprache und Literatur, 1974), 103 and 131.

50. Paul Whitfield White, "Theater and Religious Culture," in *A New History of Early English Drama*, ed. John D. Cox and David Scott Kastan (New York: Columbia University Press, 1997), 133–151, esp. 150 and 151. Ian Green argues that a large number of "Protestant" publications were "of dubious orthodoxy" and were more interested in promoting good behavior than specific theological positions. This was particularly true of cheap print (including printed plays), which, Green argues, "said a great deal about God, but little about Christ." Partially as a result of government censorship, plays from the period often tended to focus on "story-telling and pious morality rather than the finer points of official doctrine." See *Print and Protestantism in Early Modern England* (Oxford: Oxford University Press, 2000), 556 and 565. See also Tessa Watt, *Cheap Print and Popular Piety, 1550–1640* (Cambridge: Cambridge University Press, 1991).

51. Thomas Dekker, Henry Chettle, and William Haughton, *The Pleasant Comodie of Patient Grissill*, in *The Dramatic Works of Thomas Dekker*, ed. Fredson Bowers, vol. 1 (Cambridge: Cambridge University Press, 1953), 212–298. All citations refer to this edition of the play.

52. The link between Grissill's return with the full pitcher and the biblical story of the woman at the well, which recurs throughout the Bible and consistently signals female piety, further underscores the Christian virtue of Dekker's heroine. See for example Genesis 24:11–28; and John 4:1–30.

53. For the importance of a closely aligned devotional genre, cases of conscious, to seventeenth-century women's piety, see Mary Ellen Lamb, "Merging the Secular and the Spiritual in Anne Halkett's Memoirs," in *Genre and Women's Life Writing in Early Modern England*, ed. Michelle M. Dowd and Julie A. Eckerle (Aldershot: Ashgate, 2007), 81–96.

54. Anne clearly realizes that her actions go against her husband's wishes and must be kept secret; delivering food to Forest, she states that "neither [her] husbands, nor [her] servants eyes have any way discovered him" (3.1).

55. Though she does not go so far as to advocate wifely disobedience, Elizabeth Egerton, Countess of Bridgewater, similarly suggests that wives can and should turn to personal piety in the face of recalcitrant husbands, arguing: "if he be fickle & various, not caring much to be with his wife at home, then thus may the wife make her owne happynesse, for then shee may give herselfe up to prayer." Huntington MS EL 8376, fo. 87r.

56. Crawford, *Women and Religion*, 204.

57. For discussions of the play's domestic disorder in terms of its Christian overtones, see Diana E. Henderson, "Many Mansions: Reconstructing *A Woman Killed with Kindness*," *Studies in English Literature 1500–1900* 26.2 (1986): 277–294, esp. 277; Michael Wentworth, "Thomas Heywood's *A Woman Killed with Kindness* as Domestic Morality," in *Traditions and Innovations: Essays on British Literature of the Middle Ages and the Renaissance*, ed. David G. Allen and Robert A. White (Newark: University of Delaware Press, 1990), 150–162, esp. 150–151; Nancy A. Gutierrez, "Exorcism by Fasting in *A Woman Killed with Kindness:* A Paradigm of Puritan Resistance?" *Research Opportunities in Renaissance Drama* 33 (1994): 43–62; and White, "Theater and Religious Culture," 149. For the link between domestic economy and moral conduct in the play, see Laura G. Bromley, "Domestic Conduct in *A Woman Killed with Kindness*," *Studies in English Literature 1500–1900* 26.2 (1986): 259–276; and Ann Christensen, "Business, Pleasure, and the Domestic Economy in Heywood's *A Woman Killed with Kindness*," *Exemplaria* 9.2 (1997): 315–340.

58. Thomas Heywood, *A Woman Killed with Kindness*, ed. Brian Scobie (London: A & C Black, 1985). All citations refer to this edition of the play. Though the play begins with a new marriage, internal evidence suggests that many years actually pass during the course of the plot. For example, in scene 13 a maid brings in two of Anne and John Frankford's children, suggesting the passage of several years over the course of their marriage.

59. See Orlin, *Private Matters and Public Culture*, 137–181, esp. 167. On the complex gender ideologies associated with hospitality, see also Felicity Heal, *Hospitality in Early Modern England* (Oxford: Clarendon Press, 1990). Heywood vividly dramatizes the implicit dangers of hospitality in *The Rape of Lucrece* (London, 1608). Lucrece's rape is represented as a direct, though unintended, consequence of her exemplary housewifery and her generosity as a hostess.

60. See Gutierrez, who relates these images specific to the rhetoric of puritan writer William Perkins ("Exorcism by Fasting," 48). See also Christensen, "Business, Pleasure, and the Domestic Economy."

61. For a discussion of the significance of both table and bed to marital relationships, see the following essays in *Staged Properties in Early Modern English Drama*, ed. Jonathan Gil Harris and Natasha Korda (Cambridge: Cambridge University Press, 2002): Catherine

Richardson, "Properties of Domestic Life: The Table in Heywood's *A Woman Killed with Kindness*," 129–152; and Sasha Roberts, " 'Let me the curtains draw': The Dramatic and Symbolic Properties of the Bed in Shakespearean Tragedy," 153–174.

62. On the servants as witnesses to Anne's sinful behavior in this scene, see Wall, *Staging Domesticity*, 202–203.

4 HOUSEHOLD PEDAGOGIES: FEMALE EDUCATORS AND THE LANGUAGE OF LEGACY

1. Ben Jonson, "To Penshurst," in *Ben Jonson and the Cavalier Poets: Authoritative Texts and Criticism*, ed. Hugh Maclean (New York: Norton, 1974), 21–23. All citations will be taken from this edition of the poem. For the poem's erasure of the manual labor necessary to maintain such a rural estate, see Raymond Williams, *The Country and the City* (New York: Oxford University Press, 1973); Thomas D. Marshall, "Addressing the House: Jonson's Ideology at Penshurst," *Texas Studies in Literature and Language* 35.1 (1993): 57–78; and Don E. Wayne, *The Semiotics of Place and the Poetics of History* (Madison: University of Wisconsin Press, 1984).

2. See Patricia Crawford, "The Construction and Experience of Maternity," 6–13; Hilda L. Smith, "Humanist Education and the Renaissance Concept of Woman," in *Women and Literature in Britain, 1500–1700*, ed. Helen Wilcox (Cambridge: Cambridge University Press, 1996); Charlton, *Women, Religion and Education*; Willen, "Women and Religion," 140–165, esp. 144–146 and 148–150.

3. *The Oxford English Dictionary Online*, entries 3.a. and 2 for education.

4. In her introduction to *Women's Education in Early Modern Europe: A History, 1500–1800*, ed. Whitehead (New York: Garland, 1999, ix–xvi), Barbara J. Whitehead argues that the definition of education as formal schooling is both historically and theoretically limiting, suggesting that scholars adapt a broader definition of education that understands it as "the means by which a body of knowledge that is required of each social member to fulfill her obligations is passed on" (xi–xii). See also Sharon D. Michalove, "Equal in Opportunity? The Education of Aristocratic Women 1450–1540," in *Women's Education in Early Modern Europe*, 47–74, esp. 53–59 and 68–70; Karen Cunningham, " 'She Learns As She Lies': Work and the Exemplary Female in English Early Modern Education," *Exemplaria* 7.1 (1995): 209–235, esp. 217; Edith Snook, " 'His open side our book': Meditation and Education in Elizabeth Grymeston's *Miscelanea Meditations Memoratives*," in *Maternal Measures: Figuring Caregiving in the Early Modern Period*, ed. Naomi J. Miller and Naomi Yavneh (Aldershot: Ashgate, 2000), 163–175, esp. 163–166; and Charlton, *Women, Religion and Education*.

5. For the imitative techniques of humanist pedagogy, see Charlton, *Women, Religion and Education*, 92–97; Rebecca W. Bushnell, *A Culture of Teaching: Early Modern Humanism in Theory and Practice* (Ithaca: Cornell University Press, 1996); Richard Halpern, *The Poetics of Private Accumulation: English Renaissance Culture and the Genealogy of Capital* (Ithaca: Cornell University Press, 1991), 19–60; and Richard Helgerson, *The Elizabethan Prodigals* (Berkeley: University of California Press, 1977), 16–43.

6. Roger Ascham, *The Scholemaster* (London, 1570). On the use of exemplars, see Charlton, *Women, Religion and Education*, 77–105; and Ian Green, *The Christian's ABC: Catechisms and Catechizing in England c. 1350–1640* (Oxford: Oxford University Press, 1996). For a discussion of Ascham's pedagogical ideas, see Lloyd Davis, " 'Sick Desires': *All's Well That Ends Well* and the Civilizing Process," in *Shakespeare Matters: History, Teaching, Performance*, ed. Lloyd Davis (Newark: University of Delaware Press, 2003), 89–102.

7. Thomas Elyot, *The Education or bringinge up of children translated oute of Plutarche* (London, 1532); and Cleaver, *A Godlie Forme of Householde Government*. See also Gouge, *Of Domesticall Duties*, Mm1r–Nn2v.

8. For inheritance practices in early modern England, see Eileen Spring, *Law, Land, and Family: Aristocratic Inheritance in England, 1300 to 1800* (Chapel Hill: University of North Carolina Press, 1993); *Family and Inheritance: Rural Society in Western Europe 1200–1800*, ed. Jack Goody, Joan Thirsk, and E.P. Thompson (Cambridge: Cambridge University Press, 1976); Lawrence Stone, *The Crisis of the Aristocracy 1558–1641* (Oxford: Oxford University Press, 1965); and Erickson, *Women and Property*. For an analysis of parental advice during the period that focuses explicitly on the relationships between fathers and sons, see R.C. Richardson, "The Generation Gap: Parental Advice in Early Modern England," *Clio* 32.1 (2002): 1–25.

9. See Erickson, *Women and Property*, 24.

10. See Thomas Becon, *The Catechism of Thomas Becon*, ed. John Ayre (Cambridge: Cambridge University Press, 1844); and Perkins, *Christian Oeconomie*.

11. See especially Korda, *Shakespeare's Domestic Economies*, 38–51; Erickson, *Women and Property*; Rose, "Where Are the Mothers," 290–314, esp. 293–294; Mary Prior, "Women and the Urban Economy: Oxford 1500–1800," in *Women in English Society 1500–1800*, ed. Prior (London: Routledge, 1991), 93–117; Amussen, *An Ordered Society*, 67–94; and Margaret J.M. Ezell, *The Patriarch's Wife: Literary Evidence and the History of the Family* (Chapel Hill: University of North Carolina Press, 1987), 9–35.

12. Harris, *English Aristocratic Women 1450–1550*, 19.

13. Erickson, *Women and Property*, 150.

14. Korda, *Shakespeare's Domestic Economies*, 27.

15. Willen, "Women and Religion," 148.
16. December 22, 1599, *Letters and Memorials of State*, ed. Arthur Collins (London, 1746), II, 153. Quoted in Wayne, *The Semiotics of Place*, 72. For a detailed discussion of Barbara Gamage's correspondence and what it reveals about her domestic and managerial duties, see Margaret P. Hannay, "'High Housewifery': The Duties and Letters of Barbara Gamage Sidney, Countess of Leicester," *Early Modern Women: An Interdisciplinary Journal* 1 (2006): 7–35.
17. Crawford, *Women and Religion*, 204. For the gradual development of the sexual division of labor in England during the eighteenth century, see Hill, *Women, Work and Sexual Politics*, 259–267.
18. William Shakespeare, *3 Henry VI*, in *The Riverside Shakespeare*, ed. G. Blakemore Evans, 2nd ed. (Boston: Houghton Mifflin, 1997), 711–747. All citations refer to this edition of the play.
19. Kathryn Schwarz, *Tough Love: Amazon Encounters in the English Renaissance* (Durham: Duke University Press, 2000), 97.
20. Thomas Bentley, *The Monument of Matrones* (London, 1582); and John Dod, *Ten sermons tending chiefly to the fitting of men for the worthy receiving of the Lords Supper* (London, 1609). All citations refer to these editions of the texts. For early modern women's significant involvement in the business of arranging suitable marriages for their children, see also Ezell, *The Patriarch's Wife*, 9–35.
21. Jean E. Howard and Phyllis Rackin, *Engendering a Nation: A Feminist Account of Shakespeare's English Histories* (London, Routledge: 1997), 87.
22. Rose, "Where Are the Mothers," 310.
23. Schwarz, *Tough Love*, 103.
24. Schwarz, *Tough Love*, 103–104.
25. See Schwarz, *Tough Love*, 103.
26. The plot of *Two Angry Women*, which involves an extended feud between two neighboring families, bears a striking resemblance to Shakespeare's *Romeo and Juliet* (written in 1595–1596), to which it can be usefully compared. Both plays feature a pair of "star-crossed" lovers and end with a reconciliation of the older generation that is brought about through the actions of the new. However, *Two Angry Women* shifts focus from the noble houses of the Capulets and Montagues to homes of two middling-sort families. And unlike Shakespeare's play, in which both mothers and fathers are at fault in the quarrel, Porter's texts places blame on the mothers alone.
27. Henry Porter, *The Two Angry Women of Abington, Nero and Other Plays*, ed. Herbert P. Horne, Havelock Ellis, Arthur Symons, and A. Wilson Verity (London: Vizetelly & Co, 1888), 97–200. All citations refer to this edition of the play. This edition has no lineation.
28. See *The Lawes Resolutions of Womens Rights* (London, 1632), E2v. For the significance of clandestine marriage to new comedy, see Lorna Hutson, *The Usurer's Daughter: Male Friendship and Fictions*

of Women in Sixteenth-Century England (London: Routledge, 1994). For the contradictions in Protestant literature about clandestine marriage and parental consent, see Mary Beth Rose, *Gender and Heroism in Early Modern English Literature* (Chicago: University of Chicago Press, 2002), 92–94.

29. Useful introductions and studies of mothers' legacy books include: Betty S. Travitsky, "The New Mother," 33–43; Sylvia Brown, "'Over Her Dead Body': Feminism, Poststructuralism, and the Mother's Legacy," in *Discontinuities: New Essays on Renaissance Literature and Criticism*, ed. Viviana Comensoli and Paul Stevens (Toronto: University of Toronto Press, 1998), 3–26; Ramona Wray, *Women Writers of the Seventeenth Century* (Tavistock: Northcote House, 2004), 38–52; Christine W. Sizemore, "Attitudes Toward the Education and Roles of Women: Sixteenth-Century Humanists and Seventeenth-Century Advice Books," *The University of Dayton Review* 15.1 (1981): 57–67; and Sizemore, "Early Seventeenth-Century Advice Books: The Female Viewpoint," *South Atlantic Bulletin* 41.1 (1976): 41–49.

30. Jocelin's *Legacie* also has a manuscript history. Jocelin's autograph manuscript, written in 1622, the year of her death, was followed by a second manuscript copy, "authorized" and edited by Thomas Goad in 1624. Both of these manuscripts are now in the British Library (BL Add. MS 27,467 and BL Add. MS 4378). All references to Jocelin that follow, however, will be taken from the first printed edition of 1624. For the textual history of the *Legacie*, see Sylvia Brown, "Elizabeth Joscelin: Introduction," in *Women's Writing in Stuart England: The Mothers' Legacies of Dorothy Leigh, Elizabeth Joscelin and Elizabeth Richardson*, ed. Brown (Phoenix Mill: Sutton, 1999), 91–105, esp. 100–102; and Jean LeDrew Metcalfe, introduction to *The Mothers Legacy to her Unborn Child*, ed. Metcalfe (Toronto: University of Toronto Press, 2000), 3–31, esp. 17–25.

31. For literary and historical explanations for the popularity of mothers' legacies during this period, see Valerie Wayne, "Advice for Women," 56–79. For the potential political and religious significances of these texts, see Catharine Gray, "Feeding on the Seed of the Woman: Dorothy Leigh and the Figure of Maternal Dissent," *ELH* 68.3 (2001): 563–592; and Michelle M. Dowd, "Structures of Piety in Elizabeth Richardson's *Legacie*," in *Genre and Women's Life Writing in Early Modern England*, ed. Dowd and Julie A. Eckerle (Aldershot: Ashgate, 2007), 115–130.

32. William Perkins, *A salve for a sicke man* (London, 1595). See also Thomas Becon, *The Sycke Mans Salve* (London, 1561). For writings about death in early modern England, see Houlbrooke, *Death, Religion*; Claire Gittings, *Death, Burial and the Individual in Early Modern England* (London: Routledge, 1984), 7–38; Lucinda McCray Beier, "The Good Death in Seventeenth-Century England,"

in *Death, Ritual, and Bereavement,* ed. Ralph Houlbrooke (London: Routledge, 1989), 43–61; Duffy, *The Stripping of the Altars,* 299–378; Bettie Anne Doebler, *"Rooted Sorrow": Dying in Early Modern England* (Rutherford: Fairleigh Dickinson University Press, 1994); Cressy, *Birth, Marriage and Death,* 379–473; and Ian Green, *Print and Protestantism.*

33. See Houlbrooke, *Death, Religion,* 185; Mendelson and Crawford, *Women in Early Modern England,* 195; Cressy, *Birth, Marriage and Death,* 390; Retha M. Warnicke, "Eulogies for Women: Public Testimony of Their Godly Example and Leadership," in *Attending to Women in Early Modern England,* ed. Betty S. Travitsky and Adele F. Seeff (Newark: University of Delaware Press, 1994), 168–186, esp. 170; and Wall, "Isabella Whitney," 35–62, esp. 42–43.

34. Philip Stubbes, *A Christal Glas for christian women* (London, 1592). All citations refer to this edition of the text.

35. For an analysis of the religious and gendered implications of Katherine's speech, see Suzanne Trill, "Religion and the Construction of Femininity," in *Women and Literature in Britain 1500–1700,* ed. Helen Wilcox (Cambridge: Cambridge University Press, 1996), 30–55, esp. 33–35; Ralph Houlbrooke, "The Puritan Death-Bed, c.1560–c.1660," in *The Culture of English Puritanism, 1560–1700,* ed. Christopher Durston and Jacqueline Eales (New York: St. Martin's, 1996), 122–144, esp. 127 and 130–134; and Patricia Phillippy, *Women, Death and Literature in Post-Reformation England* (Cambridge: Cambridge University Press, 2002), 81–108.

36. See Martha J. Craig, "'Write it upon the walles of your houses': Dorothy Leigh's *The Mothers' Blessing,*" in *Women's Life-Writing: Finding Voice/Building Community,* ed. Linda S. Coleman (Bowling Green: Bowling Green State University Press, 1997), 191–208, esp. 203–204; Kristen Poole, "'The fittest closet for all goodness': Authorial Strategies of Jacobean Mothers' Manuals," *Studies in English Literature 1500–1900* 35.1 (1995): 69–88; Beilin, *Redeeming Eve,* 266–285; Teresa Feroli, "'Infelix Simulacrum': The Rewriting of Loss in Elizabeth Jocelin's *The Mothers Legacie,*" *ELH* 61.1 (1994): 89–102; Wall, "Isabella Whitney," 35–46; and Wayne, "Advice for Women," 70–72.

37. Dorothy Leigh, *The Mothers Blessing* (London, 1616). All citations refer to this edition of the text. Very little is known about Leigh's life, including the exact date of her birth. For genealogical information on Leigh and her family, see George Ormerod, *The History of the County Palatine* (London, 1882), 662; and J. P. Earwalker, *East Cheshire: Past and Present; or A History of the Hundred of Macclesfield, in the County Palatine of Chester,* 2 vols. (London, 1877), 251.

38. In Chapter 31, for example, Leigh urges her children to be "masters of [them]selves" and not "subject to their affections" (F11v, F12v). In Chapter 41, she warns against idleness and the disorder

it can produce in households: "for whilest [a man] is idel, or using some vaine pastime out of his calling, his children & servants disobey GOD, and mispend their time, and weaken his estate, and all through his owne carelesnesse to please God" (L2r–L2v).

39. For biographical information on Jocelin, see Fran Teague, "Elizabeth Jocelin," in *An Encyclopedia of British Women Writers*, ed. Paul Schlueter and June Schlueter (New Brunswick: Rutgers University Press, 1998), 350–351.

40. Elizabeth Jocelin, *The Mothers Legacie, To her unborne Childe* (London, 1624). All citations refer to this edition of the text.

41. For example, see Vives, *A Very frutefull and pleasant boke*, esp. D2r–F2v.

42. Catholic books of hours, for example, depended heavily on the use of set prayers prescribed for specific days of the year. For disagreements between Puritans and Anglicans about the use of set prayers of the *Book of Common Prayer*, see John E. Booty, "Communion and Commonweal: The Book of Common Prayer," in *The Godly Kingdom of Tudor England: Great Books of the English Reformation*, ed. Booty (Wilton, CT: Morehouse-Barlow, 1981), 139–216; and Ramie Targoff, *Common Prayer: The Language of Public Devotion in Early Modern England* (Chicago: University of Chicago Press, 2001).

43. For another example of one of Jocelin's set prayers, see the morning prayer that begins: "In thy Name, Oh blessed Saviour, I arise" (C12r–C12v).

44. For Grymeston's source material and literary method, see Beilin, *Redeeming Eve*, 268–269; and Ruth Hughey and Philip Hereford, "Elizabeth Grymeston and Her *Miscelanea*," *The Library* 15.1 (1934): 61–69. Hughey and Hereford also provide detailed bibliographic and biographic information on Grymeston and her text.

45. Elizabeth Grymeston, *Miscelanea, Meditations, Memoratives* (London, 1604). All citations refer to this edition of the text.

46. Megan Matchinske, "Gendering Catholic Conformity," *Journal of English and Germanic Philology* 101.3 (2002): 329–357, esp. 350–351.

47. For a study of Grymeston's text as an educational model for her son, see Snook, " 'His open side our book.' "

48. For the penal laws concerning Catholic books and the complexities of their enforcement, see Frances E. Dolan, *Whores of Babylon: Catholicism, Gender and Seventeenth-Century Print Culture* (Ithaca: Cornell University Press, 1999), 66–67 and 72. In "Gendering Catholic Conformity," Matchinske argues that the revised 1606 edition of Grymeston's text should have been censored given the publication laws at the time, but that it escaped this fate largely due to the strategies of equivocation that Grymeston employs.

49. See Erickson, *Women and Property*, 139 and 24–25. See also Mary Prior, "Wives and Wills 1558-1700," in *English Rural Society*,

1500–1800: Essays in Honour of Joan Thirsk, ed. John Chartres and David Hey (Cambridge: Cambridge University Press, 1990), 201–225; Wall, "Isabella Whitney," 45; and Houlbrooke, *Death, Religion*, 83–84. For an extended study of Goad's introduction, see Sylvia Brown, "The Approbation of Elizabeth Jocelin," in *English Manuscript Studies 1100–1700*, vol. 9, ed. Peter Beal and Margaret J.M. Ezell (London: British Library, 2000), 129–164.

50. See Wall, "Isabella Whitney," 45.

51. On early modern wills, see Erickson, *Women and Property*, 32–33 and 204; Richard T. Vann, "Wills and the Family in an English Town: Banbury, 1550–1800," *Journal of Family History* 4.4 (1979): 346–367, esp. 346–348; Nesta Evans, "Inheritance, Women, Religion and Education in Early Modern Society as Revealed by Wills," in *Probate Records and the Local Community*, ed. Philip Riden (London: Alan Sutton, 1985), 53–70.

52. No recorded will has been found for Leigh. She is not listed in the *Dictionary of National Biography*, and very little of her biography is known outside of the *Blessing* itself. See Travitsky, "The New Mother," 38; Craig, "Write it upon the walles," 195; and Sylvia Brown, "Introduction to Dorothy Leigh: *The Mothers Blessing* (1616)," in *Women's Writing in Stuart England: The Mothers' Legacies of Dorothy Leigh, Elizabeth Jocelin and Elizabeth Richardson*, ed. Brown (Phoenix Mill: Sutton, 1999), 3–14.

53. Erickson, *Women and Property*, 221. For women's wills as evidence of gift-giving within a "gendered social network" rather than the "lineal descent of property" that characterized men's wills, see also J.S.W. Helt, "Women, Memory and Will-Making in Elizabethan England," in *The Place of the Dead: Death and Remembrance in Late Medieval and Early Modern Europe*, ed. Bruce Gordon and Peter Marshall (Cambridge: Cambridge University Press, 2000), 188–205, esp. 199–201.

54. Erickson, *Women and Property*, 221.

55. See Erickson, *Women and Property*, 24–28.

56. William Shakespeare, *All's Well That End's Well*, ed. G.K. Hunter (London: Methuen and Co., 1959). All citations refer to this edition of the play. For the focus on mourning and nostalgia in the play, see Lynne M. Simpson, "The Failure to Mourn in *All's Well That Ends Well*," *Shakespeare Studies* 22 (1994): 172–187.

57. On Shakespeare's addition of the Countess, see David J. Palmer, "Comedy and the Protestant Spirit in Shakespeare's *All's Well That Ends Well*," *Bulletin of the John Rylands University Library of Manchester* 71 (1989): 95–107, esp. 95–97; Susan Snyder, "'The King's not here': Displacement and Deferral in *All's Well*," *Shakespeare Quarterly* 43.1 (1992): 20–32; and Adelman, *Suffocating Mothers*, 80.

58. Rose, "Where are the Mothers," 310.

59. See Jane Freeman, "Life-Long Learning in Shakespeare's *All's Well That Ends Well*," *Renascence* 56.2 (2004): 67–85, esp. 70–73.

60. William Kempe, *The Education of children in learning* (London, 1588).

61. For Bertram's failed social education and ethical development, see Davis, " 'Sick Desires.' "

62. See, for example, William Perkins, *The Whole Treatise of the Cases of Conscience*, comp. Thomas Pickering (Cambridge, 1606).

63. For discussions of problem comedies, see F.S. Boas, *Shakespeare and His Predecessors* (New York: Charles Scribner's Sons, 1896); William Witherle Lawrence, *Shakespeare's Problem Comedies* (New York: Macmillan, 1931); E.M. Tillyard, *Shakespeare's Problem Plays* (Toronto: University of Toronto Press, 1950); and Richard Hillman, *William Shakespeare: The Problem Plays* (New York: Twayne, 1993). For the particular comedic problems of *All's Well* and Shakespeare's representation of Helena, see David Scott Kastan, *"All's Well That Ends Well* and the Limits of Comedy," *ELH* 52.3 (1985): 575–589; Susan Snyder, *"All's Well That Ends Well* and Shakespeare's Helens: Text and Subtext, Subject and Object," *English Literary Renaissance* 18.1 (1988): 66–77; and Kathryn Schwarz, " 'My intents are fix'd': Constant Will in *All's Well That Ends Well,"* *Shakespeare Quarterly* 58.2 (2007): 200–227.

64. Hillman, *William Shakespeare*, 7. On the bed trick, see also Lawrence, *Shakespeare's Problem Plays*, 51; Tillyard, *Shakespeare's Problem Plays*, 97; Adelman, *Suffocating Mothers*, 77; Marliss C. Desens, *The Bed-Trick in English Renaissance Drama: Explorations in Gender, Sexuality, and Power* (Newark: University of Delaware Press, 1994), 59–92; and Peggy Munoz Simonds, "Sacred and Sexual Motifs in *All's Well That Ends Well,"* *Renaissance Quarterly* 42.1 (1989): 55–57.

65. For a discussion of Helena's inheritance from her father and the paradoxical treatment of her knowledge in the play, see Lisa Jardine, "Cultural Confusion and Shakespeare's Learned Heroines: 'These are old paradoxes,' " *Shakespeare Quarterly* 38.1 (1987): 1–18.

66. For the parable of the talents, see Matthew 25:14–30. For Helena's active transformation of her father's legacy, see Garrett A. Sullivan Jr., " 'Be this Sweet Helen's knell, and now forget her': Forgetting, Memory, and Identity in *All's Well That Ends Well,"* *Shakespeare Quarterly* 50.1 (1999): 51–69; and Schwarz, " 'My intents are fix'd.' "

67. For a summary of the changes in women's property and inheritance rights that had taken effect by the eighteenth century, see Erickson, *Women and Property*, 230–232.

68. *A Hundred Godly Lessons. That a Mother on her Death-Bed gave to her Children* (London, 1674).

69. George Booth, *Considerations upon the Institution of Marriage* (London, 1739).

EPILOGUE

1. White, *The Content of the Form*, 24.
2. William Congreve, *The Way of the World*, ed. Kathleen M. Lynch (Lincoln: University of Nebraska Press, 1965). All citations refer to this edition of the play.
3. For eighteenth-century domestic service, see Hill, *Women, Work and Sexual Politics*, 125–147.
4. Edward Rainbowe, Lord Bishop of Carlisle, *A Sermon Preached At the Funeral of the Right Honorable Anne Countess of Pembroke, Dorset, and Montgomery* (London, 1677). All citations refer to this edition of the text. Carlisle also emphasizes the importance of educating servants, specifically citing Clifford's gifts of books to her servants and her "building them up in the most holy Faith" (E1r).
5. See especially Gouge, *Of Domesticall Duties*; and Perkins, *Christian Oeconomie*.
6. For changes in housework in eighteenth-century England, when it became "almost exclusively women's work," see Hill, *Women, Work and Sexual Politics*, 260.
7. For the ability of narratives to cut across a given terrain, see de Certeau, *The Practice of Everyday Life*, 129.
8. For the emphasis on interiority, see, for example, Catherine Belsey, *The Subject of Tragedy: Identity and Difference in Renaissance Drama* (London: Routledge, 1985); Francis Barker, *The Tremulous Private Body: Essays in Subjection* (London: Routledge, 1984); Katherine Eisaman Maus, *Inwardness and Theater in the English Renaissance* (Chicago: University of Chicago Press, 1995); and Elizabeth Hanson, *Discovering the Subject in Renaissance England* (Cambridge: Cambridge University Press, 1998). Michael C. Schoenfeldt's *Bodies and Selves in Early Modern England: Physiology and Inwardness in Spenser, Shakespeare, Herbert, and Milton* (Cambridge: Cambridge University Press, 1999) focuses on interiority as it relates to the humoral body. On the humoral body, see Paster, *The Body Embarrassed*.
9. Garthine Walker, "Expanding the Boundaries of Female Honour in Early Modern England," *Transactions of the Royal Historical Society* 6 (1996): 235–245.
10. Alexandra Shepard, "Manhood, Credit and Patriarchy in Early Modern England c.1580–1640," *Past and Present* 167.1 (2000): 75–106, esp. 92.
11. Rachel Speght, *A Dream, Mortalities Memorandum* (London, 1621), A4r–C1r. All citations refer to this edition of the text.
12. The phrase "*labor omnia vincet*" alludes to Virgil's *Georgics* 1.145, but it also recalls the phrase "*omnia vincit amor*" from Virgil's *Eclogue* 10.69 and the Prioress's motto "*Amor vincit omnia*" from the General Prologue to Chaucer's *Canterbury Tales* 1.162. For the poem's

revision of romance conventions, see Barbara Lewalski's introduction to *The Polemics and Poems of Rachel Speght*, ed. Lewalski (New York: Oxford University Press, 1996), xi–xxxvi, esp. xxviii–xxx.

13. See Barbara Ehrenreich, *Nickel and Dimed: On (Not) Getting By in America* (New York: Metropolitan Books, 2001); and Mary Romero, *Maid in the U.S.A.* (New York: Routledge, 1992).

BIBLIOGRAPHY

PRIMARY SOURCES

Manuscripts

British Library, London
> Add. MS 27,467. "A mother's legacy to her unborn child," by Elizabeth Jocelin. 1622.
> Add. MS 4378. "The mother's legacy to her unborn child," by Elizabeth Jocelin. 1624.
> MS Egerton 2614. Diary of Lady Margaret Hoby. 1599–1603.

Folger Shakespeare Library, Washington, D.C.
> MS V.a. 468. Cookery book of Elizabeth Fowler. Late seventeenth century.
> MS V.a. 347. Sermons, receipts, and family records. c. 1616.

Huntington Library, San Marino, CA
> MS EL 8376. Papers of Elizabeth Egerton, Countesse of Bridgewater. c. 1663.

Printed Primary Sources

Ascham, Roger. *The Scholemaster*. London, 1570.

Beadle, John. *The Journal or Diary of a Thankful Christian*. London, 1656.

Becon, Thomas. *The Catechism of Thomas Becon*. Ed. John Ayre. Cambridge: Cambridge University Press, 1844.

———. *The Sycke Mans Salve*. London, 1561.

Bentley, Thomas. *The Monument of Matrones*. London, 1582.

Booth, George. *Considerations upon the Institution of Marriage*. London, 1739.

Cleaver, Robert. *A Godlie Forme of Householde Government: For the Ordering of Private Families, according to the direction of Gods word*. London, 1598.

Clifford, Anne. *The Diaries of Lady Anne Clifford*. Ed. D.J.H. Clifford. Phoenix Mill: Sutton, 1990.

Clinton, Elizabeth. *The Countesse of Lincolnes Nurserie*. The English Experience. Vol. 720. Amsterdam: Walter J. Johnson, Inc., 1975.

Congreve, William. *The Way of the World*. Ed. Kathleen M. Lynch. Lincoln: University of Nebraska Press, 1965.

Culpepper, Nicholas. *A Directory for Midwives*. London, 1651.

Darell, Walter. *A Short discourse of the life of Servingmen*. London, 1578.

Dekker, Thomas, Henry Chettle, and William Haughton. *The Pleasant Comodie of Patient Grissill*. In *The Dramatic Works of Thomas Dekker*, ed. Fredson Bowers. Vol. 1. Cambridge: Cambridge University Press, 1953. 212–298.

Dekker, Thomas, John Ford, and William Rowley. *The Witch of Edmonton*. Ed. Arthur F. Kinney. London: A & C Black, 1998.

Dekker, Thomas, and John Webster. *Westward Ho!* In *The Dramatic Works of Thomas Dekker*, ed. Fredson Bowers. Vol. 2. Cambridge: Cambridge University Press, 1955. 318–403.

Dod, John. *Ten sermons tending chiefly to the fitting of men for the worthy receiving of the Lords Supper*. London, 1609.

The Down-right Wooing of Honest John and Betty. Bodleian, Douce Ballads. Vol. 1 (63a). London, 1671–1704?

Elyot, Thomas. *The Education or bringinge up of children translated oute of Plutarche*. London, 1532.

Erasmus, Desiderius. *The New Mother*. In *Collected Works of Erasmus: Colloquies*, trans. Craig R. Thompson. Vol. 39. Toronto: University of Toronto Press, 1997. 590–618.

Featley, John. *A Fountaine of Teares*. London, 1646.

Gouge, William. *Of Domesticall Duties*. London, 1622.

Grymeston, Elizabeth. *Miscelanea, Meditations, Memoratives*. London, 1604.

Herbert, George. "Business." *The Temple*. In *The Complete English Poems*, ed. John Tobin. London: Penguin, 1991. 105–106.

———. "The Church Porch." *The Temple*. In *The Complete English Poems*, ed. John Tobin. London: Penguin, 1991. 6–22.

———. "Discipline." *The Temple*. In *The Complete English Poems*, ed. John Tobin. London: Penguin, 1991. 168–169.

———. "The Elixir." *The Temple*. In *The Complete English Poems*, ed. John Tobin. London: Penguin, 1991. 174.

———. "The Family." *The Temple*. In *The Complete English Poems*, ed. John Tobin. London: Penguin, 1991. 128.

Heywood, Thomas (?). *The Fair Maid of the Exchange*. Ed. Arthur Brown. Oxford: Malone Society Reprints, 1962–1963.

Heywood, Thomas. *The Rape of Lucrece*. London, 1608.

———. *A Woman Killed with Kindness*. Ed. Brian Scobie. London: A & C Black, 1985.

Heywood, Thomas, and William Rowley. *Fortune By Land and Sea*. In *The Dramatic Works of Thomas Heywood*, ed. R.H. Shepherd. Vol. 6. London: John Pearson, 1874. 359–435.

A Hundred Godly Lessons. That a Mother on her Death-Bed gave to her Children. London, 1674.

Jocelin, Elizabeth. *The Mothers Legacie, To her unborne Childe*. London, 1624.

Jonson, Ben. *The Magnetic Lady.* Ed. Peter Happé. Manchester: Manchester University Press, 2000.

———. "To Penshurst." In *Ben Jonson and the Cavalier Poets: Authoritative Texts and Criticism,* ed. Hugh Maclean. New York: W.W. Norton, 1974. 21–23.

Kempe, William. *The Education of children in learning.* London, 1588.

The Lawes Resolutions of Womens Rights. London, 1632.

Leigh, Dorothy. *The Mothers Blessing.* London, 1616.

A Letter sent by the Maydens of London, to the vertuous Matrones & Mistresses of the same. London, 1567.

M., I. *A Health to the Gentlemanly profession of Servingmen.* London, 1598.

Markham, Gervase. *The English Housewife.* Ed. Michael R. Best. Kingston: McGill-Queen's University Press, 1986.

Middleton, Thomas, and William Rowley. *The Changeling.* Ed. Joost Daalder. London: A & C Black, 1990.

Moulsworth, Martha. "The Memorandum of Martha Moulsworth Widdowe." In *"My Name Was Martha": A Renaissance Woman's Autobiographical Poem,* ed. Robert C. Evans and Barbara Wiedemann. West Cornwall, CT: Locust Hill, 1993. 4–8.

Newcome, Henry. *The Compleat Mother. Or An Earnest Perswasive to all Mothers (especially those of Rank and Quality) to Nurse their own Children.* London, 1695.

Perkins, William. *Christian Oeconomie: Or, A Short Survey of the Right Manner of erecting and ordering a Familie, according to the Scriptures.* London, 1609.

———. *A salve for a sicke man.* London, 1595.

———. *The Whole Treatise of the Cases of Conscience.* Comp. Thomas Pickering. Cambridge, 1606.

Philips, Katherine. "In memory of that excellent person Mrs. Mary Lloyd of Bodidrist." In *The Collected Works of Katherine Philips, The Matchless Orinda,* ed. Patrick Thomas. Vol. 1. Essex: Stump Cross Books, 1990. 111–114.

Porter, Henry. *The Two Angry Women of Abington.* In *Nero and Other Plays,* ed. Herbert P. Horne, Havelock Ellis, Arthur Symons, and A. Wilson Verity. London: Vizetelly & Co., 1888. 97–200.

Rainbowe, Edward, Lord Bishop of Carlisle. *A Sermon Preached At the Funeral of the Right Honorable Anne Countess of Pembroke, Dorset, and Montgomery.* London, 1677.

Raynalde, Thomas. *The Byrth of mankynd, otherwyse named the womans Boke.* London, 1552.

Rogers, Richard. *Seven Treatises.* London, 1603.

Shakespeare, William. *All's Well That End's Well.* Ed. G.K. Hunter. London: Methuen and Co., 1959.

———. *As You Like It.* In *The Riverside Shakespeare,* ed. G. Blakemore Evans. 2nd ed. Boston: Houghton Mifflin, 1997. 403–436.

Shakespeare, William. *3 Henry VI*. In *The Riverside Shakespeare*, ed. G. Blakemore Evans. 2nd ed. Boston: Houghton Mifflin, 1997. 711–747.

———. *The Merchant of Venice*. In *The Riverside Shakespeare*, ed. G. Blakemore Evans. 2nd ed. Boston: Houghton Mifflin, 1997. 288–319.

———. *Romeo and Juliet*. Ed. Brian Gibbons. London: Arden, 1980.

———. *Titus Andronicus*. In *The Riverside Shakespeare*, ed. G. Blakemore Evans. 2nd ed. Boston: Houghton Mifflin, 1997. 1069–1100.

———. *Twelfth Night*. Ed. J.M. Lothian and T.W. Craik. London: Methuen, 1975.

Sharp, Jane. *The Midwives Book or the Whole Art of Midwifry Discovered*. Ed. Elaine Hobby. New York: Oxford University Press, 1999.

Smith, Henry. *A Preparative to Mariage*. London, 1591.

Speght, Rachel. *A Dream*. In *Mortalities Memorandum*. London, 1621. A4r–C1r.

Spenser, Edmund. *A View of the Present State of Ireland*. In *The Works of Edmund Spenser*, ed. R. Morris. London: Macmillan, 1902. 609–683.

Stirling, William Alexander, Earl of. *Recreations with the Muses*. London, 1637.

Stubbes, Philip. *A Christal Glas for christian women*. London, 1592.

Tusser, Thomas. *Five hundreth points of good husbandry united to as many of good husswiferie*. London, 1573.

Vives, Juan Luis. *A Very frutefull and pleasant boke called the Instruction of a Christen Woman*. Trans. Richard Hyrde. London, 1529.

Webster, John. *The Duchess of Malfi*. Ed. Elizabeth M. Brennan. New York: W.W. Norton, 1993.

Whitney, Isabella. *A Sweet Nosgay*. London, 1573.

Wilson, Thomas. *The Arte of Rhetorique*. London, 1553.

A Womans Work is never done. Roxburge Ballads I. Fo.534. London, 1660?

Woolley, Hannah. *The Compleat Servant-Maid; Or, The Young Maidens Tutor*. London, 1677.

———. *The Gentlewomans Companion; Or, a Guide to the Female Sex*. London, 1673.

———. *A Supplement to the Queen-Like Closet; Or, A Little of Everything*. London, 1674.

SECONDARY SOURCES

Acheson, Katherine Osler. "The Modernity of the Early Modern: The Example of Anne Clifford." In *Discontinuities: New Essays on Renaissance Literature and Criticism*, ed. Viviana Comensoli and Paul Stevens. Toronto: University of Toronto Press, 1998. 27–51.

Adelman, Janet. *Suffocating Mothers: Fantasies of Maternal Origin in Shakespeare's Plays, Hamlet to the Tempest*. New York: Routledge, 1992.

Althusser, Louis. "Ideology and Ideological State Apparatuses (Notes towards an Investigation)." In *Lenin and Philosophy and Other Essays*, trans. Ben Brewster. New York: Monthly Review, 1971. 127–186.

Amussen, Susan Dwyer. *An Ordered Society: Gender and Class in Early Modern England*. New York: Columbia University Press, 1988.

———. "Punishment, Discipline, and Power: The Social Meanings of Violence in Early Modern England." *Journal of British Studies* 34.1 (1995): 1–34.

Anderson, Linda. *A Place in the Story: Servants and Service in Shakespeare's Plays*. Newark: University of Delaware Press, 2005.

Archer, Ian W. *The Pursuit of Stability: Social Relations in Elizabethan London*. Cambridge: Cambridge University Press, 1991.

Barker, Francis. *The Tremulous Private Body: Essays in Subjection*. London: Routledge, 1984.

Barroll, Leeds. "The Court of the First Stuart Queen." In *The Mental World of the Jacobean Court*, ed. Linda Levy Peck. Cambridge: Cambridge University Press, 1991. 191–208.

Barthes, Roland. "The Discourse of History." Trans. Stephen Bann. *Comparative Criticism* 3 (1981): 7–20.

Beauchamp, Virginia Walcott, Elizabeth H. Hageman, and Margaret Mikesell. Introduction to *The Instruction of a Christen Woman*, by Juan Luis Vives. Ed. Beauchamp, Hageman, and Mikesell. Urbana: Illinois University Press, 2002. xv–xciii.

Beier, A.L. *Masterless Men: The Vagrancy Problem in England in 1560–1640*. London: Methuen, 1985.

Beier, A.L., and Roger Finlay, eds. *London 1500–1700: The Making of the Metropolis*. London: Longman, 1986.

Beier, Lucinda McCray. "The Good Death in Seventeenth-Century England." In *Death, Ritual, and Bereavement*, ed. Ralph Houlbrooke. London: Routledge, 1989. 43–61.

Beilin, Elaine V. *Redeeming Eve: Women Writers of the English Renaissance*. Princeton: Princeton University Press, 1987.

Bell, Ilona. "In Defense of Their Lawful Liberty: A Letter sent by the Maydens of London." In *Women, Writing, and the Reproduction of Culture in Tudor and Stuart Britain*, ed. Mary E. Burke, Jane Donawerth, Linda L. Dove, and Karen Nelson. Syracuse: Syracuse University Press, 2000. 177–192.

Belsey, Catherine. *The Subject of Tragedy: Identity and Difference in Renaissance Drama*. London: Routledge, 1985.

Ben-Amos, Ilana Krausman. *Adolescence and Youth in Early Modern England*. New Haven: Yale University Press, 1994.

Bennett, Judith M. *Ale, Beer, and Brewsters in England: Women's Work in a Changing World 1300–1600*. Oxford: Oxford University Press, 1996.

———. "'History That Stands Still': Women's Work in the European Past." *Feminist Studies* 14.2 (1988): 269–283.

Bennett, Judith M., and Amy M. Froide. "A Singular Past." In *Singlewomen in the European Past, 1250–1800*, ed. Bennett and Froide. Philadelphia: University of Pennsylvania Press, 1999. 1–37.

———, eds. *Singlewomen in the European Past, 1250–1800*. Philadelphia: University of Pennsylvania Press, 1999.

Berry, Ralph. *Shakespeare and Social Class*. Atlantic Highlands, NJ: Humanities International, 1988.

Bicks, Caroline. *Midwiving Subjects in Shakespeare's England*. Aldershot: Ashgate, 2003.

Bloch, Chana. *Spelling the Word: George Herbert and the Bible*. Berkeley: University of California Press, 1985.

Blumenfeld-Kosinski, Renate. *Not of Woman Born: Representations of Caesarean Birth in Medieval and Renaissance Culture*. Ithaca: Cornell University Press, 1990.

Boas, F.S. *Shakespeare and His Predecessors*. New York: Charles Scribner's Sons, 1896.

Booty, John E. "Communion and Commonweal: The Book of Common Prayer." In *The Godly Kingdom of Tudor England: Great Books of the English Reformation*, ed. Booty. Wilton, CT: Morehouse-Barlow, 1981. 139–216.

Botelho, Lynn, and Pat Thane, eds. *Women and Aging in British Society Since 1500*. Harlow, England: Longman, 2001.

Botonaki, Effie. "Seventeenth-Century Englishwomen's Spiritual Diaries: Self-Examination, Covenanting, and Account Keeping." *Sixteenth Century Journal* 30.1 (1999): 3–21.

Bouwsma, William J. *John Calvin: A Sixteenth-Century Portrait*. Oxford: Oxford University Press, 1988.

Brenner, Robert. *Merchants and Revolution: Commercial Change, Political Conflict, and London's Overseas Traders, 1550–1653*. Cambridge: Cambridge University Press, 1993.

Brodsky, Vivien. "Single Women in the London Marriage Market: Age, Status and Mobility, 1598–1619." *The Newberry Papers in Family and Community History* 80.2 (1980): 1–29.

Bromley, Laura G. "Domestic Conduct in *A Woman Killed with Kindness*." *Studies in English Literature 1500–1900* 26.2 (1986): 259–276.

Brown, Elizabeth A. "Companion Me With My Mistress: Cleopatra, Elizabeth I, and Their Waiting Women." In *Maids and Mistresses, Cousins and Queens: Women's Alliances in Early Modern England*, ed. Susan Frye and Karen Robertson. New York: Oxford University Press, 1999. 131–145.

Brown, Sylvia. "The Approbation of Elizabeth Jocelin." In *English Manuscript Studies 1100–1700: Writings by Early Modern Women*, ed. Peter Beal and Margaret J.M. Ezell. Vol. 9. London: The British Library, 2000. 129–164.

———. "Elizabeth Joscelin: Introduction." In *Women's Writing in Stuart England: The Mothers' Legacies of Dorothy Leigh, Elizabeth Joscelin and Elizabeth Richardson*, ed. Brown. Phoenix Mill: Sutton, 1999. 91–105.

———. "Introduction to Dorothy Leigh: *The Mothers Blessing* (1616)." In *Women's Writing in Stuart England: The Mothers' Legacies of Dorothy Leigh, Elizabeth Joscelin and Elizabeth Richardson*, ed. Brown. Phoenix Mill: Sutton, 1999. 3–14.

———. "'Over Her Dead Body': Feminism, Poststructuralism, and the Mother's Legacy." In *Discontinuities: New Essays on Renaissance Literature and Criticism*, ed. Viviana Comensoli and Paul Stevens. Toronto: University of Toronto Press, 1998. 3–26.

Bruster, Douglas. "Shakespeare and the Composite Text." In *Renaissance Literature and Its Formal Engagements*, ed. Mark David Rasmussen. New York: Palgrave, 2002. 43–66.

Burford, E.J., and Joy Wotton. *Private Vices—Public Virtues: Bawdry in London from Elizabethan Times to the Regency*. London: Robert Hale, 1995.

Burke, Victoria E. "Women and Early Seventeenth-Century Manuscript Culture: Four Miscellanies." *The Seventeenth Century* 12.2 (1997): 135–150.

Burnett, Mark Thornton. *Masters and Servants in English Renaissance Drama and Culture: Authority and Obedience*. New York: St. Martin's, 1997.

Bushnell, Rebecca W. *A Culture of Teaching: Early Modern Humanism in Theory and Practice*. Ithaca: Cornell University Press, 1996.

Butler, Judith. *Bodies That Matter: On the Discursive Limits of "Sex."* New York: Routledge, 1993.

———. "Performative Acts and Gender Constitution: An Essay in Phenomenology and Feminist Theory." In *Performing Feminisms: Feminist Critical Theory and Theatre*, ed. Sue-Ellen Case. Baltimore: Johns Hopkins University Press, 1990. 270–282.

Butler, Martin. *Theatre and Crisis, 1632–1642*. Cambridge: Cambridge University Press, 1984.

Cahn, Susan. *Industry of Devotion: The Transformation of Women's Work in England, 1500–1660*. New York: Columbia University Press, 1987.

Callaghan, Dympna. "The Ideology of Romantic Love: The Case of *Romeo and Juliet*." In *The Weyward Sisters: Shakespeare and Feminist Politics*, ed. Callaghan, Lorraine Helms, and Jyotsna Singh. Oxford: Oxford University Press, 1994. 59–101.

———. *Shakespeare Without Women*. London: Routledge, 2000.

Cavallo, Sandra, and Lyndan Warner, eds. *Widowhood in Medieval and Early Modern Europe*. Harlow, England: Longman, 1999.

Charlton, Kenneth. *Women, Religion and Education in Early Modern England*. London: Routledge, 1999.

Chartier, Roger, ed. *A History of Private Life: Passions of the Renaissance*. Vol. 3. Cambridge, MA: Harvard University Press, 1989.

Chatman, Seymour. *Story and Discourse: Narrative Structure in Fiction and Film*. Ithaca: Cornell University Press, 1978.

Christensen, Ann. "Business, Pleasure, and the Domestic Economy in Heywood's *A Woman Killed with Kindness*." *Exemplaria* 9.2 (1997): 315–340.

Clark, Alice. *Working Life of Women in the Seventeenth Century*. London: Routledge, 1919; 3rd ed., 1992.

Clark, Andrew. *Domestic Drama: A Survey of the Origins, Antecedents, and Nature of the Domestic Play in England, 1500–1640.* Salzburg: Institut für Englische Sprache und Literatur, 1975.

Clark, Sandra S. "Glauce." In *The Spenser Encyclopedia*, ed. A.C. Hamilton. London: Routledge, 1990. 333.

Clarke, Elizabeth. "Diaries." In *A Companion to English Renaissance Literature and Culture*, ed. Michael Hattaway. Malden, MA: Blackwell, 2000. 609–613.

———. "Women's Manuscript Miscellanies in Early Modern England." In *Teaching Tudor and Stuart Women Writers*, ed. Susanne Woods and Margaret P. Hannay. New York: MLA, 2000. 52–60.

Clifford, D.J.H. Introduction to *The Diaries of Lady Anne Clifford*. Ed. Clifford. Phoenix Mill: Sutton, 1990. x–xvi.

———. Prologue to *The Diaries of Lady Anne Clifford*. Ed. Clifford. Phoenix Mill: Sutton, 1990. 1–18.

———. "The Years Between, 1620–1649." In *The Diaries of Lady Anne Clifford*, ed. Clifford. Phoenix Mill: Sutton, 1990. 83–102.

Cody, Lisa Forman. "The Politics of Reproduction: From Midwives' Alternative Public Sphere to the Public Spectacle of Man Midwifery." *Eighteenth-Century Studies* 32.4 (1999): 477–495.

Cohen, Stephen. "Between Form and Culture: New Historicism and the Promise of a Historical Formalism." In *Renaissance Literature and Its Formal Engagements*, ed. Mark David Rasmussen. New York: Palgrave, 2002. 17–42.

Cohen, Walter. *Drama of a Nation: Public Theater in Renaissance England and Spain*. Ithaca: Cornell University Press, 1985.

Collinson, Patrick. *The Birthpangs of Protestant England: Religious and Cultural Change in the Sixteenth and Seventeenth Centuries*. Basingstoke: Macmillan, 1988.

Comensoli, Viviana. *"Household" Business: Domestic Plays of Early Modern England*. Toronto: University of Toronto Press, 1996.

Comilang, Susan. "English Noblewomen and the Organization of Space: Gardens, Mourning Posts, and Religious Recesses." Ph.D. diss., The George Washington University, 2001.

Cook, Ann Jennalie. *Making a Match: Courtship in Shakespeare and His Society*. Princeton: Princeton University Press, 1991.

Correll, Barbara. "Malvolio at Malfi: Managing Desire in Shakespeare and Webster." *Shakespeare Quarterly* 58.1 (2007): 65–92.

Craig, Martha J. " 'Write it upon the walles of your houses': Dorothy Leigh's *The Mothers Blessing*." In *Women's Life-Writing: Finding Voice/Building Community*, ed. Linda S. Coleman. Bowling Green: Bowling Green State University Press, 1997. 191–208.

Crawford, Patricia. "Attitudes to Menstruation in Seventeenth-Century England." *Past and Present* 91 (1981): 47–73.

———. "The Construction and Experience of Maternity in Seventeenth-Century England." In *Women as Mothers in Pre-Industrial England: Essays in Memory of Dorothy McLaren*, ed. Valerie Fildes. London: Routledge, 1990. 3–38.

———. *Women and Religion in England 1500–1720*. London: Routledge, 1993.

———. "Women's Published Writings 1600–1700." In *Women in English Society 1500–1800*, ed. Mary Prior. London: Routledge, 1986. 211–282.

Cressy, David. *Birth, Marriage and Death: Ritual, Religion, and the Life-Cycle in Tudor and Stuart England*. Oxford: Oxford University Press, 1997.

———. *Bonfires and Bells: National Memory and the Protestant Calendar in Elizabethan and Stuart England*. London: Weidenfeld and Nicolson, 1989.

Culler, Jonathan. *The Pursuit of Signs: Semiotics, Literature, Deconstruction*. London: Routledge, 1981. 169–187.

Cunningham, Karen. "'She Learns As She Lies': Work and the Exemplary Female in English Early Modern Education." *Exemplaria* 7.1 (1995): 209–235.

Dabhoiwala, Faramerz. "The Pattern of Sexual Immorality in Seventeenth- and Eighteenth-Century London." In *Londinopolis: Essays in the Cultural and Social History of Early Modern London*, ed. Paul Griffiths and Mark S.R. Jenner. Manchester: Manchester University Press, 2000. 86–106.

Davies, Kathleen M. "Continuity and Change in Literary Advice on Marriage." In *Marriage and Society: Studies in the History of Marriage*, ed. R.B. Outhwaite. New York: St. Martin's, 1981. 58–80.

Davis, Lloyd. "'Sick Desires': *All's Well That Ends Well* and the Civilizing Process." In *Shakespeare Matters: History, Teaching, Performance*, ed. Lloyd Davis. Newark: University of Delaware Press, 2003. 89–102.

Davis, Natalie Zemon. "Women in the Crafts in Sixteenth-Century Lyon." In *Women and Work in Preindustrial Europe*, ed. Barbara A. Hanawalt. Bloomington: Indiana University Press, 1986. 167–197.

de Certeau, Michel. *The Practice of Everyday Life*. Trans. Steven Rendall. Berkeley: University of California Press, 1984.

Desens, Marliss C. *The Bed-Trick in English Renaissance Drama: Explorations in Gender, Sexuality, and Power*. Newark: University of Delaware Press, 1994.

Diehl, Huston. *Staging Reform, Reforming the Stage: Protestantism and Popular Theater in Early Modern England*. Ithaca: Cornell University Press, 1997.

Doebler, Bettie Anne. *"Rooted Sorrow": Dying in Early Modern England*. Rutherford: Fairleigh Dickinson University Press, 1994.

Dolan, Frances E. "Marian Devotion and Maternal Authority in Seventeenth-Century England." In *Maternal Measures: Figuring Caregiving in the Early Modern Period*, ed. Naomi J. Miller and Naomi Yavneh. Aldershot: Ashgate, 2000. 282–292.

———. "Reading, Work, and Catholic Women's Biographies." *English Literary Renaissance* 33.3 (2003): 328–357.

Dolan, Frances E. *Whores of Babylon: Catholicism, Gender and Seventeenth-Century Print Culture*. Ithaca: Cornell University Press, 1999.

Dollimore, Jonathan, and Alan Sinfield, eds. *Political Shakespeare: New Essays in Cultural Materialism*. Ithaca: Cornell University Press, 1985.

Donker, Marjorie, and George M. Mulldrow. *Dictionary of Literary-Rhetorical Conventions of the English Renaissance*. Westport, CT: Greenwood, 1982.

Dowd, Michelle M. "Structures of Piety in Elizabeth Richardson's *Legacie*." In *Genre and Women's Life Writing in Early Modern England*, ed. Dowd and Julie A. Eckerle. Aldershot: Ashgate, 2007. 115–130.

Dowd, Michelle M., and Julie A. Eckerle, eds. *Genre and Women's Life Writing in Early Modern England*. Aldershot: Ashgate, 2007.

Duffy, Eamon. *The Stripping of the Altars: Traditional Religion in England 1400–1580*. New Haven: Yale University Press, 1992.

Durston, Christopher, and Jacqueline Eales. "Introduction: The Puritan Ethos, 1560–1700." In *The Culture of English Puritanism, 1560–1700*, ed. Durston and Eales. New York: St. Martin's, 1996. 1–31.

Earle, Peter. "The Female Labour Market in London in the Late Seventeenth and Early Eighteenth Centuries." *The Economic History Review* 42.3 (1989): 328–353.

Earwalker, J.P. *East Cheshire: Past and Present: or A History of the Hundred of Macclesfield, in the County Palatine of Chester*. 2 vols. London, 1877.

Eccles, Audrey. *Obstetrics and Gynaecology in Tudor and Stuart England*. London: Croom Helm, 1982.

Ehrenreich, Barbara. *Nickel and Dimed: On (Not) Getting By in America*. New York: Metropolitan Books, 2001.

Ellinghausen, Laurie. "Literary Property and the Single Woman in Isabella Whitney's *A Sweet Nosgay*." *Studies in English Literature 1500–1900* 45.1 (2005): 1–22.

Erickson, Amy Louise. Introduction to *Working Life of Women in the Seventeenth Century*, by Alice Clark. London: Routledge, 1992. vii–lv.

———. *Women and Property in Early Modern England*. London: Routledge, 1993.

Evans, Nesta. "Inheritance, Women, Religion and Education in Early Modern Society as Revealed by Wills." In *Probate Records and the Local Community*, ed. Philip Riden. London: Alan Sutton, 1985. 53–70.

Evenden, Doreen. "Mothers and Their Midwives in Seventeenth-Century London." In *The Art of Midwifery: Early Modern Midwives in Europe*, ed. Hilary Marland. London: Routledge, 1993. 9–26.

Everett, Barbara. *Young Hamlet: Essays on Shakespeare's Tragedies*. Oxford: Oxford University Press, 1989. 152–165.

Evett, David. *Discourses of Service in Shakespeare's England*. New York: Palgrave, 2005.

Ezell, Margaret J.M. *The Patriarch's Wife: Literary Evidence and the History of the Family*. Chapel Hill: University of North Carolina Press, 1987.

————. *Writing Women's Literary History.* Baltimore: Johns Hopkins University Press, 1993.

Fabian, Johannes. *Time and the Other: How Anthropology Makes Its Object.* New York: Columbia University Press, 1983.

Felski, Rita. *Beyond Feminist Aesthetics: Feminist Literature and Social Change.* Cambridge, MA: Harvard University Press, 1989.

Ferguson, Margaret W. "A Room Not Their Own: Renaissance Women as Readers and Writers." In *The Comparative Perspective on Literature: Approaches to Theory and Practice,* ed. Clayton Koelb and Susan Noakes. Ithaca: Cornell University Press, 1988. 93–116.

Feroli, Teresa. " 'Infelix Simulacrum': The Rewriting of Loss in Elizabeth Jocelin's *The Mothers Legacie.*" *ELH* 61.1 (1994): 89–102.

Fildes, Valerie. *Breasts, Bottles and Babies: A History of Infant Feeding.* Edinburgh: Edinburgh University Press, 1986.

————. *Wet Nursing: A History from Antiquity to the Present.* Oxford: Basil Blackwell, 1988.

Fish, Stanley. *The Living Temple: George Herbert and Catechizing.* Berkeley: University of California Press, 1978.

Fissell, Mary E. *Vernacular Bodies: The Politics of Reproduction in Early Modern England.* Oxford: Oxford University Press, 2004.

Fletcher, Anthony. *Gender, Sex and Subordination in England 1500–1800.* New Haven: Yale University Press, 1995.

Forman, Valerie. "Material Dispossessions and Counterfeit Investments: The Economies of *Twelfth Night.*" In *Money and the Age of Shakespeare: Essays in New Economic Criticism,* ed. Linda Woodbridge. New York: Palgrave, 2003. 113–127.

Freeman, Jane. "Life-Long Learning in Shakespeare's *All's Well That Ends Well.*" *Renascence* 56.2 (2004): 67–85.

Froide, Amy M. *Never Married: Singlewomen in Early Modern England.* Oxford: Oxford University Press, 2005.

Frye, Northrop. *Anatomy of Criticism.* Princeton: Princeton University Press, 1971.

Fuchs, Barbara. "Faithless Empires: Pirates, Renegadoes, and the English Nation." *ELH* 67.1 (2000): 45–69.

Fumerton, Patricia. *Unsettled: The Culture of Mobility and the Working Poor in Early Modern England.* Chicago: University of Chicago Press, 2006.

Gittings, Claire. *Death, Burial, and the Individual in Early Modern England.* London: Routledge, 1984.

Goldberg, Jonathan. *Writing Matter: From the Hands of the English Renaissance.* Stanford: Stanford University Press, 1990.

Goodich, Michael. "*Ancilla Dei*: The Servant as Saint in the Late Middle Ages." In *Women of the Medieval World: Essays in Honor of John H. Mundy,* ed. Julius Kirshner and Suzanne F. Wemple. Oxford: Basil Blackwell, 1985. 119–136.

Goody, Jack, Joan Thirsk, and E.P. Thompson, eds. *Family and Inheritance: Rural Society in Western Europe 1200–1800*. Cambridge: Cambridge University Press, 1976.

Gowing, Laura. *Common Bodies: Women, Touch and Power in Seventeenth-Century England*. New Haven: Yale University Press, 2003.

———. *Domestic Dangers: Women, Words, and Sex in Early Modern London*. Oxford: Clarendon Press, 1996.

———. "'The freedom of the streets': Women and Social Space, 1560–1640." In *Londinopolis: Essays in the Cultural and Social History of Early Modern London*, ed. Paul Griffiths and Mark S.R. Jenner. Manchester: Manchester University Press, 2000. 130–151.

Graham, Elspeth. "Women's Writing and the Self." In *Women and Literature in Britain 1500–1700*, ed. Helen Wilcox. Cambridge: Cambridge University Press, 1996. 209–233.

Graham, Elspeth, Hilary Hinds, Elaine Hobby, and Helen Wilcox. Introduction to *Her Own Life: Autobiographical Writings by Seventeenth-Century Englishwomen*. Ed. Graham, Hinds, Hobby, and Wilcox. London: Routledge, 1989. 1–27.

Gray, Catharine. "Feeding on the Seed of the Woman: Dorothy Leigh and the Figure of Maternal Dissent." *ELH* 68.3 (2001): 563–592.

Green, Ian. *The Christian's ABC: Catechism and Catechizing in England*. Oxford: Clarendon Press, 1996.

———. *Print and Protestantism in Early Modern England*. Oxford: Oxford University Press, 2000.

Green, Juana. "The Sempster's Wares: Merchandising and Marrying in *The Fair Maid of the Exchange* (1607)." *Renaissance Quarterly* 53.4 (2000): 1084–1118.

Greenblatt, Stephen. *Shakespearean Negotiations: The Circulation of Social Energy in Renaissance England*. Berkeley: University of California Press, 1988.

Griffiths, Paul. *Youth and Authority: Formative Experiences in England 1560–1640*. Oxford: Clarendon Press, 1996.

Gurr, Andrew. *Playgoing in Shakespeare's London*. Cambridge: Cambridge University Press, 1996.

———. *The Shakespearean Stage 1574–1642*. Cambridge: Cambridge University Press, 1992.

Gutierrez, Nancy A. "Exorcism by Fasting in *A Woman Killed with Kindness*: A Paradigm of Puritan Resistance?" *Research Opportunities in Renaissance Drama* 33 (1994): 43–62.

Hafter, Daryl M., ed. *European Women and Preindustrial Craft*. Bloomington: Indiana University Press, 1995.

Halpern, Richard. *The Poetics of Private Accumulation: English Renaissance Culture and the Genealogy of Capital*. Ithaca: Cornell University Press, 1991.

Hanawalt, Barbara. "Peasant Women's Contribution to the Home Economy in Late Medieval England." In *Women and Work in Preindustrial Europe*, ed. Hanawalt. Bloomington: Indiana University Press, 1986. 3–19.

————, ed. *Women and Work in Preindustrial Europe*. Bloomington: Indiana University Press, 1986.

Hannay, Margaret P. "'High Housewifery': The Duties and Letters of Barbara Gamage Sidney, Countess of Leicester." *Early Modern Women: An Interdisciplinary Journal* 1 (2006): 7–35.

————. "'O Daughter Heare': Reconstructing the Lives of Aristocratic Englishwomen." In *Attending to Women in Early Modern England*, ed. Betty S. Travitsky and Adele F. Seeff. Newark: University of Delaware Press, 1994. 35–63.

Hanson, Elizabeth. *Discovering the Subject in Renaissance England*. Cambridge: Cambridge University Press, 1998.

Harbage, Alfred. *Shakespeare and the Rival Traditions*. New York: Macmillan, 1952.

Harley, David. "Provincial Midwives in England: Lancashire and Cheshire, 1660–1760." In *The Art of Midwifery: Early Modern Midwives in Europe*, ed. Hilary Marland. London: Routledge, 1993. 27–48.

Harris, Barbara. *English Aristocratic Women 1450–1550: Marriage and Family, Property and Careers*. Oxford: Oxford University Press, 2002.

Havens, Earle. *Commonplace Books: A History of Manuscripts and Printed Books from Antiquity to the Twentieth Century*. New Haven: Yale University Press, 2001.

Heal, Felicity. *Hospitality in Early Modern England*. Oxford: Clarendon Press, 1990.

Heinemann, Margot. *Puritanism and Theater: Thomas Middleton and Opposition Drama under the Early Stuarts*. Cambridge: Cambridge University Press, 1982.

Helgerson, Richard. *The Elizabethan Prodigals*. Berkeley: University of California Press, 1976.

Helt, J.S.W. "Women, Memory and Will-Making in Elizabethan England." In *The Place of the Dead: Death and Remembrance in Late Medieval and Early Modern Europe*, ed. Bruce Gordon and Peter Marshall. Cambridge: Cambridge University Press, 2000. 188–205.

Henderson, Diana E. "Many Mansions: Reconstructing *A Woman Killed with Kindness*." *Studies in English Literature 1500–1900* 26.2 (1986): 277–294.

————. "The Theater and Domestic Culture." In *A New History of Early English Drama*, ed. John D. Cox and David Scott Kastan. New York: Columbia University Press, 1997. 173–194.

Herman, David. "Introduction: Narratologies." In *Narratologies: New Perspectives on Narrative Analysis*, ed. Herman. Columbus: Ohio State University Press, 1997. 1–30.

Hettinger, Madonna J. "Defining the Servant: Legal and Extra-Legal Terms of Employment in Fifteenth-Century England." In *The Work of Work: Servitude, Slavery, and Labor in Medieval England*, ed. Allen J. Frantzen and Douglass Moffat. Glasgow: Bruithne, 1994. 206–228.

Hill, Bridget. *Servants: English Domestics in the Eighteenth Century*. Oxford: Oxford University Press, 1996.

Hill, Bridget. *Women, Work and Sexual Politics in Eighteenth-Century England*. Montreal: McGill-Queen's University Press, 1989.

Hill, Christopher. *Society and Puritanism in Pre-Revolutionary England*. New York: St. Martin's, 1997.

Hillman, Richard. *William Shakespeare: The Problem Plays*. New York: Twayne, 1993.

Hobby, Elaine. *Virtue of Necessity: English Women's Writing 1649–88*. London: Virago, 1988.

Hodgkins, Christopher. *Authority, Church, and Society in George Herbert: Return to the Middle Way*. Columbia: University of Missouri Press, 1993.

Honeyman, Katrina, and Jordan Goodman. "Women's Work, Gender Conflict, and Labour Markets in Europe, 1500–1900." *The Economic History Review* 44.4 (1991): 608–628.

Horwich, Richard. "Wives, Courtesans, and the Economics of Love in Jacobean City Comedy." In *Drama in the Renaissance: Comparative and Critical Essays*, ed. Clifford Davidson, C.J. Gianakaris, and John H. Stroupe. New York: AMS, 1986. 255–273

Houlbrooke, Ralph. *Death, Religion and the Family in England 1480–1750*. Oxford: Clarendon Press, 1998.

———. "The Puritan Death-Bed, c.1560–c.1660." In *The Culture of English Puritanism, 1560–1700*, ed. Christopher Durston and Jacqueline Eales. New York: St. Martin's, 1996. 122–144.

Howard, Jean E. *The Stage and Social Struggle in Early Modern England*. London: Routledge, 1994.

———. *Theater of a City: The Places of London Comedy, 1598–1642*. Philadelphia: University of Pennsylvania Press, 2007.

———. "Women, Foreigners, and the Regulation of Urban Space in *Westward Ho*." In *Material London, ca.1600*, ed. Lena Cowen Orlin. Philadelphia: University of Pennsylvania Press, 2000. 150–167.

Howard, Jean E., and Phyllis Rackin. *Engendering a Nation: A Feminist Account of Shakespeare's English Histories*. London: Routledge, 1997.

Howell, Martha C. *The Marriage Exchange: Property, Social Place, and Gender in Cities of the Low Countries, 1300–1550*. Chicago: University of Chicago Press, 1998.

Hughey, Ruth, and Philip Hereford. "Elizabeth Grymeston and Her *Miscelanea*." *The Library* 15.1 (1934): 61–94.

Hutson, Lorna. *The Usurer's Daughter: Male Friendship and Fictions of Women in Sixteenth-Century England*. London: Routledge, 1994.

Ingram, Martin. " 'Scolding Women Cucked or Washed': A Crisis in Gender Relations in Early Modern England?" In *Women, Crime and the Courts in Early Modern England*, ed. Jenny Kermode and Garthine Walker. Chapel Hill: University of North Carolina Press, 1994. 48–80.

Iser, Wolfgang. *The Fictive and the Imaginary: Charting Literary Anthropology*. Baltimore: Johns Hopkins University Press, 1993.

Jameson, Fredric. *The Political Unconscious: Narrative as a Socially Symbolic Act*. Ithaca: Cornell University Press, 1981.

Jardine, Lisa. "Cultural Confusion and Shakespeare's Learned Heroines: 'These are old paradoxes.'" *Shakespeare Quarterly* 38.1 (1987): 1–18.

———. *Still Harping on Daughters: Women and Drama in the Age of Shakespeare*. New York: Columbia University Press, 1983.

Jenner, Mark S.R., and Paul Griffiths. Introduction to *Londinopolis: Essays in the Cultural and Social History of Early Modern London*. Ed. Griffiths and Jenner. Manchester: Manchester University Press, 2000. 1–23.

Johnson, Marilyn L. *Images of Women in the Works of Thomas Heywood*. Salzburg: Institut für Englische Sprache und Literatur, 1974.

Jones, Ann Rosalind. "Maidservants of London: Sisterhoods of Kinship and Labor." In *Maids and Mistresses, Cousins and Queens: Women's Alliances in Early Modern England*, ed. Susan Frye and Karen Robertson. New York: Oxford University Press, 1999. 21–32.

Jones, Ann Rosalind, and Peter Stallybrass. *Renaissance Clothing and the Materials of Memory*. Cambridge: Cambridge University Press, 2000.

Karras, Ruth Mazo. *Common Women: Prostitution and Sexuality in Medieval England*. Oxford: Oxford University Press, 1996.

Kastan, David Scott. "*All's Well That Ends Well* and the Limits of Comedy." *ELH* 52.3 (1985): 575–589.

———. *Shakespeare After Theory*. New York: Routledge, 1999.

Kastan, David Scott, and Peter Stallybrass, eds. *Staging the Renaissance: Reinterpretations of Elizabethan and Jacobean Drama*. New York: Routledge, 1991.

King, Margaret L. *Women of the Renaissance*. Chicago: University of Chicago Press, 1991.

Korda, Natasha. "Labours Lost: Women's Work and Early Modern Theatrical Commerce." In *From Script to Stage in Early Modern England*, ed. Peter Holland and Stephen Orgel. Houndmills, Basingstoke: Palgrave, 2004. 195–230.

———. *Shakespeare's Domestic Economies: Gender and Property in Early Modern England*. Philadelphia: University of Pennsylvania Press, 2002.

Kowaleski, Maryanne. "Singlewomen in Medieval and Early Modern Europe: The Demographic Perspective." In *Singlewomen in the European Past, 1250–1800*, ed. Judith M. Bennett and Amy M. Froide. Philadelphia: University of Pennsylvania Press, 1999. 38–82.

———. "Women's Work in a Market Town: Exeter in the Late Fourteenth Century." In *Women and Work in Preindustrial Europe*, ed. Barbara A. Hanawalt. Bloomington: Indiana University Press, 1986. 145–164.

Kussmaul, Ann. *Servants in Husbandry in Early Modern England*. Cambridge: Cambridge University Press, 1981.

Kusunoki, Akiko. "'Their Testament at Their Apron-strings': The Representation of Puritan Women in Early-Seventeenth-Century England." In *Gloriana's Face: Women, Public and Private, in the English Renaissance*, ed. S.P. Cerasano and Marion Wynne-Davies. New York: Harvester Wheatsheaf, 1992. 185–204.

Lake, Peter. "Defining Puritanism—Again?" In *Puritanism: Transatlantic Perspectives on a Seventeenth-Century Anglo-American Faith*, ed. Francis J. Bremer. Boston: Massachusetts Historical Society, 1993. 3–29.

———. *Moderate Puritans and the Elizabethan Church*. Cambridge: Cambridge University Press, 1982.

Lamb, Mary Ellen. "The Agency of the Split Subject: Lady Anne Clifford and the Uses of Reading." *English Literary Renaissance* 22.3 (1992): 347–368.

———. "Margaret Hoby's Diary: Women's Reading Practices and the Gendering of the Reformation Subject." In *Pilgrimage for Love: Essays in Early Modern Literature in Honor of Josephine A. Roberts*, ed. Sigrid King. Tempe: ACMR, 1999. 63–94.

———. "Merging the Secular and the Spiritual in Anne Halkett's Memoirs." In *Genre and Women's Life Writing in Early Modern England*, ed. Michelle M. Dowd and Julie A. Eckerle. Aldershot: Ashgate, 2007. 81–96.

———. "Tracing a Heterosexual Erotics of Service in *Twelfth Night* and the Autobiographical Writings of Thomas Whythorne and Anne Clifford." *Criticism* 40.1 (1998): 1–25.

Lanham, Richard A. *A Handlist of Rhetorical Terms*. 2nd ed. Berkeley: University of California Press, 1991.

Laqueur, Thomas. *Making Sex: Body and Gender from the Greeks to Freud*. Cambridge, MA: Harvard University Press, 1990.

Laurence, Anne. *Women in England 1500–1760: A Social History*. London: Phoenix Giant, 1996.

Lawrence, William Witherle. *Shakespeare's Problem Comedies*. New York: MacMillan, 1931.

Leinwand, Theodore B. *The City Staged: Jacobean Comedy, 1603–1613*. Madison: University of Wisconsin Press, 1986.

Lewalski, Barbara K. "Emblems of the Religious Lyric; George Herbert and Protestant Emblematics." *Hebrew University Studies in Literature* 6 (1978): 32–56.

———. Introduction to *The Polemics and Poems of Rachel Speght*. Ed. Lewalski. New York: Oxford University Press, 1996. xi–xxxvi.

———. *Writing Women in Jacobean England*. Cambridge, MA: Harvard University Press, 1993.

Luecke, Marilyn. "The Reproduction of Culture and the Culture of Reproduction in Elizabeth Clinton's *The Countesse of Lincolnes Nurserie*." In *Women, Writing, and the Reproduction of Culture in Tudor and Stuart Britain*, ed. Mary E. Burke, Jane Donawerth, Linda L. Dove, and Karen Nelson. Syracuse: Syracuse University Press, 2000. 238–252.

Malcolmson, Cristina. *Heart-Work: George Herbert and the Protestant Ethic*. Stanford: Stanford University Press, 1999.

———. "'What You Will': Social Mobility and Gender in *Twelfth Night*." In *The Matter of Difference: Materialist Feminist Criticism of Shakespeare*, ed. Valerie Wayne. Ithaca: Cornell University Press, 1991. 29–57.

Marcus, Leah S. "George Herbert and the Anglican Plain Style." In *'Too Rich to Clothe the Sunne': Essays on George Herbert*, ed. Claude J. Summers and Ted-Larry Pebworth. Pittsburgh: University of Pittsburgh Press, 1980. 179–193.

Marshall, Thomas D. "Addressing the House: Jonson's Ideology at Penshurst." *Texas Studies in Literature and Language* 35.1 (1993): 57–78.

Matchinske, Megan. "Gendering Catholic Conformity." *Journal of English and Germanic Philology* 101.3 (2002): 329–357.

———. "Serial Identity: History, Gender, and Form in the Diary Writing of Lady Anne Clifford." In *Genre and Women's Life Writing in Early Modern England*, ed. Michelle M. Dowd and Julie A. Eckerle. Aldershot: Ashgate, 2007. 65–80.

Maus, Katherine Eisaman. *Inwardness and Theater in the English Renaissance*. Chicago: University of Chicago Press, 1995.

McIntosh, Marjorie Keniston. "Servants and the Household Unit in an Elizabethan English Community." *Journal of Family History* 9.1 (1984): 3–23.

———. *Working Women in English Society, 1300–1620*. Cambridge: Cambridge University Press, 2005.

McLaren, Dorothy. "Marital Fertility and Lactation 1570–1720." In *Women in English Society 1500–1800*, ed. Mary Prior. London: Methuen, 1985. 22–53.

McLuskie, Kathleen. "The Act, the Role, and the Actor: Boy Actresses on the Elizabethan Stage." *New Theatre Quarterly* 3 (1987): 120–130.

———. *Dekker and Heywood: Professional Dramatists*. London: St. Martin's, 1994.

McNeil, Fiona. *Poor Women in Shakespeare*. Cambridge: Cambridge University Press, 2007.

Meads, Dorothy M., ed. *The Diary of Lady Margaret Hoby 1599–1605*. London: Routledge, 1930.

Mei, Huang. *Transforming the Cinderella Dream: From Frances Burney to Charlotte Brontë*. New Brunswick: Rutgers University Press, 1990.

Meldrum, Tim. *Domestic Service and Gender 1660–1750*. Harlow, England: Pearson, 2000.

———. "London Domestic Servants from Depositional Evidence, 1660–1750: Servant-Employer Sexuality in the Patriarchal Household." In *Chronicling Poverty: The Voices and Strategies of the English Poor, 1640–1840*, ed. Tim Hitchcock, Peter King, and Pamela Sharpe. New York: St. Martin's, 1997. 47–69.

Mendelson, Sara Heller. *The Mental World of Stuart Women*. Amherst: University of Massachusetts Press, 1987.

Mendelson, Sara Heller. "Stuart Women's Diaries and Occasional Memoirs." In *Women in English Society 1500–1800*, ed. Mary Prior. London: Routledge, 1985. 181–201.

Mendelson, Sara, and Patricia Crawford. *Women in Early Modern England 1550–1720*. Oxford: Clarendon Press, 1998.

Metcalfe, Jean LeDrew. Introduction to *The Mothers Legacy to her Unborn Child*. Ed. Metcalfe. Toronto: University of Toronto Press, 2000. 3–31.

Michalove, Sharon D. "Equal in Opportunity? The Education of Aristocratic Women 1450–1540." In *Women's Education in Early Modern Europe: A History, 1500–1800*, ed. Barbara J. Whitehead. New York: Garland, 1999. 47–74.

Mink, Louis O. "Everyman His or Her Own Annalist." In *On Narrative*, ed. W.J.T. Mitchell. Chicago: University of Chicago Press, 1980. 233–239.

Montrose, Louis. *The Purpose of Playing: Shakespeare and the Cultural Politics of the Elizabethan Theatre*. Chicago: University of Chicago Press, 1996.

Moody, Joanna. Introduction to *The Private Life of an Elizabethan Lady: The Diary of Lady Margaret Hoby 1599–1605*. Ed. Moody. Phoenix Mill: Sutton, 1998. xv–lii.

———, ed. *The Private Life of an Elizabethan Lady: The Diary of Lady Margaret Hoby 1599–1605*. Phoenix Mill: Sutton, 1998.

Morgan-Russell, Simon. " 'No Good Thing Even Comes Out of It': Male Expectation and Female Alliance in Dekker and Webster's *Westward Ho*." In *Maids and Mistresses, Cousins and Queens: Women's Alliances in Early Modern England*, ed. Susan Frye and Karen Robertson. Oxford: Oxford University Press, 1998. 70–84.

Moss, Ann. *Printed Commonplace-Books and the Structuring of Renaissance Thought*. Oxford: Clarendon Press, 1996.

Mullaney, Steven. *The Place of the Stage: License, Play, and Power in Renaissance England*. Ann Arbor: University of Michigan Press, 1988.

Neill, Michael. *Putting History to the Question: Power, Politics, and Society in English Renaissance Drama*. New York: Columbia University Press, 2000.

———. " 'A woman's service': Gender, Subordination, and the Erotics of Rank in the Drama of Shakespeare and his Contemporaries." *Shakespearean International Yearbook* 5 (2005): 127–144.

Newcomb, Lori Humphrey. "The Romance of Service: The Simple History of *Pandosto's* Servant Readers." In *Framing Elizabethan Fictions: Contemporary Approaches to Early Modern Narrative Prose*, ed. Constance C. Relihan. Kent, OH: Kent State University Press, 1996. 117–139.

Newman, Karen. *Fashioning Femininity and English Renaissance Drama*. Chicago: University of Chicago Press, 1991.

Nussbaum, Felicity A. *The Autobiographical Subject: Gender and Ideology in Eighteenth-Century England*. Baltimore: John Hopkins University Press, 1989.

O'Connor, Mary. "Representations of Intimacy in the Life-Writing of Anne Clifford and Anne Dormer." In *Representations of the Self from the*

Renaissance to Romanticism, ed. Patrick Coleman, Jayne Lewis, and Jill Kowalik. Cambridge: Cambridge University Press, 2000. 79–96.

Orgel, Stephen. "Nobody's Perfect: Or Why Did the English Stage Take Boys for Women?" *The South Atlantic Quarterly* 88 (1989): 7–29.

Orlin, Lena Cowen. "Boundary Disputes in Early Modern London." In *Material London, ca. 1600*, ed. Orlin. Philadelphia: University of Pennsylvania Press, 2000. 345–376.

———. *Elizabethan Households*. Washington, D.C.: Folger Shakespeare Library, 1995.

———. Introduction to *Material London, ca. 1600*. Ed. Orlin. Philadelphia: University of Pennsylvania Press, 2000. 1–13.

———. *Private Matters and Public Culture in Post-Reformation England*. Ithaca: Cornell University Press, 1994.

Ormerod, George. *The History of the County Palatine*. London, 1882.

Ostovich, Helen. "The Appropriation of Pleasure in *The Magnetic Lady*." In *Maids and Mistresses, Cousins and Queens: Women's Alliances in Early Modern England*, ed. Susan Frye and Karen Robertson. Oxford: Oxford University Press, 1999. 98–113.

Palmer, David J. "Comedy and the Protestant Spirit in Shakespeare's *All's Well That Ends Well*." *Bulletin of the John Rylands University Library of Manchester* 71 (1989): 95–107.

Parker, Patricia. *Literary Fat Ladies: Rhetoric, Gender, Property*. New York: Methuen, 1987.

Paster, Gail Kern. *The Body Embarrassed: Drama and the Disciplines of Shame in Early Modern England*. Ithaca: Cornell University Press, 1993.

Pearson, Lu Emily. *Elizabethans at Home*. Stanford: Stanford University Press, 1957.

Perry, Ruth. "Colonizing the Breast: Sexuality and Maternity in Eighteenth-Century England." *Eighteenth-Century Life* 16 (1992): 185–213.

Peters, Christine. *Patterns of Piety: Women, Gender and Religion in Late Medieval and Reformation England*. Cambridge: Cambridge University Press, 2003.

Pfeiffer, Doug. " 'A life beyond life': The Rise of English Literary Biography." Ph.D. diss., Columbia University, 2005.

Phillippy, Patricia. *Women, Death and Literature in Post-Reformation England*. Cambridge: Cambridge University Press, 2002.

Pollack, Linda A. "Embarking on a Rough Passage: The Experience of Pregnancy in Early-Modern Society." In *Women as Mothers in Pre-Industrial England: Essays in Memory of Dorothy McLaren*, ed. Valerie Fildes. London: Routledge, 1990. 39–67.

Poole, Kristin. " 'The fittest closet for all goodness': Authorial Strategies of Jacobean Mothers' Manuals." *Studies in English Literature 1500–1900* 35.1 (1995): 69–88.

Prescott, Anne Lake. "Marginally Funny: Martha Moulsworth's Puns." In *"The Muses Females Are": Martha Moulsworth and Other Women Writers of the English Renaissance*, ed. Robert C. Evans and Anne C. Little. West Cornwall, CT: Locust Hill, 1995. 85–90.

Prior, Mary. "Wives and Wills 1558–1700." In *English Rural Society, 1500–1800: Essays in Honour of Joan Thirsk*, ed. John Chartres and David Hey. Cambridge: Cambridge University Press, 1990. 201–225.

———. "Women and the Urban Economy: Oxford 1500–1800." In *Women in English Society 1500–1800*, ed. Prior. London: Routledge, 1991. 93–117.

Quilligan, Maureen. "Completing the Conversation." *Shakespeare Studies* 25 (1997): 42–49.

Raoul, Valerie. "Women and Diaries: Gender and Genre." *Mosaic* 22.3 (1989): 57–65.

Rappaport, Steve. *Worlds Within Worlds: Structures of Life in Sixteenth-Century London*. Cambridge: Cambridge University Press, 1989.

Rasmussen, Mark David. "New Formalisms?" In *Renaissance Literature and Its Formal Engagements*, ed. Rasmussen. New York: Palgrave, 2002. 1–14.

Richardson, Catherine. "Properties of Domestic Life: The Table in Heywood's *A Woman Killed with Kindness*." In *Staged Properties in Early Modern English Drama*, ed. Jonathan Gil Harris and Natasha Korda. Cambridge: Cambridge University Press, 2002. 129–152.

Richardson, R.C. "The Generation Gap: Parental Advice in Early Modern England." *Clio* 32.1 (2002): 1–25.

Roberts, Sasha. "'Let me the curtains draw': The Dramatic and Symbolic Properties of the Bed in Shakespearean Tragedy." In *Staged Properties in Early Modern English Drama*, ed. Jonathan Gil Harris and Natasha Korda. Cambridge: Cambridge University Press, 2002. 153–174.

Romero, Mary. *Maid in the U.S.A.* New York: Routledge, 1992.

Roper, Lyndal. *The Holy Household: Women and Morals in Reformation Augsburg*. Oxford: Clarendon Press, 1989.

Rose, Mary Beth. "Gender, Genre, and History: Seventeenth-Century English Women and the Art of Autobiography." In *Women in the Middle Ages and the Renaissance: Literary and Historical Perspectives*, ed. Rose. Syracuse: Syracuse University Press, 1986. 245–278.

———. *Gender and Heroism in Early Modern English Literature*. Chicago: University of Chicago Press, 2002.

———. "Where Are the Mothers in Shakespeare? Options for Gender Representation in the English Renaissance." *Shakespeare Quarterly* 42 (1991): 291–314.

Salmon, Marylynn. "The Cultural Significance of Breastfeeding and Infant Care in Early Modern England and America." *Journal of Social History* 28.2 (1994): 247–269.

Sanders, Eve Rachele. *Gender and Literacy on Stage in Early Modern England*. Cambridge: Cambridge University Press, 1998.

Sanders, Julie. "Midwifery and the New Science in the Seventeenth Century: Language, Print and the Theatre." In *At the Borders of the Human: Beasts, Bodies and Natural Philosophy in the Early Modern Period*, ed. Erica Fudge, Ruther Gilbert, and Susan Wiseman. London: Macmillan, 1999. 74–90.

Schalkwyk, David. "Love and Service in *Twelfth Night* and the Sonnets." *Shakespeare Quarterly* 56.1 (2005): 76–100

Schoenfeldt, Michael C. *Bodies and Selves in Early Modern England: Physiology and Inwardness in Spenser, Shakespeare, Herbert, and Milton.* Cambridge: Cambridge University Press, 1999.

Schwarz, Kathryn. "Missing the Breast: Desire, Disease, and the Singular Effect of Amazons." In *The Body in Parts: Fantasies of Corporeality in Early Modern Europe,* ed. David Hillman and Carla Mazzio. New York: Routledge, 1997. 147–169.

———. " 'My intents are fix'd': Constant Will in *All's Well That Ends Well.*" *Shakespeare Quarterly* 58.2 (2007): 200–227.

———. *Tough Love: Amazon Encounters in the English Renaissance.* Durham: Duke University Press, 2000.

Scott, Joan W. *Gender and the Politics of History.* New York: Columbia University Press, 1988.

Seelig, Sharon Cadman. *Autobiography and Gender in English Modern Literature: Reading Women's Lives, 1600–1680.* Cambridge: Cambridge University Press, 2006.

Sharpe, Pamela, ed. *Women's Work: The English Experience 1650–1914.* London: Arnold, 1998.

Shepard, Alexandra. "Manhood, Credit and Patriarchy in Early Modern England c.1580–1640." *Past and Present* 167.1 (2000): 75–106.

Shikoda, Mitsuo. "Juliet, the Nursling of the Nurse." *Shakespeare Studies* (Tokyo) 25 (1987): 25–39.

Simonds, Peggy Munoz. "Sacred and Sexual Motifs in *All's Well That Ends Well.*" *Renaissance Quarterly* 42.1 (1989): 33–59.

Simpson, Lynne M. "The Failure to Mourn in *All's Well That Ends Well.*" *Shakespeare Studies* 22 (1994): 172–188.

Sizemore, Christine W. "Attitudes Toward the Education and Roles of Women: Sixteenth-Century Humanists and Seventeenth-Century Advice Books." *The University of Dayton Review* 15.1 (1981): 57–67.

———. "Early Seventeenth-Century Advice Books: The Female Viewpoint." *South Atlantic Bulletin* 41.1 (1976): 41–49.

Smith, Hilda. "Gynecology and Ideology in Seventeenth-Century England." In *Liberating Women's History: Theoretical and Critical Essays,* ed. Berenice A. Carroll. Urbana: University of Illinois Press, 1976. 97–114.

———. "Humanist Education and the Renaissance Concept of Woman." In *Women and Literature in Britain 1500–1700,* ed. Helen Wilcox. Cambridge: Cambridge University Press, 1996. 9–29.

Snook, Edith. "Fellowshippe in their apparel, [. . .] obedience in their fashions': Clothing the Subject in Lady Mary Wroth's *Countess of Montgomery's Urania.*" Unpublished essay, 2004.

———. " 'His open side our book': Meditation and Education in Elizabeth Grymeston's *Miscelanea Meditations Memoratives.*" In *Maternal Measures: Figuring Caregiving in the Early Modern Period,* ed. Naomi J. Miller and Naomi Yavneh. Aldershot: Ashgate, 2000. 163–175.

Susan Snyder. "*All's Well That Ends Well* and Shakespeare's Helens: Text and Subtext, Subject and Object." *English Literary Renaissance* 18.1 (1988): 66–77.

———. "'The King's not here': Displacement and Deferral in *All's Well*." *Shakespeare Quarterly* 43.1 (1992): 20–32.

Spring, Eileen. *Law, Land, and Family: Aristocratic Inheritance in England, 1300–1800*. Chapel Hill: University of North Carolina Press, 1993.

Spufford, Margaret. *Small Books and Pleasant Histories: Popular Fiction and its Readership in Seventeenth-Century England*. Athens: University of Georgia Press, 1981.

Stachniewski, John. *The Persecutory Imagination: English Puritanism and the Literature of Religious Despair*. Oxford: Clarendon Press, 1991.

Stevens, Martin. "Juliet's Nurse: Love's Herald." *Papers on Language and Literature* 2.3 (1966): 195–206.

Stone, Lawrence. *The Crisis of the Aristocracy 1558–1641*. Oxford: Oxford University Press, 1965.

Sullivan Jr., Garrett A. "'Be This Sweet Helen's Knell, and Now Forget Her': Forgetting, Memory, and Identity in *All's Well That Ends Well*." *Shakespeare Quarterly* 50.1 (1999): 51–69.

Summit, Jennifer. "Writing Home: Hannah Wolley, the Oxinden Letters, and Household Epistolary Practice." In *Women, Property, and the Letters of the Law in Early Modern England*, ed. Nancy E. Wright, Margaret W. Ferguson, and A.R. Buck. Toronto: University of Toronto Press, 2004. 201–218.

Targoff, Ramie. *Common Prayer: The Language of Public Devotion in Early Modern England*. Chicago: University of Chicago Press, 2001.

Taylor, Lou. *Mourning Dress: A Costume and Social History*. London, George Allen and Unwin, 1983.

Teague, Fran. "Elizabeth Jocelin." In *An Encyclopedia of British Women Writers*, ed. Paul Schlueter and June Schlueter. New Brunswick: Rutgers University Press, 1998. 350–351.

Theophano, Janet. *Eat My Words: Reading Women's Lives through the Cookbooks They Wrote*. New York: Palgrave, 2002.

Thirsk, Joan. *Economic Policy and Projects: The Development of a Consumer Society in Early Modern England*. Oxford: Clarendon Press, 1978.

Tillyard, E.M. *Shakespeare's Problem Plays*. Toronto: University of Toronto Press, 1950.

Todd, Janet. *Feminist Literary History*. New York: Routledge, 1988.

Todd, Margo. *Christian Humanism and the Puritan Social Order*. Cambridge: Cambridge University Press, 1987.

Traub, Valerie. *Desire and Anxiety: Circulations of Sexuality in Shakespearean Drama*. London: Routledge, 1992.

Travitsky, Betty S. "The New Mother of the English Renaissance." In *The Lost Tradition: Mothers and Daughters in Literature*, ed. Cathy N. Davidson and E.M. Broner. New York: F. Ungar, 1980. 33–43.

———. "The 'Wyll and Testament' of Isabella Whitney." *English Literary Renaissance* 10.1 (1980): 76–94.

Trill, Suzanne. "Religion and the Construction of Femininity." In *Women and Literature in Britain 1500–1700*, ed. Helen Wilcox. Cambridge: Cambridge University Press, 1996. 30–55.

Trubowitz, Rachel. "'But Blood Whitened': Nursing Mothers and Others in Early Modern Britain." In *Maternal Measures: Figuring Caregiving in the Early Modern Period*, ed. Naomi J. Miller and Naomi Yavneh. Aldershot: Ashgate, 2000. 82–101.

Turner, Henry S. *The English Renaissance Stage: Geometry, Poetics, and the Practical Spatial Arts 1580–1630*. Oxford: Oxford University Press, 2006.

Tuve, Rosemond. *A Reading of George Herbert*. Chicago: University of Chicago Press, 1978.

Underdown, David. "The Taming of the Scold: The Enforcement of Patriarchal Authority in Early Modern England." In *Order and Disorder in Early Modern England*, ed. Anthony Fletcher and John Stevenson. Cambridge: Cambridge University Press, 1985. 116–136.

Vann, Richard T. "Wills and the Family in an English Town: Banbury, 1550–1800." *Journal of Family History* 4.4 (1979): 346–367.

Vendler, Helen. *The Poetry of George Herbert*. Cambridge, MA: Harvard University Press, 1975.

Waldman, Marilyn Robinson. "'The Otherwise Unnoteworthy Year 711': A Reply to Hayden White." In *On Narrative*, ed. W.J.T. Mitchell. Chicago: University of Chicago Press, 1980. 240–248.

Wales and the Marches: Catalog of Stanley Crowe, Bookseller and Printseller. No. 64. London: Stanley Crowe, 1960.

Walker, Claire. "Combining Martha and Mary: Gender and Work in Seventeenth-Century English Cloisters." *Sixteenth Century Journal* 30.2 (1999): 397–417.

Walker, Garthine. "Expanding the Boundaries of Female Honour in Early Modern England." *Transactions of the Royal Historical Society* 6 (1996): 135–145.

———. "Rereading Rape and Sexual Violence in Early Modern England." *Gender and History* 10.1 (1998): 1–25.

Wall, Wendy. "Isabella Whitney and the Female Legacy." *ELH* 58.1 (1991): 35–62.

———. *Staging Domesticity: Household Work and English Identity in Early Modern Drama*. Cambridge: Cambridge University Press, 2002.

Walsham, Alexandra. *Providence in Early Modern England*. Oxford: Oxford University Press, 1999.

Warnicke, Retha M. "Eulogies for Women: Public Testimony of Their Godly Example and Leadership." In *Attending to Women in Early Modern England*, ed. Betty S. Travitsky and Adele F. Seeff. Newark: University of Delaware Press, 1994. 168–186.

Watkins, Owen C. *The Puritan Experience: Studies in Spiritual Autobiography*. New York: Schocken Books, 1972.

Watt, Tessa. *Cheap Print and Popular Piety, 1550–1640*. Cambridge: Cambridge University Press, 1991.

Wayne, Don E. *Penshurst: The Semiotics of Place and the Poetics of History.* Madison: University of Wisconsin Press, 1984.

Wayne, Valerie. "Advice for Women from Mothers and Patriarchs." In *Women and Literature in Britain 1500–1700*, ed. Helen Wilcox. Cambridge: Cambridge University Press, 1996. 56–79.

Weil, Judith. *Service and Dependency in Shakespeare's Plays.* Cambridge: Cambridge University Press, 2005.

Wells, Stanley. "Juliet's Nurse: The Use of Inconsequentiality." In *Shakespeare's Styles: Essays in Honour of Kenneth Muir*, ed. Philip Edwards, Inga-Stina Ewbank, and G.K. Hunter. Cambridge: Cambridge University Press, 1980. 51–66.

Wentworth, Michael. "Thomas Heywood's *A Woman Killed with Kindness* as Domestic Morality." In *Traditions and Innovations: Essays on British Literature of the Middle Ages and the Renaissance*, ed. David G. Allen and Robert A. White. Newark: University of Delaware Press, 1990. 150–162.

White, Hayden. *The Content of the Form: Narrative Discourse and Historical Representation.* Baltimore: Johns Hopkins University Press, 1987.

White, Paul Whitfield. "Theater and Religious Culture." In *A New History of Early English Drama*, ed. John D. Cox and David Scott Kastan. New York: Columbia University Press, 1997. 133–151.

———. *Theatre and Reformation: Protestantism, Patronage, and Playing in Tudor England.* Cambridge: Cambridge University Press, 1993.

Whitehead, Barbara J. Introduction to *Women's Education in Early Modern Europe: A History, 1500–1800.* Ed. Whitehead. New York: Garland, 1999. ix–xvi.

Wiesner, Merry E. *Women and Gender in Early Modern Europe.* Cambridge: Cambridge University Press, 1993.

Wilcox, Helen. "Entering *The Temple:* Women, Reading, and Devotion in Seventeenth-Century England." In *Religion, Literature and Politics in Post-Reformation England, 1540–1688*, ed. Donna B. Hamilton and Richard Strier. Cambridge: Cambridge University Press, 1996. 187–207.

———. "Private Writing and Public Function: Autobiographical Texts by Renaissance Englishwomen." In *Gloriana's Face: Women, Public and Private, in the English Renaissance*, ed. S.P. Cerasano and Marion Wynne-Davies. New York: Harvester Wheatsheaf, 1992. 47–62.

———, ed. *Women and Literature in Britain 1500–1700.* Cambridge: Cambridge University Press, 1996.

Willen, Diane. "Women and Religion in Early Modern England." In *Women in Reformation and Counter-Reformation Europe: Public and Private Worlds*, ed. Sherrin Marshall. Bloomington: Indiana University Press, 1989. 140–165.

Williams, Raymond. *The Country and the City.* New York: Oxford University Press, 1973.

———. *Marxism and Literature.* Oxford: Oxford University Press, 1977.

Wilson, Adrian. "The Ceremony of Childbirth and Its Interpretation." In *Women as Mothers in Pre-Industrial England: Essays in Memory of Dorothy McLaren*, ed. Valerie Fildes. London: Routledge, 1990. 68–107.

Wray, Ramona. *Women Writers of the Seventeenth Century.* Tavistock: Northcote House, 2004.

Wright, Sue. "'Churmaids, Huswyfes, and Hucksters': The Employment of Women in Tudor and Stuart Salisbury." In *Women and Work in Pre-Industrial England*, ed. Lindsey Charles and Lorna Duffin. London: Croom Helm, 1985. 100–121.

Wrightson, Keith. *Earthly Necessities: Economic Lives in Early Modern Britain.* New Haven: Yale University Press, 2000.

———. *English Society 1580–1680.* New Brunswick: Rutgers University Press, 1982.

INDEX